Lecture Notes in Artificial Intelligence   2831

Edited by J. G. Carbonell and J. Siekmann

Subseries of Lecture Notes in Computer Science

T0226308

Springer
Berlin
Heidelberg
New York
Hong Kong
London
Milan
Paris
Tokyo

Michael Schillo   Matthias Klusch
Jörg Müller   Huaglory Tianfield (Eds.)

Multiagent System Technologies

First German Conference, MATES 2003
Erfurt, Germany, September 22-25, 2003
Proceedings

 Springer

Series Editors

Jaime G. Carbonell, Carnegie Mellon University, Pittsburgh, PA, USA
Jörg Siekmann, University of Saarland, Saarbrücken, Germany

Volume Editors

Michael Schillo
Matthias Klusch
DFKI GmbH
German Research Center for Artificial Intelligence
Stuhlsatzenhausweg 3, 66123 Saarbrücken, Germany
E-mail: {schillo;klusch}@dfki.de

Jörg Müller
Siemens AG
CT, IC 6, Otto-Hahn-Ring 6, 81730 München, Germany
E-mail: joerg.p.mueller@siemens.com

Huaglory Tianfield
Glasgow Caledonian University
70 Cowcaddens Road, Glasgow, G4 0BA, UK
E-mail: h.tianfield@gcal.ac.uk

Cataloging-in-Publication Data applied for

A catalog record for this book is available from the Library of Congress.

Bibliographic information published by Die Deutsche Bibliothek
Die Deutsche Bibliothek lists this publication in the Deutsche Nationalbibliografie;
detailed bibliographic data is available in the Internet at <http://dnb.ddb.de>.

CR Subject Classification (1998): I.2, C.2.4, D.2.12, D.1.3, J.1

ISSN 0302-9743
ISBN 3-540-20124-6 Springer-Verlag Berlin Heidelberg New York

Springer-Verlag Berlin Heidelberg New York
a member of BertelsmannSpringer Science+Business Media GmbH

http://www.springer.de

© Springer-Verlag Berlin Heidelberg 2003
Printed in Germany

Typesetting: Camera-ready by author, data conversion by PTP-Berlin GmbH
Printed on acid-free paper   SPIN: 10958933   06/3142   5 4 3 2 1 0

Preface

These are the proceedings of the German conference on Multiagent System Technologies (MATES 2003), which was the first conference organized by the German special interest group on Distributed Artificial Intelligence to promote the theory and application of agents and multiagent systems. Its goals were to cover the whole range from the theory to applications of agent and multiagent technology and reflect the national and international state of the art. The conference provided an excellent interdisciplinary forum for both researchers and members of business and industry to present and discuss the latest advances in theoretical work on and prototyped or fielded systems of intelligent agents.

Building on the sequence of agent-related events in Germany in the past, such as VDI 1998 (Chemnitz), VertIS 2001 (Bamberg), and KI 2002 (Aachen), MATES 2003 was exclusively devoted to agents and multiagent systems, and the cross-fertilization between agent theory and application. In addition, it built on the success of the past international workshop on "Agent Technology and Software Engineering (AgeS 2002)", and the international symposium on "Multiagent Systems, Large Complex Systems, and E-Businesses" (MALCEB 2002). MATES 2003 was co-located with the fourth international Net.ObjectDays conference in an exciting event held in Erfurt during September 22–24.

The MATES 2003 conference featured a sequence of regular and invited talks of excellence given by leading experts in the field. Among these were two keynotes, an invited talk and 18 paper presentations selected from 49 submissions. The conference talks covered a broad area of topics of interest, such as the semantic web and issues of interoperability, agent-based engineering, systems and applications, models and architectures, and issues of collaboration and negotiation. The result of the review of all contributions by an international program committee is included in these proceedings, rich in interesting, inspiring, and advanced work on research and development of multiagent systems. During the conference, tutorials were held on adaptive agents, agents and the semantic web, and interaction protocol design in multiagent systems.

The MATES 2003 conference was organized in cooperation with the Distributed Artificial Intelligence chapter of the German Computing Society (GI). In addition, we are very much indebted to our sponsors, whose financial support helped to make this event possible and contributed to its success. The sponsors of MATES 2003 were:

NET.OBJECT DAYS
KTWEB

We are also grateful to the authors and invited speakers for contributing to this conference, as well as to all the members of the program committee and the external reviewers for their very careful, critical, and thoughtful reviews of all submissions. Finally, our thanks go to each of the brave members of the local organization team of Net.ObjectDays in Erfurt for their hard work in providing MATES 2003 with a modern, comfortable location, and an exclusive social program.

We hope you enjoyed MATES 2003, and will help us to make MATES a successful conference series with many events to come!

July 2003   Michael Schillo, Matthias Klusch,
                                                    Jörg Müller, Huaglory Tianfield

Program Co-chairs

Matthias Klusch   DFKI, Germany
Jörg Müller   Siemens AG, Germany
Michael Schillo   DFKI, Germany
Huaglory Tianfield   Glasgow Caledonian University, UK

Local Chair

Rainer Unland   University of Duisburg-Essen, Germany

Program Committee

Elisabeth Andre   University of Augsburg, Germany
Bernhard Bauer   University of Augsburg, Germany
Wolfgang Benn   Technical University, Chemnitz, Germany
Michael Berger   Siemens AG, Germany
Hans-Dieter Burkhard   Humboldt University, Berlin, Germany
Wilfried Brauer   Technical University, München, Germany
Cristiano Castelfranchi NRC Rome, Italy
Paolo Ciancarini   University of Bologna, Italy
Rosaria Conte   NRC Rome, Italy
Hans Czap   University of Trier, Germany
Kerstin Dautenhahn   University of Hertfordshire, UK
Klaus Fischer   DFKI Saarbrücken, Germany
Norbert Fuhr   University of Dortmund, Germany
Ulrich Furbach   University of Koblenz-Landau, Germany
Petra Funk   Whitestein Technologies, Switzerland
Otthein Herzog   University of Bremen, Germany
Michael Huhns   University of South Carolina, USA
Heinrich Hussmann   Technical University, Dresden, Germany
Matthias Jarke   RWTH Aachen, Germany
Liz Kendall   Monash University, Australia
Stefan Kirn   Technical University, Ilmenau, Germany
Franziska Klügl   University of Würzburg, Germany
Ryszard Kowalczyk   Swinburne University of Technology, Australia
Gerhard Kraetzschmar   University of Ulm, Germany
Karl Kurbel   University of Frankfurt/Oder, Germany
Gerhard Lakemeyer   RWTH Aachen, Germany
Winfried Lamersdorf   University of Hamburg, Germany
Jürgen Lind   Iteratec GmbH, Germany
Gabriele Lindemann   Humboldt University, Berlin, Germany
Jiming Liu   Hong-Kong Baptist University, China
Kecheng Liu   University of Reading, UK

Jürgen Müller	BeeBetter GmbH, Germany
James Odell	James Odell Associates, USA
Lin Padgham	RMIT, Australia
Mike Papazoglou	University of Tilburg, The Netherlands
Anna Perini	ITC Trento, Italy
Paolo Petta	Technical University, Wien, Austria
Frank Puppe	University of Würzburg, Germany
Giovanni Rimassa	University of Parma, Italy
Michael Rovatsos	Technical University, München, Germany
Rudi Studer	University of Karlsruhe, Germany
Ingo Timm	Technical University, Ilmenau, Germany
Robert Tolksdorf	Technical University, Berlin, Germany
Mihaela Ulieru	University of Calgary, Canada
Gerhard Weiss	Technical University, München, Germany
Mike Wooldridge	University of Liverpool, UK
Hong Zhu	Oxford Brookes University, UK

External Reviewers

Matthias Nickles	Technical University, München, Germany
Stefan Römer	Technical University, München, Germany
Christian Zirpins	University of Hamburg, Germany

Table of Contents

Engineering Agent-Based Systems

Systems and Applications (1)

Systems and Applications (2)

Models and Architectures

The Semantic Web and Issues of Inter-operability

Issues of Collaboration and Negotiation

The AgentComponent Approach, Combining Agents, and Components

Richard Krutisch, Philipp Meier, and Martin Wirsing

Ludwig-Maximilians-Universtität München
{krutisch, meierp, wirsing}@informatik.uni-muenchen.de

Abstract. In this paper we introduce a new approach, the so-called AgentComponent (AC) approach which combines component and agent technology. A multi agent system (MAS) is composed of AC instances, each AC instance consists of a knowledge base, storing the beliefs of an AC instance, of slots, storing the communication partners of an AC instance, of a set of ontologies, that represent domain specific languages for certain contexts, and of so-called ProcessComponents (PC) representing the behaviours of an AC instance. The AC is a generic component that can be reused (instantiated ACs) and parametrized by customizing the communication partners (slots), the ontologies and the behaviours (PCs) that can be added and removed from any AC instance. Hereby we achieve added value for agents and components. Agents can be easily composed, customized and reused whereas components get enhanced communication and interaction facilities from agents. We present this approach in detail, show how to construct a component-based MAS by a simple example and present a graphical tool for composing systems of AgentComponents.

1   Introduction

Software agents and software components are two emerging fields in software development. Each concept has its advantages and disadvantages but both concepts are improving the way large scaled software is built. While components focus more on reusability aspects of software, agents (MAS) focus on processing complex tasks as a community.

Agents. In agent software development we distinguish basic kinds of agent systems: Reactive systems, MAS (interaction-driven systems) and Belief-Desire-Intention systems. Reactive systems define the simplest form of agent systems. Such systems can easily be described by state machines, that react on events by triggering certain actions. MAS focus mainly on the interaction aspects of a system of agents that collaboratively execute complex tasks. In the BDI model agents have beliefs and plans and can trigger different plans to reach certain defined goals. In this paper we focus on building MAS. And therefore we shortly want to name the properties of agents in such a system [14,13]. Agents must be able to react on direct events (reactivity), moreover agents must be able to react on indirect events (proactivity) such as changes in the environment

M. Schillo et al. (Eds.): MATES 2003, LNAI 2831, pp. 1–12, 2003.

or changes of the plans of an agent. Moreover agents should execute their tasks autonomously (autonomy) i.e. there should not be too much interaction with the user during process/task execution. And of course agents must be able to interact and exchange data and information by using certain protocols and ontologies (interaction, communication, social behaviour).

Components. To find a common definition for *components* is quite a big problem [6]. And in this paper we only point out the properties of components we think are useful for this approach. In [4] is stated: *"Component (in code): A coherent package of software implementation that (a) can be independently developed and delivered, (b) has explicit and well-specified interfaces for the services it provides, (c) has explicit and well-specified interfaces for services it expects from others, and (d) can be composed with other components, perhaps customizing some of their properties, without modifying the components themselves."* Considering components, one of the most important aspects is the reusability of the component in different contexts. And to provide certain functionality even for contexts which were not intended to be contexts for this component. To provide reusability we need to specify properly the components' interfaces, so that we are able to compose and exchange components in a component based software system. The interior of a component can be considered as a blackbox that is invisible for the user. Whereas the interfaces of a component describe, the services/methods a component provides and the services/methods it needs. Moreover it does not matter who a component provides. As long as a component is well specified it can easily be composed with other components to a more complex system.

Combining Agents and Components. Many similarities can be found between agent and component technology [11]. But we are more interested in the complementary concepts of these technologies, because these are the concepts that make the profit of combining agents and components. We see the main purpose of agents in the communication ability, which gives us the possibility to process complex tasks by assigning single tasks to different agents. Instead components focus more on reusability and parametrisation/customization aspects for the deployment of a component in different contexts. In our opinion there exist two different concepts of combining agent and component technology. The first one, we call it "agentifying", sees component technology as starting point and tries to include agent properties into existing components. The second one, we call it "componentifying", considers agent technology as starting point and tries to add component features to existing agent technology. Our approach which is based upon the "componentifying concept" combines the main features of agents and components in the so-called AgentComponent (AC). In this way we achieve both: An AC has communication abilities (the agent as starting point) and that can be reused and parametrized (the included component features) for different contexts (see Fig. 1). With our approach we want to disburden agent software development. The component technology is a suitable instrument for this task by making certain agent concepts customizable and reusable. Here "reusable" means to have an AC that can be instantiated for every agent we need. And "customizable" means to connect AC instances, add/remove certain ontologies and add/remove behaviours graphically.

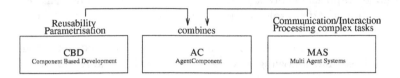

Fig. 1. Combination Profit

In section 2 we describe the basic concepts of the AC approach, where we give a simple example to illustrate these concepts. In section 3 we show how to construct AgentComponent Systems (ACS), i.e. systems composed of Agent-Components, and section 4 presents a graphical tool that helps to construct systems composed of AgentComponents. Finally, section 5 describes some related work and discusses differences to this approach, and section 6 concludes the paper.

2   AgentComponent

In general, the AC has all agent properties like autonomy, reactivity, proactivity and interaction and adds component features like reusability and customizability (according to the "componentifying concept"). An AC is a generic component that describes general services that every agent must provide and so an AC can be instantiated/reused for every agent one wants to build. A user can easily customize an AC instance for his purpose and for his context in the following ways: **(1)** Customizing the ACs' communication partners. We introduce so-called *slots* that hold information about communication partners of AC instances. Communication partners can be added to or removed from the slots of AC instances (customization of slots). **(2)** Customizing the ACs' ontologies. Ontologies can be registered or deregistered from the AC instance. **(3)** Customizing the ACs' processes. We introduce so-called *ProcessComponents* (PCs) that implement and describe simple or complex behaviours that can be added to or removed from any AC instance. With these three facilities the *appearance* and the *behaviour* of AC instances can be customized. Every AgentComponent includes the following entities for which it has to provide services. A knowledge base, slots (holding communication partners), a set of ontologies and a set of PCs:

Knowledge Base. The knowledge base is a basic element of every AC instance. An AC provides services to add, remove and get resources from the knowledge base. The following services are provided by an AC for the knowledge base concept:

(1) *retrieve* (getting knowledge from the knowledge base).

(2) *assert* (adding knowledge to the knowledge base).

(3) *retract* (removing knowledge from the knowledge base).

Ontologies. A well-known agent concept is the ontology concept that agents use to understand the content of the messages that are being sent or received. So for certain contexts ontologies must be provided that can be registered at AC instances. Instances of these ontologies can then be used as common language between AC instances and can also be asserted to, retracted or retrieved from the knowledge base. The following services are provided by the AC for the ontologies concept:

(1) *addOnto* (register an ontology at the AC instance).

(2) *removeOnto* (deregister an ontology from the AC instance).

Slots. Slots are entities of AC instances that hold information about communication partners (other agents). Communication pathways between AC instances can be created w.r.t. customized by connecting and changing slots, in this way filling the slots with the required destinations (other AC instances) for communication, and then messages can be sent and received via the created pathways. The following services are provided by the AC for the slot concept:

(1) *addSlot* (adds a slot for communication partners to AC instances).

(2) *removeSlot* (removes a slot from AC instances).

(3) *connectSlot* (fills a slot with destinations).

(4) *disconnectSlot* (removes a destination from a slot).

ProcessComponents. A PC represents a certain behaviour that can be added and removed to an AC instance.

(1) *addPC* (adds a PC to an AC instance).

(2) *removePC* (removes a PC from an AC instance).

When a PC has been added to an AC instance the PC has full use of all services that the AC provides (see Fig. 2). I.e. the PC is able to assert, retract, retrieve resources, to send and receive messages and moreover to use all the services listed in the StructuralInterface (see Fig. 2). So every PC implements an activity graph that consists of assert-, retract-, retrieve-, send-, receive-, StructuralInterface- or custom activities. In this way a PC defines which input it requires (retrieve, receive) and output it delivers (assert, retract, send, StructuralInterface services). By adding or removing PCs from an AC instance a system developer or user can determine the *appearance* (the structure of an AC instance, see StructuralInterface in Fig. 2) and the *behaviour* of an AC. That a PC determines a part of the behaviour of an AC instance is obvious, because a PC implements a certain workflow, represented by an activity graph. That a PC has the ability to determine the appearance of an AC instance is not so obvious and must be explained. We have mentioned before that a PC can use all the services that are included in the StructuralInterface. All these services define the *appearance* of an AC instance and are ment to customize the structure of an AC instance. On the one hand we want the user or system developer to do this structural customization graphically and on the other hand the PCs can implement behaviours that customize and determine the structure of an AC instance. And therefore a PC has the ability to determine the *appearance* of an AC instance by using the StructuralInterface services.

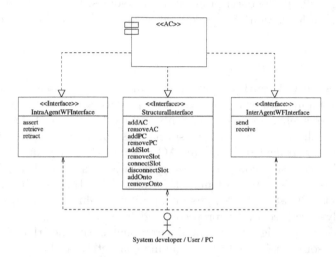

Fig. 2. AgentComponent Services

Intra-agent and Inter-agent Workflow. We have not yet talked about how AC instances or better their PCs can work together and define a workflow. This is important to explain, because we do not provide a workflow control within an AC and leave the workflow and its control to the PC implementor. The PCs themselves are supposed to work autonomously, i.e. PCs describe only their own workflow by defining what they require (receive, retrieve) and what they deliver (send, assert, retract, StructuralInterface services) not caring about the overall workflow. The way a workflow between two or more PCs is handled must be divided into two concepts, the inter-agent and the intra-agent workflow. Obviously the *inter-agent* workflow between AC instances is handled by sending and receiving messages using the pathways between AC instances. These pathways are stored in the slots and can be changed using the "connectSlot" or "disonnectSlot" service. Whereas the assert, retract and retrieve services handle the *intra-agent* workflow (workflow within an AC), by changing the knowledge base and therefore making resources available for other PCs (of the same AC instance) that wait for these resources. In this way we use the knowledge base as a "shared memory" for input and output variables, that can be used by all added PCs. The following services must be provided by an AC for the inter-agent workflow concept:

(1) *send* (sending messages to other AC instances).

(2) *receive* (receiving messages from other AC instances).

Putting all the mentioned concepts together the PC implementor has to provide:

(1) The implementation of the PC, where all services of the AC can be used to send, receive messages, to retrieve, assert and retract resources from the knowledge base and to customize the structure. **(2)** The PC description, where one must provide: (2.1) The description of all ontologies, that are required by the PC, (2.2) the information about required slots for the inter-agent communication and (2.3) the description of the workflow of the PC (mainly the description of the usage of the services), so that new PC providers understand the activities w.r.t. the behaviour of the PC.

Projects and AgentGroups. Agents are loosely coupled entities by nature, that communicate using messages and protocols and that are not directly aware of other agents around them (only indirectly via the AMS or the DF). We introduce the term *Project* as a special case of a PC. A Project normally describes an unspecified task, e.g. an AC instance does not know which other ACs are able to assist in collaboratively executing a task. So this AC has to look for one or more ACs that can handle this task. After this search they will join for this special PC at runtime and split up after finishing the Project. Projects are normally described by 1:n protocols and have a highly dynamic character. What misses in this highly dynamic environment is the fact that software systems only in some cases need such dynamic character. So, beside the Projects, we see the necessity to be able to connect the ACs directly using the before introduced slots. So we are able to build up an acquaintance net (AgentGroup) with an organization structure according to the pathways described in the slots. System developers or users will be able to create AgentGroups graphically using a tool, whereas Projects normally construct their organization structure and information pathways during runtime. The following services must be additionally provided by an AC for the AgentGroup concept:

(1) *addAC* (adds an AC to the AgentGroup of an existing AC instance).

(2) *removeAC* (removes an AC instance from an AgentGroup).

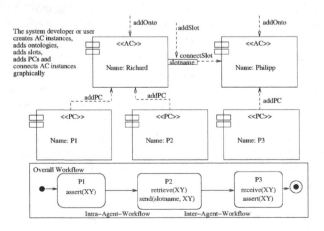

Fig. 3. Constructing a Simple AgentGroup

Example. To illustrate these basic concepts of the AC approach we describe a very small example. In this example (see Fig. 3) we describe the construction of a simple system, assuming that there exists a tool that supports the construction graphically. Furtheron, we assume that three PCs and their information description about ontologies, slots and behaviours are available. So we can use the three PCs called P1 to P3. P1 asserts an ontology object named XY to the knowledge base. P2 retrieves an XY ontology object and wants to send it to any AC instance available (we do not know to which AC instance we want to send so far, depends on the entries in the used slot). P3 receives a message containing an XY ontology object and asserts it to the ACs' knowledge base. P2 and P3 provide a description for the ontologies and for the slots they need during their workflow. First of all we create two idle AC instances named Richard and Philipp. Before we add any PC to Richard or Philipp we need to customize the structure of the both AC instances to make the intra-agent and inter-agent workflow of the PCs working. I.e. as we want to add P1 and P2 to Richard and P3 to Philipp, Richard and Philipp need the slots and the ontologies according to the PC descriptions. After creating a slot it can be filled with any destinations available, in our case we connect it with Philipp, and hereby Philipp is stored as a destination in a slot of Richard. By adding all this structural information and then adding the PCs as mentioned before we define on the one hand an intra-agent workflow where P2 requires the output (retrieve(XY)) of P1 (assert(XY)). And on the other hand we define an inter-agent workflow between P2 (send(XY)) added to Richard and P3 (receive(XY)) added to Philipp. After adding the PCs their behaviours start immediately and the workflow is executed (see Fig. 3).

Summary. We have shown an AC that provides three interfaces (InterAgentWorkflowInterface, IntraAgentWorkflowInterface and StructuralInterface) including common services every agent requires. System developers do not have to implement the AC, they just need to instantiate the AC as often as they require it. To fill the ACs with life PCs must be provided by the developers which then can be added to the AC instances. This results in an ACS (Agent Component System - assembled of ACs) which uses customized inter-agent communication (achieved by the concept of slots and ontologies) and uses customized intra-agent communication (achieved by the concept of PCs using the knowledge base).

3   Component-Oriented Development Process for AC-Systems

For constructing ACS (AgentComponent Systems) we propose a component-based software development process fully based on UML models [9]. We extend this process with the AC features and explain how we model these features. According to [9] we have four main phases in the AC development process: (1) Requirements, (2) AC Identification, (3) AC Interaction and (4) AC Specification.

We concentrate in this paper on the construction phase of ACS that mainly takes place in the AC Identification and the AC Interaction phases. As a description of all phases would go beyond the scope of this paper we will not describe the AC Specification step, because it is mainly a refinement of identification and interaction using e.g. OCL (object constraint language) to model pre- and post-conditions of PCs. For the same reason we skip the requirements phase, though it is a very important phase, as it delivers the input, like business processes, business objects, actors and use case diagrams, that we need for the design phases (identification, interaction, specification).

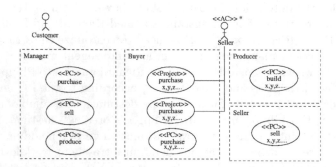

Fig. 4. Constructing AC Instances

AC Identification. Taking the input of the requirements phase we identify in this phase the agents (AC instances), roles and processes (PCs). We put all this information together to allocate the PCs to the AC instances and use UML-Use-Case diagrams [7,2] to model each AC instance with its PCs. These tailored Use-Case diagrams show AC instances and their PCs using stereotypes for AgentComponent («AC»), ProcessComponent («PC») and Project («Project»). In the example we have identified four AC instances (see Fig. 4) named Manager, Buyer, Producer and Seller and added different PCs to these AC instances. In the following we explain the Manager. In this small example we expect a Customer to order any Product at the Manager. The Manager itself has the Manager-like PCs added, that will initialize the Buyer to purchase all the parts, initialize the Producer to build any Product and initialze the Seller to sell the Product to the Customer.

Particularly the process of identifying the ACs in this example shows the way how ACS can be applied in practice. We start taking a found "real organization structure" (e.g. the organization structure of a certain company) from the requirements phase. ACS can map the "real organization structure" to the virtual organization structure where every organization element (unit,actor) is represented by an AC instance. In the example we have mapped a company structure consisting of four units Manager, Buyer, Producer and Seller to four AC instances with the same name.

AC Interaction. During this phase we describe the interaction between the AC instances we have found in the AC identification phase. We have following steps to do: (1) Modeling the organization structure, (2) defining the context ontologies and (3) describing the workflow of the identified PCs.

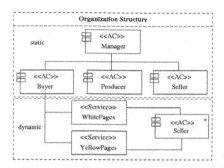

Fig. 5. Organization Structure

Modeling the organization structure. Here we describe the organization structure in an instantiated component model consisting of AC instances, yellow page services and white page services (see Fig. 5). This organization structure describes the acquaintance model (we call it AgentGroup) according to the pathways (stored in the slots) between the AC instances we have identified. Just to remember, we have identified the PCs before and therefore we have the PC description and the information which structural elements are required. For the organization structure we mainly need the slot information. The required slots must be created and filled with communication pathways (destinations) and that is what we model in this component diagram. If an AC instance (such as Buyer) includes a Project, that has dynamic behaviour and constructs its acquaintances during runtime, we model this by an association to the yellow or white pages (see Fig. 5).

Defining the context ontologies. In this step we define a context ontology for the AgentGroup. This ontology must describe all the concepts that the PCs need within their workflow. Fig. 6 provides an example ontology for purchasing, producing and selling cars modeled by a UML class diagrams.

Describing the workflow of the identified PCs. This step models the workflow of the identified PCs using UML activity diagrams [12]. In these diagrams we focus mainly on the WFInterface services *assert, retrieve, retract, receive and send* that the PCs use during their workflow. To disburden the activity diagrams we use an additional service named *change*, that models the change of an ontology instance in the knowledge base. We use one activity diagram for each PC. The ACs are represented by the swimlanes of the activity diagrams. Using these swimlanes we model the inter-agent workflow by sending objectflow states from one swimlane to another according to the created and

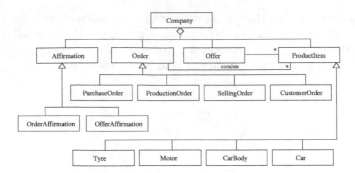

Fig. 6. Ontology example

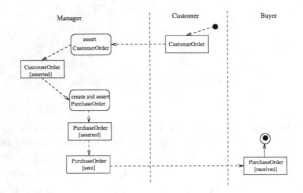

Fig. 7. Activity Diagram for PC "purchase" added to AC instance "Manager"

connected *slots*. The intra-agent communication is handled by the asserted, retracted, changed and retrieved statements. E.g. a PC waits (retrieve) until a
special ontology object has been asserted (assert) by another PC of the same
AC instance.

4   Tool Support

Currently we are developing the "AgentComponent Tool" (see Fig. 8) which
allows one to build MAS graphically consisting of ACs as introduced in this
paper (see section 2). This tool is based upon the JADE [8] framework for MAS
and already provides following features:
(1) Distributed construction and runtime customization of ACS [15],
(2) cstomizing the structure of the AC instances by different users and PCs,
(3) setting customizing permissions for different users,
(4) creating non-ACs and storing them in the slots of AC instances,
(5) using the InterAgent- and IntraAgentWorkflow services during runtime via
introspection.

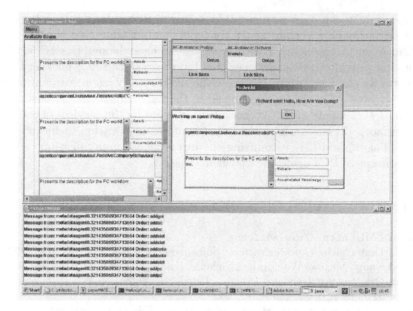

Fig. 8. AgentComponent Tool

5 Related Work

Although there exist many development and modeling approaches for agents [1, 3,10], the combination of agents and components is quite a new research field in agent technology. In our approach we borrow some concepts from existing works, e.g. the role model from [3], the activity diagram interaction protocols from [10, 12] (but in contrary to [10] we prefer a component- and model- oriented instead of a view-oriented development method) and different kinds of diagrams from the UML. And moreover we include combined agent and component technology aspects into these concepts. [5] also describes a component-based design method for agents. In contrast to [5] we have no compositional processes and knowledge, instead we have autonomously working processes (PCs). Moreover our AC provides infrastructure services but no workflow control for the processes as proposed by [5]. The AC approach does not focus on certain agent types like weak agents, strong agents or BDI-agents. The PCs can be implemented more or less *intelligently*, with beliefs, desires and goals or only with normal task execution functionality.

6 Concluding Remarks

Agent technology is a complex software technology. To make this technology easier to understand we need to encapsulate the complex concepts of agent technology in order to disburden the development of agent systems. And we found the component technology as a suitable means to disburden agent software development by making certain agent concepts customizable (see section 2) and reusable (AgentComponent). For this purpose we have defined the AC as a component that provides certain services (the interfaces of the AC) for every agent. In this way we can instantiate and reuse the AC for every agent we want to build and instantiated ACs can be customized in the following ways: (1) customizing the structural elements of the AC instance (achieved by the services of the StructuralInterface), (2) customizing the inter-agent communication (achieved by the concept of slots) and (3) customizing the intra-agent communication (achieved by the concept of PCs using the knowledge base).

References

1. Agent UML. http://www.auml.org.
2. Bernd Oesterreich. *Objektorientierte Softwareentwicklung*. Oldenbourg, 1998.
3. David Kinny, Michael Wooldridge, Nicholas Jennings. The GAIA Methodology for Agent-Oriented Analysis and Design. *Journal of Autonomous Agents and Multi-Agent Systems 3*, pages 285 – 312, 2000.
4. Desmond Francis D'Souza, Alan Cameron Wills. *Objects, Components and Frameworks With UML*. Addison Wesley, 1999.
5. Frances M.T. Brazier, Catholijn Jonker, Jan Treur. Principles of Component-Based Design of Intelligent Agents. *Data and Knowledge Engineering*, 41:1 – 28, 1998.
6. Frank Griffel. *Componentware*. dpunkt.verlag, 1998.
7. Grady Booch, James Rumbaugh, Ivar Jacobson. *The Unified Modeling Language User Guide*. Addison Wesley, 1998.
8. The JADE Programmers' Guide. http://sharon.cselt.it/projects/jade/.
9. John Cheesman, John Daniels. *UML Components, A Simple Process for Specifying Component-Based Software*. Addison Wesley, 2001.
10. Juergen Lind. The MASSIVE Development Method for Multiagent Systems. *In Proceedings of the Fifth International Conference on the Practical Application of Intelligent Agents and Multi-Agents (PAAM2000)*, 2000.
11. Juergen Lind. Relating Agent Technology and Component Models, 2001.
12. Juergen Lind. Specifying Agent Interaction Protocols with Standard UML. *In Proceedings of the Second International Workshop on Agent-Oriented Software Engineering (AOSE-2001)*, 2222, 2002.
13. M. Wooldridge and P.Ciancarini. Agent-Oriented Software Engineering: The State of the Art. *Agent-Oriented Software Engineering. Springer-Verlag Lecture Notes*, 1957, 2001.
14. Nick R. Jennings et al. Agent-Based Business Process Management. *ACM SIGMOD Record 27*, pages 32–39, 1998.
15. Philipp Meier, Martin Wirsing. Implementation Patterns for Visual Construction of Multi-Agent-Systems, Technical Report.
http://www.pst.informatik.uni-muenchen.de/publications/acpatterns.pdf.

From Simulated to Real Environments: How to Use SeSAm for Software Development

Franziska Klügl, Rainer Herrler, and Christoph Oechslein

Lehrstuhl für Künstliche Intelligenz und Angewandte Informatik
Institut für Informatik, Universität Würzburg
Am Hubland, 97074 Würzburg
{kluegl,herrler,oechslein}@informatik.uni-wuerzburg.de

Abstract. In this paper we want to show the possibilities to use agent-based modeling and simulation for software development. Therefore we present the integrated environment SeSAm and recent extensions, that allow creating simulated environments for agent based software as well as actually developing and deploying software agents.

1 Introduction

The development of agent-based software[1] is a quite hard task that incorporates difficulties like for example sophisticated software architectures, synchronization of concurrent processes with distributed control and data as well as unpredictability of interaction patterns [10]. For solving these problems, there exist not only diverse approaches for agent-oriented software engineering, but also lots of tools and frameworks for implementing agent-based software.

In spite of constant progress in agent-based software engineering the gap between specification and implementation is seldom addressed: The question is how to implement the completely designed agent system in a way that its validity and robustness is ensured? The problem here is twofold. On one hand the specification of the agent system has to be translated into executable code, on the other hand this code has to be tested thoroughly for validation and verification. We want to show in this paper, that – based on an existing simulation environment for agent-based models – tools can be provided that not only support the development of agent-based software but also the testing in different useful ways.

After going into more detail about agent-based software development, we continue in the remainder of the paper by presenting the modeling and simulation environment SeSAm, that allows visual agent modeling as well as experimenting and analyzing agent-based simulation experiments. In section 4 and

---

[1] We distinguish between "agent based software" and "agent based simulation" based on the environment the agent system is existing in. In agent based simulation the environment is also simulated and completely under the control of the modeler. Agent-based software is working in a real-world environment. Nevertheless, also developing agent-based simulations is sophisticated as well.

M. Schillo et al. (Eds.): MATES 2003, LNAI 2831, pp. 13–24, 2003.
© Springer-Verlag Berlin Heidelberg 2003

5 we describe the possibilities for using SESAM as a tool for supporting agent based software development. In the first place an approach will be proposed for modeling a simulated environment as a testbed for agent systems, afterwards we describe how to transfer automatically agent programs from simulated environments to real-world environments. We terminate with a short conclusion and outlook about further work.

2 Agent-Based Software Development and Simulation

Agent-based methodologies for engineering multi-agent systems try to direct the developers by providing process models for the single phases of development: requirement engineering, analysis and specification. They are mostly proposing graphical means for representing their outcomes. There is a huge amount of proposals that aim at supporting agent systems for distributed problem solving applications, e.g. GAIA [20], other agent-oriented software engineering methodologies are proposed specially for open agent systems, like [11]. A survey about methodologies and the problem in general can be e.g. found in [9].

However, the problem of actually producing code is left to traditional object-oriented procedures, as these methods merely stop at the design level. As another extreme, there are some formal specification frameworks that produce executable code. The earlier ones built upon temporal logic [4], BDI Logic [18] or Z schemes [14]. At least the logic-based frameworks have problems when applied to more complex problems with a lot of different agents.

More practically oriented frameworks were proposed by providing modifications and enhancements of UML specifications. The most famous is Agent UML [15] that was introduced to capture the flexible, high-level interactions between agents. Other specification languages concern class diagrams for specifying social concepts. MESSAGE/UML [2] is providing means for formulating knowledge-level concepts, like goals or roles by extending class and activity diagrams. Flake et al. [5] focus on how to generate code for a multi-agent system from UML diagrams based on a method called CASA.

On the other hand there are lots of tools for supporting the implementation by providing environments for the development of agent-based software with pre-defined building blocks of platforms according to FIPA standards. The *Agent Construction Tools* Site[2] lists (at 2003-05-11) 24 tools for mobile agents, agent infrastructure or development as commercial products and 36 products from research institutes. Another extensive, yet very heterogeneous list can be found on the AgentLink pages. Here only two environments for FIPA compliant platforms, like JADE[3] or FIPA-OS[4] should be mentioned. It seems that at least JADE is not only used by the developing institute.

Whereas there are some approaches for formal verification of agent-based software [21], testing agent-based software mostly refers to debugging issues.

---

[2] http://www.agentbuilder.com/AgentTools/

[3] http://sharon.cselt.it/projects/jade/ or [17]

[4] http://fipa-os.sourceforge.net/

There are no tools for systematic testing as e.g. are used in general modeling and simulation area for determining the sensitivity of a program to environmental changes. This is of course due to the fact that the environment in which the agent-based software will be deployed is not part of the implementation environment. If the tools provide a simulated environment in necessary detail testing agent based software would be facilitated. However, modeling and simulating the environment and also simulating the behavior of the agents in reaction to their abstracted, potentially simplified environment seems to be useful but seldomly manageable as it might require more than double work - implementing the real agent system, the simulated environment and the simulated agent system in this environment. Uhrmacher et al. propose in [19] to use reflection for adapting the agents behavior for acting in a simulated environment.

Our UML extensions (called SeSAmUML see [16]) focus on behavior-based specification of agents based on activity diagrams.It therefore share some similarities with some other specification languages or tools by also using the uml activity graph or the uml state graph (see [3,6,7]). Our approach for bridging the gap between specification and implementation is to provide a (complete) visual modeling tool that allows to build a specification based on analogous graphical primitives and afterwards implement this specification by adding additional information to render more precisely. The approach described here is different from Jade [17] or JACK [8] as it supports the simulation and the analysis of the simulation results of the implemented agent models. It also supports the visual modelling of behavior based agent type models in contrast to Jade (only a Java-framework with low-level predefined agent types) or JACK (which support BDI agent types but not continuous visual).

3   SeSAm

SeSAm stands for "Shell for Simulated Agent Systems". It provides a generic environment for modeling and experimenting with agent-based simulations. Its development was specially focused on providing a tool for the easy construction of complex models, as the main vision behind it was a tool for researchers without actual programming background [13].

In the following we want to present some important properties of SeSAm. We are currently working on a methodology for performing simulations, but have to evaluate and maybe modify it in the context of multi agent software development. Therefore we will present our results in addition to a deep evaluation and a long case study in a forthcoming paper. More information about SeSAm can obtained from http://www.simsesam.de.

3.1   SeSAmUML and Visual Agent Programming

SeSAm-Agents consist of a body that contains a set of state variables and a behavior that is implemented in form of UML-like activity diagrams. Activities (the nodes of an activity graph) are seen as scripts that are initiated and terminated by firing rules. Based on this simple concept both, a specification language and a software environment for modeling and simulation were developed.

The specification framework focuses on the representation of agent behavior especially in relation to other agents, resources or the general environment [16]. An example can be seen in figure 1. This is a part of a specification of a model about the evolution of sociality in ants. It shows the different agent classes, their behavior and interaction. Behavior graphs are augmented with class diagrams

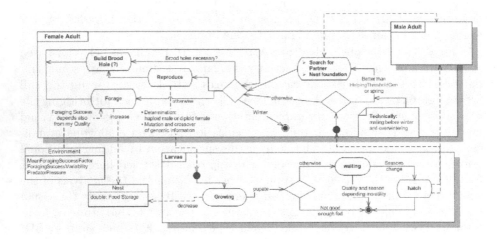

Fig. 1. Example specification of a biological model with interactions between different agents (Female, Male Adult and Larvae) and resources (Nest). Also some parameters of the general environment influence certain activities.

for the agents internal structure. Basically there is a predefined distinction between agents (active entities), resources (passive entities) and the environment (global surrounding). Only in simple models no protocol-type specification of the agents interaction is necessary. In these cases, most interaction consists mainly of implicit coordination: One agent changes the environment more or less deliberatively. Any other agent may perceive the modified surroundings and adapts its behavior according to it. More complex agent based models require a detailed specification of interaction sequences.

Such a specification of an agent-based simulation model can be directly implemented using SESAM, if the description provides sufficient details down to primitive actions and perception predicates. With every activity actions are associated which are executed when the agent is in this activity. Rules are responsible for termination and selection of activities. Actions of activities and conditions of rules can be composed from an extensive number of primitive building blocks. Figure 2 shows a screenshot of a part of the implementation of the specification shown in figure 1, namely central behavior of an agent of the class *female adult*.

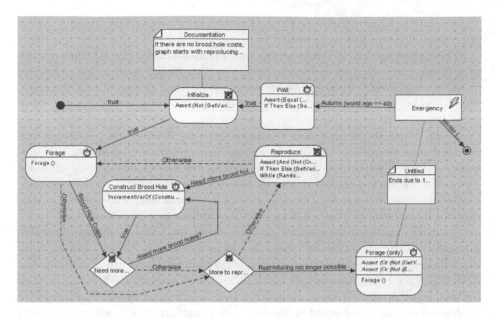

Fig. 2. Screenshot of an implemented SESAM-model: Partial behavior of an agent of the adult female class as specified in figure 1.

In addition to these normal activity nodes and rule arrows, also special forms of nodes like input or output nodes were introduce. These describe activities where the agent interacts with other agents and thus are marked for denoting this special purpose. Processing its activity graph initiates at the start node and terminates with the end node. The lifetime of an activity graph is over when the end node is selected. Activity graphs can be hierarchically organized in a way that a rule selects an activity graph instead of a simple activity. Additionally several activity graphs may determine the behavior of an agent in parallel. The agent itself is terminated when one of its activity graphs ends. Thus the implementation of rather complex behavior is possible that can even resemble the functionality of some reactive planning routines, like RAP.

As indicated in figure 2, a user is able to design visually the behavior of an agent. Analogous mechanisms are provided for specifying the static structures of an agent, an agent system or the environmental elements and their configuration. Thus a complete agent-based simulation model can be implemented visually without programming in a traditional programming language.

3.2 Modularization

Graphical modeling is built upon a set of predefined primitive elements – action primitive, perception primitive or operator primitive. They can be combined to function calls visualized in form of a tree. Such an expression can be constructed every time when needed, or can be composed into user functions with arguments.

They may represent more abstract building blocks or subroutines. Possible forms of combination are recursion, selection or composition.

The primitive actions, perceptions and operators form the interface to the underlying programming language Java. For integrating such a Java method, it has to "declared" with additional information that describe its arguments, functionality, etc. This declaration is interpreted for the visual programming integration.

A set of attributes and user functions may be defined independently and grouped to a so called "feature" representing some notion of additional non-basic abilities that can be assigned to agents (or the environmental classes). They may be implemented visually by the modeler supporting modularization. Predefined features are for example spatial representation and functions that capture movement, or gene attributes with evolutionary operators.

Another important issue is the question about the basic data types available for agents static structure and behavior implementation. In addition to standard data types, like boolean, numeric, string values there are also composed data types like hashtables or lists (with index-based access). Besides the built-in (or via features added) types a modeler can specify new types. They support sophisticated high-level agent structures and behaviors. There are two types of user types: enumerations and compositions. The range of first consists of a collection of predefined symbols, for example "female" and "male" for a data typ "gender". The value of a variable of this type is one element out of this collection, here e.g. "female". The second form of user defined data types is composition where an arbitrary number of attributes with other data types (also user defined ones) may be aggregated.

3.3 Database Interface and Ontology Import

For large input data it is neither comfortable nor useful to implement and fill complex data structures for simulation, since databases are available for the organization and storage of large data sets. Therefore a special feature provides an online interface to an JDBC database (mySQL). Attributes of agents (or the environment) can be connected to database entities. Thus, agents may read and write from and to these database entities. With this additional components real world data, e.g. weather data or task structures, may be integrated into an agent-based simulation. On the other hand, this is no one way connection. SeSAm may be used to to provide an dynamic testbed for intelligent systems that use information from the database e.g. for planning.

For complex (open) agent systems the first step for ensuring interaction abilities is to define an ontology that clarifies the common terms, relations. For certain domains, established ontologies exist. Thus grounding a simulation model on an already existing ontology increases readability and transparency of the modelled structures. This supports not only communication about the model, but also later enhancements of it. Therefore we developed an plugin for importing large parts of any ontology developed in Protege into SeSAm-models. The structures are directly converted to user data structures from where they can be converted using standard refactoring tools of SeSAm to agent or resource classes, attributes, etc.

3.4 Simulation and Experimentation Support

All information about and parts of a simulation model – from agent structure and behavior to relevant features and ready-to-run simulation run specification – are stored into a XML file based on a XML schema. Based on this model data format we developed a converter for a printable html visualization of a complete model.

Support for simulation cannot end when the model is implemented completely. Testing and executing experiments are also very demanding and effortful tasks. As there are freely configurable instruments for gathering data and scripting options for constructing simulation experiments on several computers concurrently, SeSAm is a highly valuable tool for agent based simulations.

However, due to fact, that SeSAm is made for agent based *simulations*, the programming facilities may only be used for agents in a simulated world that is completely under the control of the modeler. This does not work when aiming at agent-based software. Therefore we aim at extending the usability of SeSAm by adding new enhancements for relating SeSAm agents to real world agents. This will be presented in the following sections.

4 Simulation-Controlled MAS

Agent-based applications are part of an environment containing real world agents like users and other systems (possibly agent systems). In agent software development isolated tests are usually very difficult, instead tests have to be made under the conditions of this environment. As mentioned above, our idea was to extend SeSAm in a way that it can be used as a testbed for agent based software without re-modeling the agent for interacting with the simulated environment. Then, creating models of the global system becomes rather intuitive.

Figure 3 shows an sketch of two possible related scenarios. An agent based application is integrated in an environment consisting of additional information systems and users, that can also be seen as agents. The mapping of this scenario to a simulation controlled MAS is depicted in figure 3(b). All agents from the real-world environment are replaced by simulated agents in SeSAm. The level of detail of the simulation is depending on the requirements of the agent system. Due to the representation of the real-world in the simulated testbed the developed components can be tested both, under realistic as well as under extreme conditions. This usually cannot be done in the real world for reasons of cost or security.

4.1 Technical Base and Realization

To support connecting agent systems to SeSAm a new plugin was developed, that allows to extend SeSAm agents with FIPA compliant communication abili-

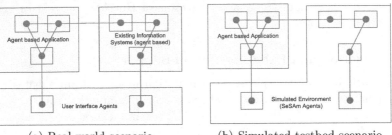

(a) Real world scenario   (b) Simulated testbed scenario

Fig. 3. Sketch of a possible development scenario where 3(a) describes the original situation and 3(b) represents the simulated environment.

ties. Extended in this way SESAM agents can interact with other agents running on any kind of FIPA platform. New primitives for registering and deregistering at a directory facilitator as well as for sending and receiving messages can be used in the SESAM models. This is supported by the ontology feature mentioned above enabling domain modelers to construct agents and message contents from ontology terms and concepts.

Thus, coupling agent applications and environment (either the real or the simulated one) is possible with less effort, since all systems use standardized interfaces.

Technically, the SESAM FIPA feature is realized by integrating and controling a complete JADE-platform. When SESAM is started the developer may start the JADE platform with special platform configuration parameters or allow the default start by SESAM. Since SESAM allows to make several simulation runs in parallel, each simulation run - when started - is associated with a single agent container within JADE. This concept is used to keep the different worlds separated.

SESAM agents in a running simulation can decide to create a representation of themselves in the associated JADE agent container. This agent can be seen as some kind of rather passive shadow. State representation and reasoning is still carried out by the SESAM agent, but all actions regarding the FIPA functionality (mainly communication tasks) are delegated to the JADE shadow. Received messages on the other hand are stored by the shadow in an incoming message queue until the SESAM agent performs a sensing action. The following primitive actions and functions were added to the SESAM primitive set:

- `StartJade()`: This function starts a local JADE platform, if it isn't already running. A window showing a view on this platform is opened.
- `CreateShadow()`: The acting agent decides to create his shadow identity. The functions described below can only be called if a shadow has been created before. Not every agent in simulation needs to have a shadow.
- `GetJadeAgentsOfName(name)`: This function returns a list of addresses of agents with a given name. When executed this function makes a query to

the directory service of the platform. The returned address (agent identifier) can be used to contact the agents.

- GetJadeAgentWithService(servicetype): This function returns a list of addresses of agents offering a certain service. The directory service at the local platform returns at matching candidates from the set of registered agents.

- IsACLMessagePending(): This boolean function returns true if the shadow agent has received at least one ACL-Messages. This message can then be received using the ReceiveACLMessage primitive.

- ReceiveACLMessage(): This function is used to receive a pending message, otherwise the simulation is blocked until a message is received. If such a blocking is not desired, one should use the IsACLMessagePending predicate before. The function returns the content of the message as well as the address of the sender for answering purposes.

- SendACLMessage(receiver, content): This function sends a message to another agent running on any FIPA agent platform.

4.2 Example Application: *Agent.Hospital*

A example of the development of a simulation controlled MAS is the integrated health care scenario *Agent.Hospital* [12]. In *Agent.Hospital* various agent based health care systems offer their services on FIPA compliant platforms. These multi agent systems have been linked together with a joint directory facilitator and have also been integrated into the worldwide network of agent platforms, named *Agentcities*.

Agent.Hospital was developed by a couple of research institutions across germany, working together in a priority research program founded by the german research foundation (DFG). For testing the participants agreed on creating a integrated simulation scenario that may be used by all systems concurrently. The central control of the integrated scenario was modelled with SESAM. An exemplified patient process was chosen, that required interaction with every projects agent system. The simulated patients were modelled by the domain experts, specifying all possible interactions with the agent applications. One prerequisite for interoperability of SESAM and the agent applications was the development of a hospital ontology [1] that was built by all the participants in advance. The final result was a simulation model of a virtual hospital, where software agents and simulated agent systems were integrated. Simulation runs can show the overall behavior of the resulting system consisting of many different multi-agent systems in whole. In addition integrating a new agent application into this overall environment shows whether the implemented interfaces are applicable.

This example application can be seen as a first evaluation even if we have to make a more representative evaluation in future. The experiment showed that it is possible and comparatively easy to create simulated testbeds for software agents.

5   SeSAm-Agents Breaking Out

SESAM development capabilities are not just limited to create environment simulations for software agents. As the language for agent behavior descriptions has the power of a programming language, it can be used for development of agent applications more directly by using the visual programming facilities for rapid agent development.

As described above, an agent behavior representation at specification level is provided, thus programming becomes quite comfortable and seems to be more like a modeling process, without any error-prone gaps between specification and running code. Therefore our idea is to take agents – implemented in SESAM – out of the simulated environment and apply them in agent based programs for real-world problem solving.

The first step towards this real-world applicability has already been made by enabling SESAM agents to communicate with FIPA agents. But this is not enough. In the next step, we let agents break out from the simulated environment. There are two possible ways of technical realization:

- **Interpreting Agent Wrapper:** A generic JADE agent was developed, that is able to load and interpret the SESAM behavior description. This generic agent wrapper works like an adapter around the agent description. We are now evaluating restrictions in SESAM behavior specification, that have to be meet for external use. Such restrictions for example are that step-wise simulation is not used implicitly for synchronization of agents or that the search for communication partners is done using a directory facilitator.
- **SeSAm to JAVA Compiler:** In some cases developers may prefer creating source code. This is a very common practice especially for building graphical user interface or code generation from UML diagrams. Code generation in SESAM is not yet available at the moment, however first promising steps have been undertaken.

Both approaches are very similar in their power, but there are some issues for deciding between compilation and interpretation. One might be that compiling restricts round trip engineering, as well as dynamic use during runtime. On the other side compiling might cause faster execution and is more flexible as the compiled result can be modified and extended manually.

However, when used for software development SESAM has to compete with existing integrated development environments for (non-visual) traditional programming languages. Due to the powerful, yet pre-defined agent structure and abilities, there is a huge potential for providing e.g. online syntax consistency tests, refactoring and debugging functions. For facilitating the development on agent-based simulation models we already offer some of these features.

As a small test example we used a simple supply chain model for bicycle production. Results showed that is it possible to use the XML behavior description outside a simulated environment based on a wrapper for SESAM agent in JADE. The next steps are integrating interfaces for users and other real-world data sources. Another focus is the general applicability of this approach.

6   Conclusion and Further Work

In this paper we presented several approaches for practically relating agent-based simulation and software development. We showed, how virtual environments for agent based software can be created based on the interoperability features of SeSAm. The feasibility and utility of this approach was shown with the *Agent.Hospital* project. A more visionary proposal focused on the re-use of the powerful visual agent programming facilities of SeSAm for allowing simulated agents to be deployed in real world. The interpretation approach for the transfer of simulated agents to real-word environments is almost available, whereas the development of the compilation approach just has started. For further development of the approaches presented here, more sophisticated application scenarios are necessary and also further improvements in SeSAm concerning implementation support.

Another important point is that agent dynamics in SeSAm are just described in activity graphs, not generated based on goals and planning abilities. This would be necessary for applications of really intelligent agents. Their development would profit a lot from the abstract structures and visual interfaces provided by SeSAm. Enhancement in the SeSAm agent abilities are not only under realization for scheduling, but also planned for goal-oriented behavior.

Acknowledgement. The authors would like to thank Alexander Huber and his students from the TU Erlangen for their implementation of the database interface. The work described in this paper was partially supported by DFG under SFB 554 (Christoph Oechslein) and SPP 1083 (Rainer Herrler).

References

1. Becker, M., Heine, C., Herrler, R. and Krempels, K.H. 2002. *OntHoS - an Ontology for Hospital Scenarios*. In: Technical Report No. 300, Julius-Maximilians-Universität Würzburg, Institut für Informatik, September, 2002
2. Caire, G., Coulier, W., Garijo, F., Gomez, J., Pavon, J., Leal, F., Chainho, P., Kearney, P., Stark, J., Evans, R. and Ph. Massonet. 2001. *Agent Oriented Analysis Using Message/UML* in. Agent-Oriented Software Engineering, LNCS 2222, pp. 119ff
3. DeLoach, S.: Analysis and Design using MaSE and agentTool. In: *Proceedings of the 12th Midwest Artificial Intelligence and Cognitve Science Conference (MAICS 2001)*. Oxford, Ohio, 2001
4. Fisher, M. 1995.   Representing and Executing Agent-Based Systems.   In Wooldridge, M. and Jennings, N. R., editors, *Intelligent Agents: Proceedings of the ATAL'94*, volume 890 of *LNAI*, pages 307–323. Springer.
5. Flake, S., Geiger, Ch. and J. Küster. 2001. *Towards UML-based Analysis and Design of Multi-Agent Systems* In. International NAISO Symposium on Information Science Innovations in Engineering of Natural and Artificial Intelligent Systems (ENAIS'2001), Dubai March 2001.

6. Gervais, M.-P. ; MUSCUTARIU, F.: Towards an ADL for Designing Agent-Based Systems. In: *Proc. of Agent-Oriented Software Engineering (AOSE) 2001, Agents 2001, Montreal*, 2001, S. 49–56

7. Griss, M. ; Fonseca, S. ; Cowan, D. ; Kessler, R.: Using UML State Machine Models for More Precise and Flexible JADE Agent Behaviors. In: *Proceedings of the Third International Workshop on Agent-Oriented Software Engineering (AOSE-02), Bologna, Italy*, 2002

8. Howden, N. ; Rönnquist, R. ; Hodgson, A. ; Lucas, A.: JACK Intelligent Agents — Summary of an Agent Infrastructure. In: *5th International Conference on Autonomous Agents*, URL http://www.agent-software.com, 2001

9. Iglesias, C., Garijo, M., and J. C. Gonzales. 1999. A Survey of Agent-Oriented Methodologies. In Müller, J. P., Singh, M., and Rao, A. S., editors, *Intelligent Agents V: Proceedings of the ATAL'98*, volume 1555 of *LNAI*. Springer.

10. Jennings, N. R. 2000 On Agent-Based Software Engineering. *Artificial Intelligence*, 117:277–296, 2000.

11. Juan, T., Pearce, A. and L. Sterling. 2002. *ROADMAP: Extending the Gaia Methodology for Complex Open Systems* Proceedings of the First International Joint Conference on Autonomous Agents and Multi-Agent Systems (AAMAS 2002), Bologna, Italy, July 2002.

12. Kirn, S., Heine, C., Herrler, R. and K. H. Krempels. 2003. *Agent.Hospital - Agent-Based Open Framework for Clinical Applications* accepted at WETICE, Linz, June 2003.

13. Klügl, F. 2001. *Multi Agent Simulation - Concepts, Tools, Application*(in german), Addison Wesley, München

14. Luck, M., Griffiths, N. and M. d'Inverno. 1997. From Agent Theory to Agent Construction. In Müller, J. P., Wooldridge, M. J., and Jennings, N. R., editors, *Intelligent Agents III (= Proceedings of ATAL'96)*, volume 1193 of *Lecture Notes in Artificial Intelligence*, pages 49–63. Springer.

15. Odell, J., van Dyke Parunak, H., and B. Bauer. 2000. Extending UML for Agents. In *Proceedings of Agent-Oriented Information Systems 2000, Workshop at the AAAI 2000*.

16. Oechslein, C., Klügl, F., Herrler, R. and F. Puppe, 2002. *UML for Behavior-Oriented Multi-Agent Simulations*. In: Dunin-Keplicz, B., Nawarecki, E.: From Theory to Practice in Multi-Agent Systems, CEEMAS 2001 Cracow, Poland, September 26-29, 2001, (= LNCS 2296), Springer, Heidelberg, pp. 217ff

17. Poggi, A. ; Rimassa, R.: JADE - A FIPA-compliant agent framework. In: *Proceedings of PAAM'99, London*, 1999, S. 97–108

18. Rao, A. S. 1996. *AgentSpeak(L): BDI Agents Speak Out in a Logical Computable Language* In W. Van de Velde and J. W. Perram, editors, Agents Breaking Away: Proceedings of the 7 th 24 European Workshop on Modeling Autonomous Agents in a Multi-Agent World, (LNAI Volume 1038), 42-55. Springer-Verlag.

19. Uhrmacher, A. M., Kullick, B. and J. Lemcke. 2002. *Reflection in Simulating and Testing Agents*. In 16th European Meeting on Cybernetics and Systems Research (EMCSR 2002), 2002.

20. Wooldridge, M., Jennings, N. R., and D. Kinny. 1999. A Methodology for Agent-Oriented Analysis and Design. In *Proceedings of the 3rd Internation Conference on Autonomous Agents,1999*. ACM Press.

21. Wooldridge, M. 1997. Agent-Based Software Engineering. *IEE Proc. on Software Engineering*, 144(1):26–37, 1997.

Indicators for Self-Diagnosis: Communication-Based Performance Measures

Michael Rovatsos[1], Michael Schillo[2], Klaus Fischer[2], and Gerhard Weiß[1]

[1] Department of Informatics, Technical University of Munich,
Boltzmannstraße 3, 85748 Garching, Germany
{rovatsos, weissg}@informatik.tu-muenchen.de

[2] German Research Center for Artificial Intelligence (DFKI),
Stuhlsatzenhausweg 3, 66123 Saarbrücken, Germany
{schillo, kuf}@dfki.de

Abstract. Multiagent systems (MAS) have found their way into industrial applications in recent years and appear to be one of the most promising technologies that originated in AI research in recent years. However, evaluation standards as they are common e.g. in the scheduling or database systems communities are largely amiss. In this paper, we propose *communication-based performance measurement* (CBPM) as a new method that is particularly suitable for open, communication-intensive MAS, and argue that it can be used as to design *indicators for self-diagnosis* by the MAS itself. The ability of such self-diagnosis is a prerequisite for MAS with self-repairing and self-optimising properties required by the *autonomic computing* view. CBPM is based on the idea that important aspects of the external behaviour of a MAS can be measured in terms of the communication processes within them. We present different levels of communication-based performance measurement: frequency analysis of performatives and analysis of complex message patterns. Several examples of analyses of inter-agent communication based on FIPA-ACL and the contract-net protocol in implemented, complex, market-oriented MAS demonstrate the usefulness of our approach. We conclude that these performance measures provide useful information about MAS and pave the way for devising autonomic self-improvement methods for these systems.

1 Introduction

In the last few years, multiagent systems (MAS) have been increasingly successful in industrial applications [9], particularly as a paradigm used for systems that have to operate in complex, dynamic, distributed domains. Recently, *autonomic computing* [10] has been proclaimed as a new approach to industrial systems that are capable of *self-management*, i.e. that have *self-configuring*, *self-healing*, *self-optimising* and *self-protecting* capabilities. It is believed that this can be achieved through a peer-to-peer collaboration of *managers* that control the use of computational resources (databases, networks, storage facilities, etc.), measure system properties and decide what steps to take to improve performance, usability or security in the system.

From a MAS perspective, these managers can be seen as agents that observe the system and take appropriate action. However, this can be particularly difficult in *open*,

M. Schillo et al. (Eds.): MATES 2003, LNAI 2831, pp. 25–37, 2003.

communication-intensive systems (cf. Internet agents, ubiquitous computing) where the internal design of system components is highly encapsulated and hence not always accessible for manager agents. The increasing popularity of technologies such as Web Services and open platforms for agent-based service deployment such as Agentcities [1] calls for methods to measure and influence the behaviour of system resources at the level of *communication* rather than direct control.

Starting from this observation, this paper develops methods for *communication-based performance measurement* (CBPM) for MAS that are based on an analysis of the communication processes that unfold during operation of these systems. We claim that these measures have the potential to become valuable *performance indicators* when such systems are analysed by manager agents, and that this *self-diagnosis* is capable of providing useful guidance in trying to meet external requirements such as *self-repair* and *self-optimisation*. To this end, we propose several such performance measures and illustrate their usefulness with practical examples.

The remainder of the paper is structured as follows: Section 2 describes briefly our intuitions regarding communication-based performance measurement and the general ideas behind it. Then, in Section 3, we introduce the generic model of MAS that we use to define measures. Section 4 provides detailed definitions for the proposed performance measures. This is followed by illustrative examples in Sections 5 and 6. Finally, we sum up with a discussion in Section 7.

2   Why Communication-Based Performance Measurement?

In the process of designing and developing software systems, developers have several attributes of the final product in mind, such as e.g. availability, security, modifiability. Ideally, software engineering methods should give off-the-shelf advice on how to proceed in the process of engineering the system in order to achieve these requirements. This is a core aspect of *performance engineering* [5], where it is common practice to distinguish between

- *internal attributes* of the product (i.e. those which can be measured purely in terms of the product itself) and
- *external attributes* of the product (i.e. those which can only be measured with respect to how the product relates to its environment).

In general, internal attributes are more domain-independent and easy to measure, which does not hold for external attributes. Therefore, it is highly desirable to predict the values of external attributes (e.g. usability and comprehensibility) on the basis of measurements regarding internal attributes (such as resource load, errors during stress testing, etc). From the standpoint of autonomic computing, manager agents take over the role of the performance engineer during operation of the system: they must measure *internal* attributes of the system (such as exchange of information between components, data storage strategies etc.) to be able to predict *external* attributes, such as optimal responsiveness, data security, etc.

When dealing with open systems of communicating agents, managers are additionally confronted with systems in which the precise operation of computational sub-processes (agents) cannot be predicted *a priori*: achieving effective measurement and control is very difficult in the absence of full knowledge of the internal design of other agents. It is therefore not surprising that the issue of *performance measurement* of MAS has been largely avoided[1] despite the fact that successful engineering methods have been proposed for MAS in recent years by researchers in the field of *agent-oriented software engineering* [7,13].

Effectively, all we are left with as a basis for performance measurement in open MAS is the *communication* observed in the system, and this is the central idea behind *communication-based performance measurement* (CBPM): to use *communication data* between agents in the system as data material that is suitable for performance measurement, and then defining appropriate measures for this kind of data. Thereby, we define any data as communication that is either (a) a textual message passed between two or more agents or (b) some (physical) action that an agent performs publicly, i.e. an action that can be observed by at least one agent other than itself.

Although open systems "force" us to take such an approach by the encapsulation of agent internal computation, two fundamental properties of MAS, namely that

- MAS are (usually) based on deliberative, knowledge-based agents, and that
- agents in MAS communicate using high-level languages such as KQML [8] or FIPA-ACL [6]

also suggest that the approach offers several *advantages*:

1. Even if reliable mental models of the agents are not available in open systems, high-level ACLs allow us to derive the states of social commitments, the intentions of agents etc. to a certain degree. This is due to the semantics we *impute* on the ACL performatives – even if they are violated by agents, this will eventually become evident in observable agent behaviour (e.g. if a promise is not kept). Thus, high-level ACLs allow for a tracing of much more abstract types of interactions and dependencies than, for example, low-level network communication.
2. This kind of measurement allows us to abstract from non-communicative properties of the system so that we can immensely reduce the global complexity of the system. Knowing that agents are able to process knowledge-level representations (of tasks, environment states, etc.) allows us to ignore the details of their internal reasoning (in fact, in open systems, we have no other choice); at the same time, we can expect at least those aspects that are relevant to the interaction between components to become visible in the contents of messages, and hence open to an analysis by the manager agent (who is a knowledge-based agent in turn).

Motivated by these advantages, we need to identify and precisely define concrete measures. As a prerequisite for these definitions, we first introduce the underlying model of MAS.

---

[1] Rare and only application-specific exceptions include work on resource management for grid computing [3] or on mobile agents, where performance measures concentrate on computation overhead for message passing and agent migration [4].

3   A Generic MAS Model

Our MAS consists of a set of agents $\mathcal{A} = \{a, b, c, \dots\}$ (that need not be fixed over time), which (among other things) are able to communicate with each other by using a speech-act based agent communication language (like KQML [8] or FIPA-ACL [6]) the semantics of which is accessible to every agent[2].

Furthermore, we assume that the MAS has to perform tasks taken from a fixed set of possible tasks $\mathcal{T}$ and that they "arrive" at the system at arbitrary points in time (they may enter the system via some central "manager" agent or through different agents). To allow for a more detailed evaluation, we assume that a real-valued measure

$$c : \mathcal{T} \to \mathbb{R}$$

for the cost of the tasks is defined by the observer of the system that is measuring its performance.

The general view that we have of such task-based MAS is that when tasks come in, a negotiation process is initiated, which leads to either agreement or conflict. In the case of agreement, agents agree on a coordinated joint plan which they then execute. Otherwise, the task fails and the next task is processed. If agents reach consensus on how to perform the task, they execute the joint plan, and enter additional negotiation loops in case of further conflicts. Also, in some cases, plans may fail during execution.

In the following definitions, we will assume that a FIPA-ACL-subset of speech acts is used by the agents and we will use a simplified syntax for messages of the format

performative(sender, receiver, content)

where sender and receiver are symbolic names for agents and content is either some other message or some first-order logic formula. As the set of performatives we define for the scope of this paper

$$\begin{aligned}
\text{performative} \in \{ \ &\text{inform}, \text{inform\_done}, \text{inform\_ref}, \\
&\text{agree}, \text{accept\_proposal}, \text{request}, \\
&\text{cfp}, \text{reject\_proposal}, \text{propose}, \\
&\text{failure}, \text{not\_understood}, \text{refuse} \}
\end{aligned}$$

which is a subset of the performatives defined by FIPA [6]. In real-world applications, this set is usually extended or restricted according to the requirements of the interaction protocols used.

Finally, and maybe most importantly, in all measures we define we will use *message-time* as the underlying time-scale, i.e. instead of measuring (real) time, we measure all quantities with respect to the *total number of messages* ($TNOM$) that have occurred during operation. In the following, let

---

[2] Otherwise agents have to make huge efforts to "understand" communication, a topic which opens a whole new dimension of complexity and is not regarded here. However, obeying *semantics* by no means implies benevolence regarding *pragmatics*.

$$M = \{m_1, m_2, \ldots m_n\}$$

denote the set of all messages ($TNOM = |M|$). If needed, we can partition M into sets

$$M_T = \{m_{T_1}, \ldots m_{T_{n_i}}\}$$

for task $T \in \mathcal{T}_{curr}$ where $\mathcal{T}_{curr} \subseteq \mathcal{T}$ is the set of past processed tasks (including the task currently processed) such that

$$M = \biguplus_{T \in \mathcal{T}_{curr}} M_T$$

The advantage that measuring messages offers compared to measuring time directly is that we can (a) quantify communicative phenomena in relation to the total amount of communication so as to assess their importance in the context of all ongoing communication, (b) neglect time spent on intra-agent reasoning, and hence be able to concentrate on crucial (social) properties of the system. Although this is an abstraction, the loss of accuracy can be neglected in many deployed systems, as the time spend for communication between agents (on different machines) dominates other processes.

4   Communication-Based Performance Measures

4.1   Basic Measures

Basic measures rely on counting messages and atomic message types (i.e. certain performatives) and are therefore the simplest CBPM measures that serve as a starting point for any analysis of social system properties. The first measure we introduce is *messages per task and cost* ($MPTC$) and is computed by using the formula

$$MPTC = \sum_{T \in \mathcal{T}_{curr}} \frac{M_T}{c(T)}$$

Here the quantity $MPTC$ reflects how much communication is "spent" on a task per cost. In order to obtain comparable quantities of $MPTC$, the numbers of messages M_T are normalised with the cost of the tasks, following the intuition that it is justified for more expensive tasks to require more communication than cheaper ones. Normally, we expect MAS to be operating most efficiently, for which $MPTC$ is minimal (except, of course, if $MPTC$ takes on *extremely* small values which would mean that tasks are completed or fail without almost any communication – in which case communication does not make a difference or is not working properly).

This measure can be further refined by distinguishing assigned tasks between "failed" and "successfully completed" tasks

$$\mathcal{T}_{curr} = \mathcal{T}_{succ} \uplus \mathcal{T}_{failed}$$

and computing a "fail-fast" variant of $MPTC$

$$\text{ff\_}MPTC = \alpha \cdot \sum_{T \in \mathcal{T}_{succ}} \frac{M_T}{c(T)} + \beta \cdot \sum_{T \in \mathcal{T}_{failed}} \frac{M_T}{c(T)}$$

By using $0 \leq \alpha \ll \beta \leq 1$ we can weigh the amount of communication spent on failed tasks stronger than that spent on tasks successfully completed, thus implicitly expecting effectively communicating agents (that minimise ff_$MPTC$) to realise at an early stage that a task cannot be completed.

Looking more closely at the properties of messages exchanged rather than only counting them, we can determine the average usage of certain message *types* if we assume that the set of relevant performatives has been partitioned into such types according to certain criteria. For the scope of this paper we suggest the following partition for the list of performatives given above:

- *Type1* = {request} for messages that indicate when agents require non-local information from others,
- *Type2* = {inform, inform_done, inform_ref} for messages that can only be a reply to some question and hence indicate propagation of information among agents, or are used for synchronisation,
- *Type3* = {cfp, propose} to denote messages that indicate offers to accept a task or calls for such offers,
- *Type4* = {reject_proposal, refuse} for messages that indicate when *Type3* messages fail,
- *Type5* = {accept_proposal, agree} for messages that indicate when *Type3* messages succeed, and finally
- *Type6* = {not_understood, failure} for messages indicating either messages that are not understood or requests that cannot be handled.

In analogy to a frequency analysis of each performative (which we will come back to later), we define the *mean message type usage (MMTU)* to be

$$MMTU(x) = \frac{1}{|\mathcal{T}_{curr}|} \sum_{T \in \mathcal{T}_{curr}} \frac{|\{m \in M_i | type(m) = x\}|}{|M_T|}$$

for $x \in \{Type1, Type2, Type3, Type4, Type5, Type6\}$ to compute the average percentage of a certain message type per task. Using these values, a visualisation called *message type partition chart* can be derived that provides us with a message type profile for a specific MAS as shown in the example in Figure 1. In this example, we are dealing with a MAS in which the largest portion of all messages is spent on gathering non-local information, i.e. agents are very busy attempting to obtain information from their peers. The chart also reveals that many of these questions go unanswered ($MMTU(Type2) < MMTU(Type1)$) so obviously "information exchange" is not efficient in this system (either questions are posed that cannot be answered, or agents refuse to answer too often).

Apart from asking other agents, the agents in this system are also very busy offering and asking for services (*Type3*), and these attempts are much more often unsuccessful than successful ($MMTU(Type4) > MMTU(Type5)$). Quite often, there is no reaction at all, which is reflected by

$$MMTU(Type4) + MMTU(Type5) < MMTU(Type3)$$

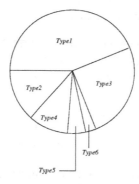

Fig. 1. A message type partition chart.

Obviously, such measurements are valuable starting points for improving system performance. Moreover, $MMTU$ can be easily further refined, which makes it a very flexible and powerful measure. As an example, we might compute its value also depending on task cost as in

$$MMTU(x, c_1, c_2) = \frac{1}{|\mathcal{T}_{curr}^{c_1, c_2}|} \sum_{T \in \mathcal{T}_{curr}^{c_1, c_2}} \frac{|\{m \in M_i | type(m) = x\}|}{|M_T|}$$

where

$$\mathcal{T}_{curr}^{c_1, c_2} = \{T \in \mathcal{T}_{curr} | c_1 \leq c(T) \leq c_2\}$$

is the set of all tasks that whose cost lies in the interval between c_1 and c_2. This would allow us to make more precise statements with respect to the distribution of message types, and the same would be the case if we parametrise $MMTU$ with e.g. certain subsets of agents, of agent types, spatial regions in a network, etc.

4.2   Measuring Complex Message Patterns

The measures introduced above already provide useful information about the amount of communication and its distribution over classes of performatives, but they do not allow for a *syntactic* analysis of entire dialogues and protocols. To achieve such an analysis, we introduce *message patterns* where we interpret sequences of messages as lists of strings and use upper-case variables $A, B, \ldots$ to denote messages or message fields that may be referred to by later messages in the same sequence. Furthermore, we use $*$ as a wildcard symbol that stands for an arbitrary message sequence. For example, a pattern

$$p = [\texttt{accept}(A, B, \texttt{do}(A, X)), *, \texttt{do}(A, X)]$$

describes a set of messages that starts with an acceptance of agent A towards agent B to perform action X and ends with A actually performing X [3]. Likewise,

---

[3] Remember that this is only a communication if the execution of X is observable for both parties – the performative do (which is not part of the language definition, in the sense of FIPA-ACL) is used to signify such observable action execution.

$$q = [\texttt{accept}(A, B, \texttt{do}(A, X)), (\neg\texttt{do}(A, X))^n]$$

stands for the set of sequences in which A does not fulfil its commitment for at least n steps after committing itself to do X.

Clearly, such patterns can be efficiently matched against messages in a message log. Hence, for any such pattern p we can measure the average length of its occurrence

$$mean\_length(p) = \frac{1}{\mathcal{T}_{curr}} \sum_{matches(m,p) \wedge m \in M} length(m)$$

where $matches(m, p)$ is a boolean function that returns $\texttt{true}$ iff pattern p matches message sequence m and $length(m)$ is the number of messages in sequence m. Alternatively, we can define the *task-relative* average length of p as

$$mean\_length(p) = \frac{1}{\mathcal{T}_{curr}} \sum_{matches(m,p) \wedge m \in M} \frac{length(m)}{|M_T|}$$

and, of course, also its frequency

$$frequency(p) = \frac{|\{m \in M | matches(m, p)\}|}{|M|}$$

Average lengths and frequencies can be used to define a number of other useful performance measures. For instance, consider a MAS in which agents exchange proposals concerning a multiagent plan to execute a task and where their peers can either $\texttt{agree}$ to a proposed plan or reject a proposed plan by $\texttt{reject\_proposal}$. Assume further that for a plan to be executed, all agents have to accept it. We can then define

$$p_a = \bigcap_{Q \in \mathcal{A}}[\texttt{propose}(P, Q, X), *, \texttt{accept}(Q, P, X)],$$
$$p_c = \bigcup_{Q \in \mathcal{A}}[\texttt{propose}(P, Q, X), *, \texttt{reject}(Q, P, X))]$$

as the set of sequences in which *all* agents (*at least one* agent) Q eventually accept/reject P's proposal X. Accordingly, we can define

$$MTTA = mean\_length(p_a),$$
$$MTTC = mean\_length(p_c)$$

where $MTTA$ stands for *mean time to agreement* and $MTTC$ stands for *mean time to conflict*. Likewise, patterns can be defined for task allocation, resource allocation, conflict resolution, negotiation processes, etc. In particular, if a specific set of *interaction protocols* is used in the MAS, properties of enacted instances of these protocols can be quantified, e.g. the number of bids in an auction, the *mean time to accepted bid* etc. Quite evidently, these kinds of measures can be superior when it comes to predicting the behaviour of external attributes: if we consider *responsiveness* as a required external attribute in a parallel execution environment for agents, surely $MTTA$ is more expressive than $TNOM$, as probably many messages are sent in parallel while we are interested in the length of the sequence until an agreement is reached.

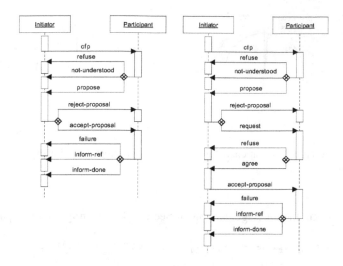

Fig. 2. Sequence diagrams for the contract-net (left) and contract-net-with-confirmation (right) protocols.

5   Example 1: Evaluating Interaction Protocols

To see how applying measures of different complexity can be useful, we now demonstrate the usage of the above classes of measures in the context of a practical and relevant problem. Suppose a specific *protocol manager agent* in the MAS has to decide on the task assignment method used in the system, and that there are one hundred *task manager* agents each of which needs to find a *bidder agent* for a task it has to assign. Suppose for simplicity all bidder agents have identical capabilities, i.e. any bidder can execute any task in principle, yet only a *single* task at a time and the communication deadlines are at the same time. Assume further that the protocol manager agent may choose between the contract-net protocol (CNP) [12] and the contract-net-with-confirmation protocol (CNCP) (for a detailed description, see [11]). Let us further suppose that he has tried both mechanisms on comparable problem instances. In a (representative) experiment with our implemented system, the *assigned tasks ratio* (ATR) (i.e. the ratio between tasks successfully assigned and the total number of tasks) was 1.0 using the CNCP while the CNP had an ATR of only 0.65.

How is this possible? The sequence diagrams of the protocols (see Figure 2) do not reveal the crucial difference in the sense that they could be used as the starting point for an informed decision between the two protocols. Let us now apply the measures introduced in the previous sections. First, we evaluate $TNOM$ (20130 for CNP, 30768 for CNCP) and perform an $MMTU$ analysis of the communication that occurred during the experiments (Figure 3). Although it is obvious that the protocols influence the occurrence of certain performatives, in this particular case $TNOM$ and $MMTU$ bring us no closer to an explanation why the ATR of the CNCP is so much higher.

Fig. 3. Message type partition chart for the the same problem solved using CNP (left) and the CNCP (right).

Remembering the message patterns of Section 4.2, we might look at pattern

$$p = [\texttt{propose}(A, B, X, \{\}), *, \texttt{reject\_proposal}(B, A, X)]$$

This means we search agent communication logs for unconditional proposals (side condition is $\{\}$) implying resource allocations (i.e. commitments to be able to perform a task in the future) which are followed by rejection and measure *mean rejected resource allocations* $MRRA = frequency(p)$[4]. And indeed, in our example we find that $MRRA$ equals *zero* in the CNCP case, and 0.35 in the CNP case. The former case indicates that with the CNCP no resources are allocated before it is clear that they are going to be used, while the latter represents the missing allocations expressed by the low ATR of the CNP. This shows at a glance the superiority of the CNCP in the respect that it never produces the sequence "allocating resources" $\rightarrow$ "rejecting this allocation".

This example illustrates that a more complex measure can explain the correlation between an internal attribute $MRRA$ and the external attribute ATR when simpler measures, such as $MPTC$ and $MMTU$ are not.

6   Example 2: Evaluating the Optimal Amount of Communication

Next, picture the situation of a manager agent who maintains the platform on which the above multiagent system is running, with the decision on using the CNCP instead of the CNP already made due to the above considerations. To make the scenario more interesting, assume that the manager agent has no control over the participating agents, which we call *clients* (previously managers), and *service providers* (previously bidders) but it can set the standard protocol to be used. Of course, costs for providing a service may vary, as may the price preferences of clients, i.e. there is no guarantee that tasks get assigned at all. Also, suppose that, for reasons of publicity (and to raise banner advertisement prices), the platform owner is interested in having as many "deals fixed" (tasks assigned) as possible. To reduce bandwidth, one of the parameters the platform may prescribe to participating agents is the maximum number of *contacted agents*,

---

[4] This is a simplified version of the pattern used for $MTTC$ in which negotiation only occurs between one manager and one bidder, and it is adapted to the needs of CNP-like negotiation by additionally requiring the empty side condition.

Table 1. r_1 and r_2 in different simulations.

r_1	Clients			r_2	Clients		
n	90	100	110	n	90	100	110
10	0.21	0.25	0.29	10	0.51	0.61	0.69
20	0.10	0.15	0.20	20	0.50	0.67	0.75

i.e. the maximal number n of calls-for-proposals/proposals (for clients/service providers, respectively). Now assume that the platform manager observes six different series of MAS runs. In the first three runs, 100 service providers and 90, 100, and 110 clients participate with $n = 10$; in another three runs, the same configurations apply, but now $n = 20$ allows for more communication. The platform manager agent, wants to know whether the cost induced by doubling the admissible amount of communication has paid off. To this end, it analyses the patterns

$$p_p = [\mathtt{cfp}(P, Q, X), \mathtt{propose}(Q, P, Y), \mathtt{request}(P, Q, Y)]$$
$$p_r = [\mathtt{cfp}(P, Q, X), *, \mathtt{refuse}(Q, P, X)]$$
$$p_d = [\mathtt{cfp}(P, Q, X), *, \mathtt{accept\_proposal}(Q, P, Y)]$$

p_p represents situations in which a proposal is followed by a request, sequences that match p_r represent "failures" of service providers (in which they cannot perform a task although they bid for it because they committed to some other task in the meantime). Sequences that match p_d, finally, mark "deals", i.e. assigned tasks that are properly carried out. Table 1 shows the values of the following quantities in the six runs we obtained from experiments in the described configurations:

$$r_1 = frequency(p_p) \text{ and } r_2 = \frac{frequency(p_r)}{frequency(p_p)}$$

Two central observations can be made: while an increase of client population from 90 to 110 causes an increase in probability r_1 (i.e. the ratio of proposals that are accepted by the client) by less than 50% in the $n = 10$ case (from 0.21 to 0.29), it *doubles* r_1 in the $n = 20$ case (from 0.10 to 0.20). Of course, it is only natural that if more clients are present, the probability increases with which the price they are willing to pay is met by some service provider. However, it looks as if being allowed to contact more potential partners increases this probability super proportional, when a bigger choice of clients is available.

On the other hand, the second table shows that the probability r_2 of not being able to perform a task although requested to do so by the client increases *stronger* in the case of $n = 20$ (from 0.5 to 0.75) than if $n = 10$ (from 0.5 to 0.69), which makes the benefits of allowing for more communication smaller; at the end of the day, $frequency(p_d) = 0.044$ in the case of $n = 20$ while $frequency(p_d) = 0.084$ in the case of $n = 10$ (with 110 clients). In other words, doubling the amount of communication (and their cost) leads to 98 assigned (and performed tasks), which is only little more than the 93 reached with $n = 10$.

Apparently, increasing the number of calls for proposals and proposals each agent may make is not very advantageous, because it makes service providers send more proposals than they are able to achieve tasks, which limits the benefits incurred by increasing the number of "matches" between clients' and providers' prices.

Therefore, the platform manager should maybe look for alternatives to increasing n if the number of participating clients increases, such as, for example, introducing "match-making" agents that find suitable service providers for clients with less communication. This is another example of how using CBPM as an analytical tool may help meet design objectives that cannot be achieved by merely tuning the system in a trial-and-error fashion.

7 Conclusion

In this paper, we suggested *communication-based performance measurement* (CBPM) for multiagent systems, a novel approach to measuring system performance based on measurements of communicative processes among agents. We argued that CBPM measures are particularly suitable as *indicators* for the self-diagnosis of autonomic computing systems, where manager agents conduct these measurements and take appropriate steps to spawn *self-repair* and *self-optimisation* processes.

Our examples of measurements in implemented, large-scale, market-based MAS proved that these measurements provide guidance for such managers, and that they can help improve system performance in *open* systems even without direct access to agents' internal control mechanisms. When employing the full analytical power of CBPM, even simple actions such as reducing message limits or adopting different protocols for the system may significantly influence the global behaviour of the system.

The problem that remains is the online derivation of these performance measures for any given domain. Obviously, this is not an easy enterprise, and much of this process will still rely on the experience of the software engineer. So far, however, we can state that at least for the decisions to be made in our examples, the framework of CBPM supports the process of evaluation. Future work will focus on how agents can be designed that embody elaborate self-diagnosing capabilities and that are able to effectively monitor and improve system behaviour *automatically*. More specifically, we aim at combining the CBPM approach with more elaborate methods for communication analysis at a more *semantic* level, in a similar way as that proposed for the evolutionary development of open MAS through human designers in the EXPAND [2] method.

References

1. AgentCities. http://www.agentcities.org, 2003.
2. W. Brauer, M. Nickles, M. Rovatsos, G. Weiß, and K. F. Lorentzen. Expectation-Oriented Analysis and Design. In *Proceedings of the 2nd Workshop on Agent-Oriented Software Engineering (AOSE-2001) at the Autonomous Agents 2001 Conference*, volume 2222 of *LNAI*, Montreal, Canada, May 29 2001. Springer-Verlag, Berlin.

3. J. Cao, D. J. Kerbyson, and G. R. Nudd. Performance evaluation of an agent-based resource management infrastructure for grid computing. In *Proceedings of the 1st IEEE/ACM International Symposium on Cluster Computing and the Grid, Brisbane, Australia,* pages 311–318, 2001.
4. M. Dikaiakos, M. Kyriakou, and G. Samaras. Performance evaluation of mobile-agent middleware: A hierarchical approach. In G. P. Picco, editor, *Proceedings of the 5th IEEE International Conference on Mobile Agents*, volume 2240 of *Lecture Notes in Computer Science*, pages 244–259, Berlin et al., 2001. Springer-Verlag.
5. R. Dumke, C. Rautenstrauch, A. Schmietendorf, and A. Scholz, editors. *Performance Engineering*, volume 2047 of *Lecture Notes in Computer Science*. Springer-Verlag, Berlin et al., 2001.
6. FIPA. FIPA (Foundation for Intelligent Agents), http://www.fipa.org, 2003.
7. N.R. Jennings. On agent-based software engineering. *Artificial Intelligence*, 117:277–296, 2000.
8. Y. Labrou and T. Finin. A Proposal for a new KQML Specification. Technical Report TR CS-97-03, Computer Science and Electrical Engineering Department, University of Maryland Baltimore County, Baltimore, MD, February 1997.
9. V. Parunak. Industrial and practical applications of DAI. In G. Weiss, editor, *Multiagent Systems*, pages 377–421. The MIT Press, Cambridge et al., 1999.
10. IBM Research. Autonomic computing, http://www.research.ibm.com/autonomic/, 2003.
11. M. Schillo, C. Kray, and K. Fischer. The Eager Bidder Problem:A Fundamental Problem of DAI and Selected Solutions. In *Proceedings of the First International Conference on Autonomous Agents and Multiagent Systems (AAMAS '02)*, pages 599–607, 2002.
12. R.G. Smith and R. Davis. Frameworks for cooperation in distributed problem solving. *IEEE Transactions on Systems, Man, and Cybernetics*, SMC-11(1):61–70, 1981.
13. M. J. Wooldridge. Agent-based software engineering. *IEE Proceedings on Software Engineering*, 144(1):26–37, 1997.

The AEP Toolkit for Agent Design and Simulation

Joscha Bach and Ronnie Vuine

Institut für Informatik, Humboldt-Universität zu Berlin
Unter den Linden 6, 10099 Berlin, Germany
bach|vuine@informatik.hu-berlin.de

Abstract. The design of artificial agents that are meant to model behavioral, cognitive, economic or social structures asks for tools that aid in layout and implementation of agent architectures. To implement agents based on Dörner's Psi theory of emotion and cognition, our group has introduced a toolkit that assists in designing modular architectures, as well as representational structures, such as semantic networks, control scripts and connectionist structures by means of a graphical editor. At the same time, the framework supports the inclusion of functionality written in a native programming language. This paper gives an overview over the implementation of agents according to Dörner's theory, and while it also aims at giving an insight into the functioning of these agents (which we call "MicroPsi" agents), its main purpose is the explanation of the use of the toolkit.

1   Introduction

The modeling of cognition, emotion, sociality and behavior with multi-agent systems has become an important tool to test and develop hypotheses or to represent a slice of a given reality. Our group is especially concerned with the design of a model of human emotion in the context of an AI agent architecture. The resulting architecture is called MicroPsi and represents a 'broad and shallow approach' (as suggested for instance by Bates, Loyall and Reilly [5]). MicroPsi is based on theoretical work by the psychologist Dietrich Dörner [7,8,9]. Applications of MicroPsi include experiments on learning in complex environments, modeling of emotion in interaction with humans and simple cognitive modeling.

The concepts of MicroPsi have been described in earlier publications by the authors ([1,2,3]). MicroPsi is based on a network formalism ("node nets") that aids as a general method for specifying the architectural components, individual functionality of cognitive modules, representation of actuatoric and sensoric schemata and so on. To support the design of such agents, we have developed a toolkit, which we current-ly call the "AEP framework" (for *Artificial Emotion Project*), but which lends itself to the design of agents with different, not necessarily emotional architectures as well.

The AEP framework [4,14] consists of several components that support the design of individual agents (the node net editor and simulator), the multi-agent simulation environment (the world editor and simulator), the interaction between agents and human actors (the visualization tools) and the integration of the former parts (the AEP

M. Schillo et al. (Eds.): MATES 2003, LNAI 2831, pp. 38–49, 2003.

server and console). This paper briefly describes the node net formalism and then sets out to explain the implementation of several modules of MicroPsi agents. The paper concludes with a note on distributed simulation, a short outlook and examples of applications of the framework.

2   Node Nets

2.1   Representation with Nodes

In his work on modeling human emotional and cognitive behavior, Dörner suggests the use of a kind of neural network for the representation of control structures, declarative and protocol memory. [7] Dörner asks for a mechanism that can represent both symbolic knowledge and connectionist configurations with the same data structures. Such representations could for instance be implemented as influence or belief networks (see, for instance [13]) with some additional logic to make them executable and interpretable.

In MicroPsi agents, these representations are directional spreading activation networks called *node nets*. These networks consist of units with inputs ("slots"), outputs ("gates"), propagation and node functions. Units may become active, causing them to execute their node functions. Activation is stored in the gates, which also possess threshold and amplification values. The arcs or links between units connect gates with slots, and activation may spread between units.

The most common node type used to represent semantic relationships is called "concept nodes". These have nine different gates: general activation (*gen*), links for causal relations forwards (*por*) and backwards (*ret*), for *part-of* and *contains* relations (*sur*, *sub*), for membership (*cat*, *exp*), and for naming (*sym*, *ref*). Of these, *por*, *ret*, *sur* and *sub* are part of the original description of the Psi theory and derived from a theory of representation by Klix [11]; the others have been added to simplify the implementation and notation. Usually, concept nodes are symmetrically linked (i.e. for every *ret* link, there is a *por* link in the opposite direction, and so on.)

Concept nodes may be connected to special nodes, so-called "directional activators" which are connected to all individual gates of a certain type. Gates may only transmit an activation, if their corresponding activator is active, which allows for a *spreading activation* mechanism. A set of nodes that is connected to the same set of directional activators is called a *node space*.

By choosing appropriate weights and thresholds, links between nodes can express logical AND and OR terms. It can be demonstrated that this notation is suitable to express first order logic [9]. On the other hand, information retrieval with node spaces is very similar to using hierarchical Case Retrieval Networks with directional activation [12].

The current implementation of MicroPsi comes with a graphical front-end that allows to define, maintain and execute node nets. The resulting networks can be saved in XML format.

2.2   Definition of Node Nets

Node nets consist of sets of net entities U, which are called nodes and modules, and which are connected to each other by links V and to the agent environment by a vector of *DataSources* and *DataTargets*.

$$NN = \{ U, V, DataSources, DataTargets, f_{net} \}$$

where f_{net} is a propagation function calculating the transition from one state of the node net to the next.

$$U = \{(id, type, I, O, \alpha, f_{act}, f_{node})\}$$

Generally speaking, an entity $u \in U$ consists of a vector I of *slots*, a vector O of *gates*, an activation α, an activation function $f_{act} : I \rightarrow \alpha$ and a node function f_{node}: $NN \rightarrow NN$ (that is to say, there are no real limits to what the node function can do to the node net). The *id* makes it possible to uniquely identify a net entity.

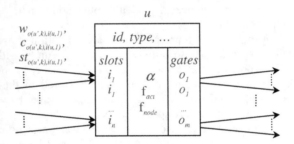

Fig. 1. Node net entity.

Entities come about in different *types*, such as register nodes, concept nodes and so on, which will be explained below.

Nodes may be grouped into *node spaces*:

$$S = \{ U, ^S DataSources, ^S DataTargets, ^S f_{net}^S \}$$

By mapping the *DataSources*^{S} of a node space to slots, the *DataTargets*^{S} to gates and the local net function f_{net}^S to a node function, it is possible to embed a node space into a single node entity, called a *node space module*. Thus, hierarchies of node spaces may be created.

Often, node spaces contain a number of nodes that have special properties, such as *Activators*$^S \subset U^S$; *Activators*$^S = \{ u_{gateType_1}, ..., u_{gateType_n} \}$. Activators may influence the way activation spreads within a node space and are explained later on.

$$V = \{(o_i^{u_1}, i_j^{u_2}, w, c\, st)\}$$

Note that nodes (u_1 and u_2) can be connected by more than one link. Links are defined by the gate $o_i^{u_1}$ and the slot $i_j^{u_2}$, which they connect, and are annotated by a weight $w \in \mathbb{R}_{[-1, 1]}$, a certainty value $c \in \mathbb{R}_{[0,1]}$, and a vector $st \in \mathbb{R}^4$; $st = (x, y, z, t)$ containing spatial-temporal values.

$$O = \{(gate\ Type,\ out,\ q,\ amp,\ min,\ max, f_{out})\}$$

Gates provide the output of net entities and consist of an output activation $out \in \mathbb{R}$, a threshold θ, an amplification factor amp, upper and lower boundaries on the activation min and max and an output activation function f_{out}: $\alpha \times O \times Activators \rightarrow out$ that calculates the values of the gates, usually by:

$$out = \begin{cases} min\left(max\left(amp \times \alpha \times act_{gateType_o}, min\right), max\right), & if\ \alpha \times act_{gateType_o} > \theta \\ 0,\ else \end{cases}$$

where $act_{gateType_o}$ is the output activation out of the activator node $u_{gateType_o} \in Activators^s$, of the respective node space. (This calculation can be replaced by other functions, using for instance a sigmoid, which is useful for implementing a variety of neural network learning functions.) By triggering an activator, the spreading of activation from gates of the particular gate type is enabled.

Input to the nodes is provided using an array of slots:

$$I = \{(slotType, in)\}$$

The value of each slot i_j^u is calculated using f_{net}, typically as the weighted sum of its inputs. Let $(v_1,...,v_k)$ be the vector of links that connect i_j^u to other nodes, and $(out_1,...,out_k)$ be the output activations of the respective connected gates:

$$in_{i_j^u} = \frac{1}{k} \sum_{n=1}^{k} w_{v_n} c_{v_n} out_n$$

2.3   Defining Specific Node Types

Concept Nodes, as mentioned before, are the typical building blocks of MicroPsi node nets. They consist of a single slot of the type gen (for "generic") and their node activation is identical with their input activation: $\alpha = in_{gen}$. Dörner's representations make use of the link types por, ret, sub and sur, which are represented by gates. Additionally, concept nodes have the gates cat, exp (for "category", denoting membership, and "exemplar", pointing to members) and sym, ref (for symbols and referenced concepts). Finally, concept nodes contain a gate gen, which makes the input activation available if it is above the threshold θ_{gen} – there is no gen activator.

Register nodes are the most basic node type. They consist of a single slot and gate, both of type gen, and like in concept nodes, their output activation amounts to $out_{gen} = [amp \cdot \alpha]_{min}^{max}$, if $\alpha > \theta$, 0 else; $\alpha = in_{gen}$

Sensor nodes are similar to register nodes, however, their activation out_{gen} is computed from an external variable $dataSource \in dataSource^s : out_{gen} = [amp\ \alpha]_{min}^{max}$, if $\alpha > \theta$, 0 else; $\alpha = in_{gen} \cdot dataSource$.

Actor nodes are extensions to sensor nodes. Using their node function, they give their input activation in_{gen} to an external variable $dataTarget \in dataTarget^s$. The external value may be available to other node spaces, or, via the technical layer of the agent, to the agent environment (e.g. the world server). In return, an input value is read that typically represents failure (-1) or success (1) of the action returned as a sensor value to out_{gen}.

Concept, register, sensor and actor nodes are the 'bread and butter' of node net representations. To *control* node nets, a number of specific register nodes have been introduced on top of that:

Activators are special registers that exist in correspondence to the gate types (*por, ret, sub, sur, cat, exp, sym* and *ref*) of concept nodes of a node space. Their output is read by the output activation function of the respective gate of their nodespace. By setting activators to zero, no activation can spread through the corresponding gates.

General activation nodes are special nodes with a single slot and gate of type *gen*, and when active, they increase the activation α of all nodes in the same node space.

General deactivation nodes are the counterpart of general activation nodes; they dampen the activation of all nodes within the same node space. They are mainly used to gradually reduce activity in a node space until only the most activated structures remain, or to end activity altogether.

Associator nodes are used to establish links between nodes in a node space. This happens by connecting all nodes with active gates, using a weight

$$w_{u_1^i u_2^j}^t = \sqrt{w_{u_1^i u_2^j}^{t-1}} + \alpha_{associator} \times associationFactor^S \times \alpha_{u_1} \times \alpha_{u_2}$$

where t is the current time step, and $associationFactor^s \in \mathbb{R}_{[0,1]}$ a node space specific constant.

Disassociator nodes are the counterpart of associator nodes; they decrease or remove links between currently active nodes in the same node space.

Additionally, there is functionality for adding and removing nodes, also encapsulated in node entities.

3   Native Modules for MicroPsi Agents

It is possible to write and execute complete programs with AEP node nets. In theory, they are sufficient to set up all behavior and control scripts of MicroPsi agents. However, the execution of scripts made up of nodes is slow, and they are hard to maintain, even using a graphical editor. This makes it desirable to add more nodes for specific tasks, and to encapsulate long scripts. This is where *native modules* come into play; they are entities with arbitrary numbers of slots and gates. In their node function f_{node} , they hide program code written in a native computer language.

In the current implementation, native modules contain Java code and can perform any kind of manipulation on the node net. By integrating Java IDE, graphical node net editor and agent runtime environment, the extension of the agents becomes quite comfortable. For the basic functions of MicroPsi agents, a number of native modules have been added, of which three will be explained here:

3.1   Script Execution

Node scripts consist of chains of concept nodes that are connected by *por/ret* links. With *sub/sur* links, macros and hierarchies are defined. This may be read as: after 'step 1' follows 'step 2' (*por*), and 'step 1' consists of 'part 1', 'part 2', 'part 3' and so on. 'Part 1' can again be the beginning of a chain or network of *por*-linked nodes.

The linking of the 'parts' determines whether they are alternatives or conjunctions. The lowest level of these hierarchies is always formed by sensor and actor nodes. Because of these structures, it is possible to execute hierarchical plans with thousand of basic actions at the lowest level and few abstract elements on the highest levels and thus reduce the computational complexity of plan construction. Such hierarchical scripts can be run using the native module "ScriptExecution". ScriptExecution has two slots – Abort and ScriptActivation – and seven gates: Current, ProgramRegister, Macro, Idle, Success, Failure and FailAbort.

Initially, the script is retrieved and linked to a register on its highest level of hierarchy. This register is connected to the ScriptExection module. The execution starts by connecting *Idle* (which is active by default and thus susceptible to the *associator*) to the first concept node of the script. ScriptExecution first deactivates and unlinks *Idle*, and the first element is linked to *Current*.

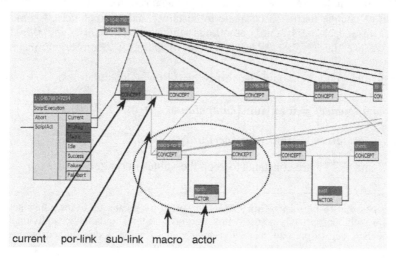

Fig. 2. Script execution.

Now, in every step, the connected concept node is activated with the value of *ScriptActivation*. If this node is the parent of a macro, that is, if it has sub links, then the sub-linked concept node with the highest activation is chosen as new current node. (Using this pre-activation mechanism, scripts can be configured to follow certain paths before execution or even during execution.) If one of the sub-linked macros was successfully executed or there are no macros at all, the *por*-linked node with the highest activation becomes the new current node – if none of the *por*-linked nodes is active, ScriptExecution waits until one of the following happens:

- a *por*-linked node becomes active, causing it to become the new current node,
- a *por*-linked node becomes active with negative activation, causing failure,
- a timeout occurs, also causing the macro to fail.

When a macro just failed or was executed successfully, the entry point to this macro will again become the current node; ScriptExecution then decides how to go on in the manner given above. Macro success and failure are signaled at the *Success* and *Failure* gates. Fig. 2 shows a very simple script with just two levels of hierarchy.[1]

3.2 Emotional Regulation

This module calculates the emotional parameters from urges, relevant signals and values from the previous step. The module maintains the following internal states: *competence, arousal, certainty*, resolution level (*resLevel*) and selection threshold (*selThreshold*). These values are directly visible at the module's gates. Any subsystem of the agent that is subject to emotional regulation is linked to these gates, receiving the current emotional parameters via f_{net} .

Additional gates signal the 'cognitive urges': *certaintyU* and *efficiencyU*, which are calculated every step simply as difference between a target value and the actual value. At the slots, the module receives the values of the 'physiological urges' (*extU$_{1.3}$*) and the amount of change that is to be made to certainty and competence, if some event occurs that influences the system's emotional state (slots *certaintyS* and *efficiencyS*). The way we use these values is very similar to Dörner's 'EmoRegul' mechanism [8,10].

At every time step *t* the module performs the following calculations:

$$competence_t = \max\left(\min\left(competence_{t-1} + in_t^{efficiencyS}, 0\right), l^{competence}\right)$$

$$certainty_t = \max\left(\min\left(certainty_{t-1} + in_t^{certaintyS}, 0\right), l^{certainty}\right)$$

($l^{competence}$ and $l^{certainty}$ are constants to keep the values in range)

---

[1] It is also possible to perform script execution solely by means of a spreading activation mechanism with appropriately adjusted link weights and thresholds. Here, individual nodes propagate their activation into the *sub*-direction, until actor nodes or sensor nodes are reached. In turn the *sub*-linked nodes propagate a small *sur*-activation to keep their parents active. If a sensor or actor succeeds, its activation is *sur*-propagated and excites their parents strong enough to allow for a overcoming the *por*-threshold. The *por*-gate in turn has to have an inhibitory link to stop the activation of its originator.

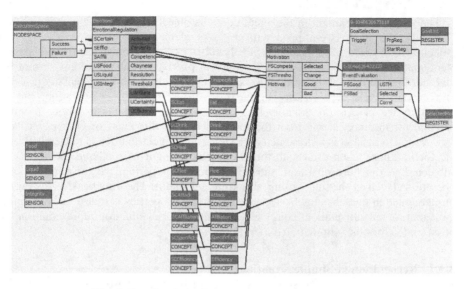

Fig. 3. Emotional regulation and motivation (editor view).

$$efficiencyU_t = target^{competence} - competence_t$$

$$certaintyU_t = target^{certainty} - certainly_t$$

($target^{certainty}$ and $target^{certainty}$ are target values representing the optimum levels of competence and certainty for the agent.)

$$arousal_t = \max\left(certaintyU_t, efficiencyU_t, in_t^{ext U}\right) - competence_t$$

$$resLevel_t = 1 - \sqrt{arousal_t}$$

$$selThreshold_t = selThreshold_{t-1} arousal_t$$

3.3 Perception

Perceptions of MicroPsi agents are organized as trees, where the root represents a situation, and the leaves are basic sensor nodes. A situation is typically represented by a chain of *por/ret* links that are annotated by spatial-temporal attributes. These attributes define how the focus of attention has to move from each element to sense the next; thus, the memory representation of an object acts as an instruction for the perception module on how to recognize this situation.

Situations may contain other situations or objects; these are connected with *sub/sur* links (that is, they are '*part of*' the parent situation). We refer to situations that consist of other situations as 'complex situations', in contrast to 'simple situations' that contain only single or chained sensor nodes *sur/sub*-linked with a single concept node.

The virtual environment of the agent contains objects representing plants and fruit. Currently, the agent is equipped with a set of elementary sensors on the level of objects (like sensors for bananas or hazel-trees). In Dörner's original design, elementary sensors are on the level of groups of pixels and colors; we have simplified this, but there is no real difference in the concept. Using more basic sensors just adds one or two levels of hierarchy in the tree of the object representation, but the algorithm for perception remains the same. All the agent learns about a virtual banana, for instance, stems from the interaction with this class of objects, i.e. after exploration, a banana is represented as a situation element that leads to a reduction in the feeding urge when used with the eat-operator, might be rendered inedible when subjected to the burn-operator, and which does not particularly respond to other operations (such as shaking, sifting, drinking and so on). The drawback of the current implementation that abstains from modeling visual properties is that it does not allow the agent to generalize about colors etc., and perhaps the situation representation will be extended for other simulation experiments.

3.3.1 Recognition of Simple Situations

Here, we look at the case of situations that have been seen before by the agent, so it already possesses a schema of the situation and uses the module "SimpleHyPercept" for recognition. (In the case of unknown situations, a different module, "Accommodation", is used to acquire a new schema.)

If the agent peeks into an external situation, elementary sensors may become active if a matching object appears. If, for instance, the agent stands in front of a banana object and happens to focus its sensors on it, the corresponding sensor node becomes active and the perception algorithm carries this activation to the concept node that is *sur*-connected with the sensor (i.e. the banana concept). If the object can only be recognized by checking several sensors, the agent retrieves all object representations containing the active sensor as part of a *por/ret* chain from memory. These chains represent for which sensors the agent has to check in which spatial relationship to the first one, to establish which of the object candidates can be assumed to lie in front of the agent (see fig. 4).

After an individual object has been found, it is checked whether it represents a part of a 'bigger picture', like a particular arrangement of bananas that has been seen in the past. This again can be determined by looking at the *sur* links of the banana concept node, which lead to known, potentially fitting situations containing bananas. The perception module builds a list of those nodes; these are the hypotheses that have to be checked.

Some of the situations in the list might be biased to be checked first, because they are considered to be more likely true. This applies especially to situations that have been recently sensed (i.e. the agent will keep his hypothesis about the environment stable, if nothing happens to disprove it).

Given that list of hypotheses, the perception module now checks one after the other. To check a hypothesis, the *por/ret*-path of the hypothesis' elements is read from memory. The sensors of the agent are then moved to the element at the beginning of the *por/ret* chain, then along the *por* path to the next position, and so on until all elements have been "looked at". After checking each element, the sensor must verify

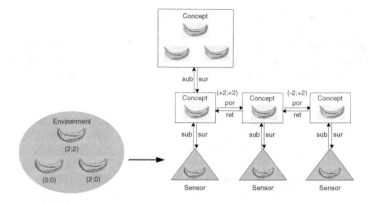

Fig. 4. A triangular arrangement of 'banana objects' is represented as a situation.

its existence in order not to disprove the hypothesis. If all elements of the situation have been successfully checked, the hypothesis is considered to be consistent with the reality of the agent environment.

If one of the elements does *not* become active, the current hypothesis is deleted from the list, and the next one is checked. If a hypothesis is checked to the end of the *por/ret* chain, it is considered to "be the case" and linked as the new current situation.

As most modules in MicroPsi agents, perception can undergo emotional modulation. Especially the resolution level matters: if it is low, fewer elements of a hypothesis need to be checked for the hypothesis to be considered true. As a result, perception is faster but inaccurate when resolution is low, but slower and precise if resolution is high.

3.3.2 Occlusion

This algorithm obviously has a problem with occlusion (which happens frequently in the real world): If one of the elements of a situation is not visible due to occlusion, or because it is outside the field of view, it won't become active, the testing of the *por/ret* chain does not succeed and the hypothesis, although possibly correct, will be discarded. The most straightforward approach to deal with that problem would be to allow a number of elements not to become active before discarding the hypothesis. Additionally, it has to be maintained that the missing elements are indeed hidden by another object at the same position, or are invisible because of blurriness, distance etc. This comes at the cost of more erroneous recognition, but in the perception of complex situations (where the occlusion problem becomes relevant) it will be a necessity.

3.3.3 Recognition of Complex Situations

Just as simple objects consist of an arrangement of sensor patterns, complex objects and situations may contain other objects. This can be represented by *sub/sur* linking them. By choosing appropriate weights on these links, alternatives and conjunctions may be expressed. The hierarchical definition of objects makes it possible to represent a face, for instance, by two eye schemas, a nose schema and a mouth schema in the correct spatial arrangement. The eye schemas may in turn consist of lid schema, brow schema, iris schema etc.

When attempting to recognize a cartoon face (like a smiley), the agent may correctly recognize the spatial arrangement of a face, but because the eyes might lack detail, discount eyelids and so on as 'occluded' and still maintain the face hypothesis. However, the more complex mechanism of conditional HyPercept has not been implemented yet by our group.

In a similar way to "ScriptExecution", "EmotionalRegulation" and "SimpleHy-Percept", native modules for protocol generation, motivation, goal selection, event evaluation, simple planning, focus control, and so on have been defined. This toolbox already enables the agent to explore its environment, memorize its experiences, attempt try-and-error strategies to satisfy its urges, learn from the results and to follow little plans.

4   Summary and Outlook

A main focus of experiments with AEP based agents will be on multi agent interaction in a complex simulated environment (although our group has also implemented an AEP based control for four-legged Sony robots).

The current AEP architecture provides a simulation server that communicates with an arbitrary number of agents, the simulation world and – via console applications – with human experimenters. All components can be distributed over a network, allowing for simulations with computationally expensive agents. Communication between AEP components is facilitated via a general protocol that exchanges objects through a communication layer and includes mechanisms for remote maintenance.

The speed of the simulation is controlled with a timer component. Although the world simulation currently only takes place in two dimensions, which are represented in a 2D viewer, a three dimensional interface improves the interaction of humans with our virtual agents. The 3D viewer simply converts the 2D environment into a three dimensional representation that is read and displayed by a graphics engine. However, this engine provides only functionality for observing the agent world (i.e. interaction is not yet possible).

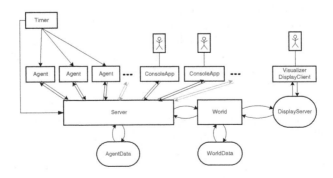

Fig. 5. MicroPsi agent and server.

MicroPsi is part of a larger effort of our group which is centered around the AEP framework. Currently, the toolkit is being used to implement classification algorithms, virtual Braitenberg vehicles [6], an artificial life simulation and to model human emotional expression.

References

1. Bach, J. (2002). *Enhancing Perception and Planning of Software Agents with Emotion and Acquired Hierarchical Categories.* In Proceedings of MASHO 02, German Conference on Artificial Intelligence KI2002: 3–12
2. Bach, J. (2003). *Emotionale Virtuelle Agenten auf der Basis der Dörnerschen Psi-Theorie.* In Burkhard, H.-D., Uthmann, T., Lindemann, G. (Eds.): ASIM 03, Workshop Modellierung und Simulation menschlichen Verhaltens, Berlin, Germany: 1–10
3. Bach, J. (2003). *The MicroPsi Agent Architecture.* Proceedings of ICCM-5, International Conference on Cognitive Modeling, Bamberg, Germany: 15–20
4. Bach, J. (2003). *Artificial Emotion Project/MicroPsi Home Page*: http://www.artificial-emotion.de
5. Bates, J., Loyall, A. B., & Reilly, W. S. (1991). *Broad agents.* AAAI spring symposium on integrated intelligent architectures. Stanford, CA: Sigart Bulletin, 2(4), Aug. 1991: 38–40
6. Braitenberg, V. (1984) *Vehicles.* Experiments in Synthetic Psychology. MIT Press.
7. Dörner, D. (1999). *Bauplan für eine Seele.* Reinbeck: Rowohlt
8. Dörner, D. (2003). *The Mathematics of Emotion.* Proceedings of ICCM-5, International Conference on Cognitive Modeling, Bamberg, Germany
9. Dörner, D., Bartl, C., Detje, F., Gerdes, J., Halcour, D., Schaub, H., & Starker, U. (2002). *Die Mechanik des Seelenwagens. Eine neuronale Theorie der Handlungsregulation.* Verlag Hans Huber, Bern
10. Dörner, D., Hamm, A., Hille, K. (1996): *EmoRegul – die Beschreibung eines Programms zur Simulation der Interaktion von Motivation, Emotion und Kognition bei der Handlungsregulation*, Memorandum des Lehrstuhls Theoretische Psychologie, Universität Bamberg
11. Klix, F. (1984). *Über Wissensrepräsentation im Gedächtnis.* In F. Klix (Ed.): Gedächtnis, Wissen, Wissensnutzung. Berlin: Deutscher Verlag der Wissenschaften.
12. Lenz, M., & Burkhard, H.-D. (1998*). Case retrieval nets: Basic ideas and extensions.* Technical report, Humboldt University, Berlin
13. Shachter, R. D. (1986). *Evaluating influence diagrams.* Operations Research, 34: 871–882
14. Vuine, R., & Bach, J. (2003). *The AEP Handbook.* http://www.artificial-emotion.de/pub/aephandbook.pdf (April 2003)

On Programming Information Agent Systems – An Integrated Hotel Reservation Service as Case Study*

Yun Ding, Heiner Litz, Rainer Malaka, and Dennis Pfisterer

European Media Laboratory,
Schloss-Wolfsbrunnenweg 33, 69118 Heidelberg, Germany
{Yun.Ding,Heiner.Litz,Rainer.Malaka,Dennis.Pfisterer}@eml.villa-bosch.de

Abstract. This paper presents our integrated hotel reservation service. Using it as a case study, we discuss the design and implementation of agent-based information systems. Taking a system as a whole, we consider not only information agents but also their interface to human users and external information sources. In particular, our focus is on the interaction behavior, which can be observed both in interactions between agents and in interactions between agents and these interface components. We show that both kinds of interaction are coordinated by the same protocol. Using our implemented hotel reservation service system, we illustrate exemplarily how this understanding can be used to systematically design and validate interaction mechanism. We explore the possibility to facilitate the rapid prototyping of information agent systems using an interaction behavior editor. Moreover, by giving insight into some details of our hotel service system, we exemplify where the difficulties in implementing information agent systems are and thus infrastructural support are desirable.

1 Introduction

The rapid growth and popularity of the World Wide Web have largely eased the access to information. At the same time, it is increasingly difficult for human people to collect, filter, evaluate and really use the vast amount of information. *Information agents* are software programs that gather information from various, heterogeneous and distributed sources on behalf of their human users to achieve their goals. For instance, they filter away irrelevant information, integrate information from different sources, proactively monitor and search for more related information, and eventually present them in an appropriate way to their users [9]. In the past, information agents have been developed for different domains such as shopping (Menczer et. al. present a good survey over existing shopping

---

* The work is funded by the Klaus Tschira Foundation, the German Federal Department for Education, Science, Research, and Technology (BMBF) in the scope of project EMBASSI under FKZ 01 IL 904 D2, and the Agentcities.NET under ACNET.02.32.

M. Schillo et al. (Eds.): MATES 2003, LNAI 2831, pp. 50–61, 2003.

agents in [20]), hotel/restaurant reservation [26,22], or portfolio management in the financial domain [9].

Information agents are just one part of an agent-based information system that additional consists of interface agents and middle agents. Interface agents interact with human users to receive their requests and deliver results. On behalf of human users, interface agents interact with information agents. Middle agents facilitate the location of agents in an open system.

In the scope of the projects EMBASSI [12] and Agentcities [1], we have developed an information system for the hotel service domain, which is called an integrated hotel reservation service. Currently, a number of hotel searching and reservation services are available on the web offering proprietary on-line searching and booking capabilities. Users have to browse through different web sites and formulate their requests anew for each of the hotel reservation systems, which normally have different user interfaces and use different terms for identical parameters. Our hotel service system uses several different vendor web sites to parallelly process a search request while offering a unified user interface and terminology.

In contrast to other related works which focus on the modeling, designing and implementation of information agents [10,8], or their low-level skills such as information extraction [18], filtering and integration, we consider the *design and implementation of interaction behavior* in an information system. Taking a system as a whole, we take into account not only information agents but also their interface to human users and external information sources. We made the following observation: When a certain interaction protocol (for example, a contract-net protocol specified by the FIPA specifications [14] for inter-agent communication) is chosen to achieve a user's goal, it coordinates not only the interaction between an interface agent and information agents but also guides the interaction between the building components of interface and information agents. This understanding is useful for systematically designing agent components. Going a step further, it might be used to construct toolkits which allow rapid prototyping of information systems and even (semi-)automatical programming. We briefly present the architecture and implementation status of our integrated hotel reservation service in section 2. Using it as a case study, the subsequent sections consider the aspects of designing interaction behavior, using ontology and agent collaboration in information systems respectively. We both describe implemented concepts for our hotel reservation service and discuss these aspects when abstracting from the particular hotel service domain. In section 6 we compare our work with related work. Section 7 sums up and points out future research directions.

2   The Case Study: Integrated Hotel Reservation Service

The architecture of our integrated hotel reservation service is illustrated in figure 1. It consists of three main parts, user interface agents, hotel service agents as information agents, and a hotel service manager as an information broker.

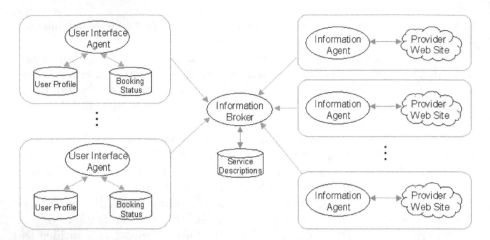

Fig. 1. System architecture of our integrated hotel reservation service

- *User interface agents:* Each user interface agent represents a human user. It trustfully keeps information such as user profiles and reservations made. On behalf of its user, it contacts hotel service agents for searching and booking a hotel or cancellation of an earlier reservation. A graphical interface (GUI) is used to navigate the interactions between the user interface agent and its user.
- *Hotel service agents:* Each hotel service agent encapsulates a web site, which provides hotel reservation services. In an open environment as the World Wide Web is located in, new web sites and thus their associated hotel service agents can dynamically join into or leave the system.
- *Hotel service manager:* The hotel service manager is designed to enable user interface agents to find the matching hotel service agents, which can handle their requests. It acts as a matchmaking middle agent [29] between them. Hotel service agents advertise and de-advertise their capabilities to the hotel service manager, while user interface agents query for matching hotel service agents to serve the requests of human users.

We implemented a prototype of integrated hotel reservation service on our agent platform *RAJA* [11]. RAJA is a FIPA [14] compliant agent platform, which is implemented on top of the well-known FIPA implementations *FIPA-OS* [15] and its lightweight version for small devices *Micro FIPA-OS* [21] as well as *JADE* [3]. The current prototype has hotel service agents for the vendors HRS (www.hrs.de), HRN (www.hoteldiscount.fr), Travelocity (www.travelocity.com) and Budgethotel (www.budgethotel.com).

3   Designing Interaction Behavior

Figure 2 shows a simplified system architecture of an agent-based information system. The interface agent interacts with a human user through a graphical

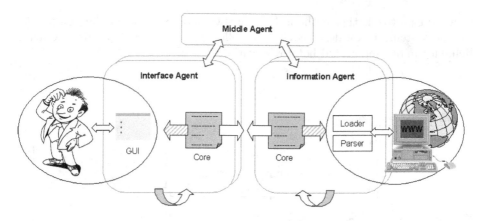

Fig. 2. Architecture of an information system and overview of interactions

interface (GUI). Information agents retrieve and parse information from the World Wide Web through their site-specific components which are called loader and parser respectively. A loader has two types of methods. One of them are used to map user-defined criteria to fields of vendor-provided forms and can be performed off-line, while the others need on-line connections to the vendor site. Methods of the second type are invoked to submit a form filled in (e.g., a form to search for hotels) or a decision from the user (e.g., accept or reject a booking proposal). Upon receiving results from vendors, which are mostly HTML-based, the task of a parser is to extract relevant information such as the names, addresses and prices of hotels from them. The core component of an interface or information agent implements the logical part/functionality of an agent. It is reusable in the sense that it is independent from the represented users and the associated external information sources. The blank arrows symbolize inter-agent interactions and interactions between an agent and its environment (i.e., a human being or an external source), while the two gray, stripy arrows symbolize interactions between the components inside an agent.

At the level of inter-agent interaction, interface agents represent human users, while information agents encapsulate external resources. However, taking the viewpoint of a user and a vendor-specific site into account, interface and information agents become new roles: (1) From the user's or the GUI's viewpoint, the associated interface agent or its core component represents the "information world", which may include several information agents and other agents. (2) From the viewpoint of a vendor-specific site or its associated loader and parser, an information agent or its core component retrieves and extracts information from it on behalf of a user. These two points consider intra-agent interactions, i.e., interactions between the GUI and the core component of an interface agent or interactions between the loader/parser and the core component of an information agent. It is not difficult to see, that the protocol for the inter-agent interaction should also guide the intra-agent interaction, which is achieved through method invocations between the components. According to the steps specified in an interaction protocol, the methods for the interactions between the components can be systematically designed. In the following, we exemplify this interaction behavior in our integrated hotel reservation service.

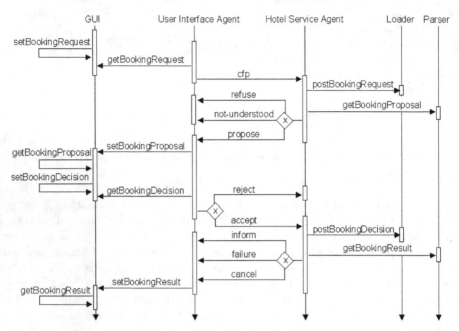

Fig. 3. Interaction diagram

Representing a vendor-specific web site, a hotel service agent interacts with a user interface agent to provide the services offered by the vendor. The interactions follow some protocols. In our system, the action "*search-hotel*" follows the FIPA-request protocol, while the actions "*book-hotel*" and "*cancel-reservation*" follow the FIPA-contract-net protocol [14]. Each action will be performed by a specialized task in its own thread. Therefore, multiple requests can be parallelly handled. For a *book-hotel* action, figure 3 shows the interaction diagram (using the notation in [23]) for the interactions among a GUI, its owning user interface agent, a hotel service agent, and its loader and parser component. The communication between a user interface agent and hotel service agents are asynchronous, since participants must not be blocked waiting for incoming messages. This enables a hotel service agent to parallelly handle requests from different users. In contrast, the communication between the components of an agent is synchronous, i.e., the `get` methods are blocking methods.

It is easy to see that the methods of the components GUI, loader and a parser are systematically derived from the interaction protocol obeyed and the domain specific ontology. This interaction behavior is useful for the rapid and systematical design and validation of interaction mechanisms for agent-based information systems. Going a step further, it might be used to construct toolkits which allow rapid prototyping of information systems and even semi-automatical programming. We are developing an *Interaction Behavior Editor*. It should allow programmers to define an interaction protocol by specifying its steps. Each step is characterized by

- a *name* and a *type*, which indicate the domain-specific issue concerned (e.g., booking_requests, proposals, decisions, and booking_results) and its data type respectively,
- a *role*, which specifies whether it is taken by the initiator or the responder of the interaction, and
- a *protocol*, which specifies the allowed actions for this step (e.g., propose, refuse, and not-understood for the second step of a contract-net protocol). The actions are related to each other by "exclusive-or", and
- its *next step*, which points to the next step of the interaction protocol.

Currently, we specify the interaction protocol in XML (an excerpt is shown in figure 4). Then, we use a set of XSL (eXtensible Stylesheet Language) style sheets to transform it into Java classes for

- the *GUI component* of the interface agent with **set** and **get** methods, whereas the **get** methods are blocking methods, and
- the *loader and parser component* for the information agent. A loader acts as an initiator of an interaction and provides **post** methods, while a parser acts as a responder and offers **get** methods. Application programmers should overwrite the abstract **post** and **get** methods for each vendor site.
- *agent behaviors/tasks* such as contract-net-initiator or contract-net-responder behavior provided by the JADE agent framework [3]. For example, an agent behavior as a contract-net-initiator offers methods `handlePropose(incoming_msg)`, `handleRefuse` and `handleNotUnderstood`, which should be overwritten by programmers.

To allow information agents to communicate with other information sources such as databases, specialized loaders can be constructed.

The effort we put into designing interaction behavior for components, which interact with the "outside world" (i.e., human user or external sources), is justified when intense feedback from the users is required to perform an action such as our *book-hotel* or *cancel-reservation* action. For simple one-shot queries, the interaction pattern is straightforward and can be easily hand-coded.

4 Using Ontology

Ontologies provide a shared and common understanding of a domain to enable the communication between people and heterogeneous and distributed application systems [17]. For a particular domain, an ontology defines its concepts (e.g., a concept of hotel for the domain of hotel service) and their associated attributes (e.g., each hotel has a name, an address, prices and a comfort category), as well as the relationships between the concepts. Using ontology is twofold. Firstly, ontologies facilitate the building of knowledge-based systems. Upon defining concepts and their relationship of a domain, individual instances of concepts can

```
<InteractionBehavior name="BookingHotel">
    <Steps>
        <step name="booking_request" role="initiator" type="HotelLanguage"
                                        next="booking_proposal">
            <protocol>  <action name="CFP" end="false"/> </protocol>
        </step>
        <step name="booking_proposal" role="responder" type="HotelLanguage"
                                        next="booking_decision">
            <protocol>
                <choice>
                    <action name="refuse" end="true"/>
                    <action name="not_understood" end="true"/>
                    <action name="propose" end="false"/>
                </choice>
            </protocol>
        </step>
        ......
    </Steps>
</InteractionBehavior>
```

Fig. 4. Specification of interaction behavior in XML: an excerpt

be created and stored in a knowledge base. The resulted knowledge base can be used with problem-solving methods to answer questions (e.g., find all hotels in the region Heidelberg with prices lower than 100$ per night) and solve problems. Secondly, for agent-based information systems, ontologies are needed both for extracting information from different sources, which often use different words for the same piece of information and for the inter-agent communication. Agents located inside an agent platform efficiently communicate via Java objects as content of messages. For inter-platform communication, string-based content languages such as KIF, SL or XML are widely used. Figure 5 outlines the steps and supporting software tools to use ontology as described above.

The ontology editor allows users to create both ontologies and individual instances of concepts into a knowledge base. The knowledge base is used by a reasoning system such as the JTP [16] or FaCT [13], while the ontologies will be translated into XML Schema to be used for the exchange of data [17] (e.g., between agents). Supports for the data exchange include (1) the automatical creating of Java classes from a XML Schema, and (2) the automatical conversion of Java objects into strings of a particular content language and vice versa.

A plug-in of the ontology editor *Protégé* called *beangenerator* [2] creates schemas and Java classes from ontologies defined using Protégé [27]. However, they can only be used within the JADE agent framework [3]. The two available XML Schema plug-ins of Protégé [28] do not produce XML Schemas, which can be subsequently used to automatically create Java classes. Apart from them, *oil2xsd* [24] converts ontologies written in OIL into XML Schema, and the source generator of the Castor project [5] automatically creates Java classes from a XML Schema. Putting it together, ontologies written in OIL can be transformed into

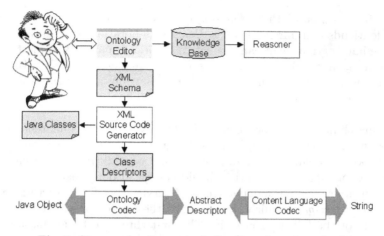

Fig. 5. Steps and software tools for the using of ontologies

Java classes using *oil2xsd* and the source generator of Castor. However, we decided to develop our ontology (or be more correct, the structure of data to be exchanged between agents) direct in XML Schema without an ontology editor, since we retrieve information from external sources instead of keeping an own knowledge base.

For the automatical conversion between Java objects and strings, we use a solution, which is slightly different from the one applied by JADE [4]. *Abstract descriptors* serve as intermediate objects between Java objects and the corresponding language-specific strings. Each Java object can be represented by an abstract descriptor that includes a number of named slots holding the values of its attributes. A *content language codec* is responsible for the conversion between strings and abstract descriptors, while an *ontology codec* converts a Java object into an abstract descriptor and vice versa. The ontology codec binds each Java class to a schema, which defines the structure of the Java class. In our approach, we use the schema encoded in the *class descriptors*, which are produced by the Castor source code generator together with the Java classes. A class descriptor provides methods to set and get the value of an attribute of the object. Therefore, we do not have to use the time-consuming Java Reflection API to inspect the Java objects, as it is done in JADE.

5 Agent Collaboration

Combinatively, five kinds of agent collaboration are conceivable in an information system. They are 1) collaboration between user interface agents, 2) between information agents, 3) between middle agents, 4) between interface and information agents, and 5) between interface, middle and information agents. The collaboration between user interface agents facilitates opinion-based filtering as used by the integrated restaurant service *IRES* [22]. When a user interface agent discovers a new restaurant or is not sure about a recommendation, it asks other user interface agents for their opinion. Trust values are used to divide agents in reliable friends and unreliable ones. Using collaboration between information agents, an information agent can delegate a request or part of a request to other information agents, if it is unable to serve the request alone [26]. Using several cooperating middle agents ensures load balancing and avoids single point of failure. Our integrated hotel reservation service employs the last two kinds of collaboration.

As a matchmaking middle agent, a hotel service manager matches *requests* from user interface agents to *capabilities* of registered hotel service agents. A challenging task is to define models of requests and capabilities. According to [10], a description of capabilities/service should consist of both basic service characteristics which are domain independent and service-specific characteristics. Our *hotel service description* which characterizes the service provided by a vendor site consists of the following criteria. The first three are basic characteristics, while the remaining ones are service-specific.

- *Popularity of a site:* summarizes how frequent human users have made use of its service, for instance, made a reservation through it.
- *Reliability:* is the likelihood of service failures,
- *Cost:* indicates the price-performance ratio it provides.
- *Service coverage and bias:* for example, the service of a vendor site may cover hotels located in Europe, Asia or worldwide. A vendor may claim a worldwide coverage but is specialized for hotels in Europe. The number of hotels found in different locations gives a hint on the coverage and bias.
- *Description of supported actions:* hotel services are provided in terms of several supported actions such as *search-hotel*, *book-hotel*, *cancel-reservation* and *change-reservation*. Each type of action is characterized by its vendor-defined cost (e.g., changing a reservation will be charged for 10$.) and its average duration.

Some characteristics in a hotel service description can be easily acquired from the vendor web site. They are, for example, the supported actions and their vendor-defined cost. Other characteristics like the duration of an action, reliability, popularity and cost of a site must be measured at runtime by user interface agents or evaluated by their associated human users. A hotel service manager stores hotel service descriptions provided by hotel service agents and updates them using the feedback from user interface agents. Each hotel service agent registers itself to the hotel service manager using a *hotel service agent description*, which includes the name of the agent, the address of the vendor site it encapsulates and the service description of the site. We model the requests from user interface agents using a *hotel service request description*. It includes

- the name of the desired action (e.g., *book-hotel*),
- the location of the searched hotels which is used to match against the service coverage and bias of hotel service agents, and
- search constraints. They specify the maximal number of expected results and preferences of the users. In response to the prevailing resource situation, e.g.,

in case of lower bandwidth, a resource-aware user interface agent would like to contact only one or two but not five or six hotel service agents. Preferences is a list of criteria on hotel service (e.g., {*reliability, price, popularity*}) which are ordered by descending importance for the user. They are used to rank the results.

6   Related Work

The bed and breakfast reservation service [26] targets the same domain as our integrated hotel service. Their approach differentiates from ours in two main aspects. Firstly, they do not use the World Wide Web as information source. Instead, hotel information is delivered by hotel providers and kept in the databases of the so-called B+B agents (Bed and Breakfast agents). Secondly, the B+B agents collaborate in order to satisfy users' requests. Whenever a B+B agent is not able to serve the user, it delegates the request to other B+B agents. In our system, a user interface agent broadcasts the user's request to several hotel service agents and gathers the results. We give human users more control over which hotel service agents to contact. For the same reason, users are asked to evaluate the services provided by different vendors.

Decker et. al. presented in [8] an architecture for information agents and described a set of reusable behaviors/tasks of these agents such as advertising, information monitoring and cloning. Rapid construction of new classes of information agents can be enabled through the reuse and combination of these existing behaviors. Their work on agent behaviors is complementary to our work on interaction behaviors.

Recently, the OpenTravel Alliance (OTA) publishes their specifications for the interoperability of travel services (e.g., hotel, flight and holiday booking or car rental) [25]. The specifications define message contents that are transferred among travel services in XML Schema. As part of future work we intend to compare our schema with the OTA schema.

In the advent of web services [19], languages and ontologies such as WSDL [6] and DAML-S [7] have been defined for describing the properties and capabilites of web services. Our *service description* and *hotel service agent description* are used by the hotel service manager to *locate* the hotel service agents, but not to invoke or activate their service. They are comparable to the service profile part of DAML-S. It is conceivable that both a single hotel service agent and the integrated hotel reservation service can participate in an open environment, which web services focus on.

7   Conclusions and Future Work

In this paper, we presented our information agent system, an integrated hotel reservation service system. Using it as a case study, we discussed the design and implementation of information agent systems.

When considering "periphery" of information agent systems such as interface to human users and external information sources, most of previous works focus on the design of human machine interface or on the task of information retrieval. They take the interaction of these components to the rest of the system as granted. However, our experience in implementing our hotel reservation services showed that it is worth investigating the *interaction behavior* when taking an agent-based information system *as a whole*. Although interactions between agents and between components of an agent are achieved in different ways, they are guided by (almost) the same protocol. Using our hotel reservation system as an example, we illustrated how this apparently trivial observation helps systematically designing and validating interaction mechanism. Then, we illustrated how to enable rapid prototyping of information systems using source code generation with XSL.

Apart from the aspect of interaction, we described how ontologies can be used in information-based agent systems. Our experience showed that it is very time-consuming to find the appropriate software tools to use ontologies. We proposed the steps to be go through to use ontologies and evaluated software tools, which automate these steps. To enable collaboration between interface and information agents through matchmaking, we have developed models, which characterize the capabilities of hotel service agents and requests issued by the users. Feedback from the users (or their associated agents) are used to dynamically adapt the capabilities modeled.

Programming agent-based information systems is inherently interdisciplinary. We take our hotel reservation service system, which is still work in progress as playground to investigate the broad range of aspects arising in information systems. For future work, we plan to develop an infrastructure, which supports the design and software reuse of information agent systems.

References

1. Project agentcities. http://www.agentcities.org.
2. *Bean generator.* http://gaper.swi.psy.uva.nl/beangenerator/content/main.php.
3. F. Bellifemine, A. Poggi, and G. Rimassa. JADE - A FIPA-compliant agent framework. In *Proc. The Practical Application of Intelligent Agents and Multi-Agents (PAAM 99)*, pages 97–108, 1999. http://sharon.cselt.it/projects/jade/.
4. G. Caire. *JADE Tutorial: Application-Defined Content Languages and Ontologies*, 2002.
5. *Castor - The Source Generator.* http://castor.exolab.org.
6. E. Christensen, F. Curbera, G. Meredith, and S. Weerawarana. *Web Services Description Language (WSDL) 1.1*, 2001. http://www.w3.org/TR/2001/NOTE-wsdl-20010315.
7. DAML-S Coalition. DAML-S: Web Service Description for the Semantic Web. In *Proc. of the first International Semantic Web Conference (ISWC)*, 2002.
8. K. Decker, A. Pannu, K. Sycara, and M. Williamson. Designing Behaviors for Information Agents. In *Proc. of the first Conference on Autonomous Agents (Agents'97)*, 1997.

9. K. Decker and K. Sycara. Intelligent Adaptive Information Agents. *Journal of Intelligent Information Agents*, 9:239–260, 1997.
10. K. Decker, K. Sycara, and M. Williamson. Modeling Information Agents: Advertisements, Organizational Roles, and Dynamic Behavior. In *Proc. of the AAAI-96 Workshop on Agent Modeling*, 1996.
11. Y. Ding, C. Kray, R. Malaka, and M. Schillo. RAJA-A Resource-Adaptive Java Agent Infrastructure. In *Proc. of the 5th International Conference on Autonomous Agents (Agents 2001)*, 2001.
12. Project EMBASSI. http://www.embassi.de.
13. The FaCT System.
    http://www.cs.man.ac.uk/ horrocks/FaCT/.
14. *Foundation for Intelligent Physical Agents. Specifications*, 2000.
    http://www.fipa.org.
15. FIPA-OS, 1999. http://fipa-os.sourceforge.net.
16. JTP: An Object-Oriented Modular Reasoning System.
    http://ksl.stanford.edu/software/jtp/.
17. M. Klein, D. Fensel, F. van Harmelen, and I. Horrocks. The relation between ontologies and xml schemas. *Electronic Trans. on Artificial Intelligence*, 2001. Special Issue on the 1st International Workshop "Semantic Web: Models, Architectures and Management".
18. N. Kushmerick and B. Thomas. Adaptive information extraction: Core technologies for information agents. In *Intelligent Information Agents R&D in Europe: An AgentLink perspective*, 2002.
19. S. McIlraith, T. Son, and H. Zeng. Semantic Web Services. *IEEE Intelligent Systems*, 16(2):46–53, 2001.
20. F. Menczer, W. Street, N. Vishwakarma, A. E. Monge, and M. Jakobsson. IntelligShopper: A Proactive, Personal, Private Shopping Assistant. In *Proc. of the first International Conference on Autonomous Agents & Multiagent Systems (AAMAS'02)*, 2002.
21. Micro FIPA-OS, 2001. http://www.cs.Helsinki.FI/group/crumpet/mfos/.
22. M. Montaner, B. Lopez, E. Acebo, S. Aciar, and I. Cuevas. *IRES: On the Integration of Restaurant Services*, 2002. Available as http://arlab.udg.es/GenialChef.pdf.
23. J. Odell, H. V. D. Parunak, and B. Bauer. Extending UML for Agents. In *Proc. of the Agent-Oriented Information Systems Workshop (AOIS) at the 17th National conference on Artificial Intelligence (AAAI)*, 2000.
24. *OIL to XML Schema Transformator.*
    http://savannah.nongnu.org/projects/oil2xsd/.
25. *OpenTravel Alliance Specification Version 2002B*, 2002.
    http://www.opentravel.org/2002b.cfm.
26. J. Padget and W. Barbera-Medina. A bed and breakfast reservation service. In *Proc. Workshop on Agentcities: Challenges in Open Agent Environments, held in conjuction with the first International Conference on Autonomous Agents & Multiagent Systems (AAMAS'02)*, 2002.
27. *The Protégé Project.* http://protege.stanford.edu/.
28. *Protégé Plug-ins Library.* http://protege.stanford.edu/plugins.html.
29. H. Wong and K. Sycara. A Taxonomy of Middle-agents for the Internet. In *Proc. of the fourth International Conference on Multi-agent Systems*, pages 465–466, 2000.

Applying Agents for Engineering of Industrial Automation Systems

Thomas Wagner

Institute of Industrial Automation and Software Engineering
University of Stuttgart
Pfaffenwaldring 47, D-70550 Stuttgart – Germany
Fax: +49 711 685 7302, Phone: +49 711 685 7295
wagner@ias.uni-stuttgart.de

Abstract. Designing, operating and maintaining industrial plants require extensive and complex engineering processes. An integrated engineering process considering all different aspects, data and workflow of plant automation design as well as interoperability to other systems is the key to more efficiency and lower costs of engineering tasks in the plant life cycle. There exists no comprehensive and satisfying solution to this problem today. However, an agent-oriented view can lead to fundamentally new and promising approaches to an integrated plant engineering process. The goal of this paper is to clearly identify the specific goals and challenges in engineering industrial plants and to show that agents are a beneficial approach to meet them. To this end, an agent-oriented solution for integrated engineering of automation systems is presented, applying the advantages of agent concepts while considering the constraints of existing automation structures.

Keywords. Automation systems, plant design & engineering, agent applications

1 Introduction

Engineering of industrial automation systems is an extensive and complex process that differs strongly from systems engineering in other application domains. This results from the fact that automation systems in industrial plants (like pharmaceutical, production or power plants) are complex, large and persistent hardware / software systems being stamped by the characteristics of the technical processes they are designed to control. Hardware and software within these systems are strongly interrelated and in designing a plant the mechanical, electrical, process and control software aspects have to be considered. The software in classical automation systems accomplishes the typical automation functions for control of the technical process [1]: control of sequences, signaling, handling, operating, monitoring and supervision. To implement this functionality, special languages with low abstraction level are applied (defined in IEC 61131-3). Examples are function building blocks and sequential function charts.

However today the software in automation systems faces new challenges. Firstly, automation systems are subject to ongoing partial modifications: rapid development and decreasing costs of high-capacity hardware components cause changes in the

M. Schillo et al. (Eds.): MATES 2003, LNAI 2831, pp. 62–73, 2003.

plant's hardware structure and functionality during its life cycle, which is up to 30 years. As existing plants cannot be rebuilt due to high investment volumes, the changes in hardware components affect particularly the software: it has to be modified continuously and its amount and complexity increases. Besides that plant operating managers increasingly require the possibility to use hardware and software components of different manufacturers and technologies in their plants [2]. Both trends result in increasing efforts for integration and configuration of the automation system. Hardware components of different manufacturers e.g. often require individual parameterization tools, resulting in a large set of tools for the engineer to handle [3].

Besides that, plant operating managers today want to manage and optimize the use and the maintenance of their assets during the operating of the plant. And finally, a strong need for the integration of functionality from enterprise management and business levels into the automation system arises (vertical integration) [2]. As automation systems have been evolved isolated from other enterprise software systems, every system has its own grown architecture and data structures and the efforts for establishing interoperability of the heterogeneous systems are high. These aspects are discussed in more detail in [4;5;6;7]. They all affect tasks and processes for the engineering of automation systems, leading to three main challenges:

1. **Faster development and modification of automation systems in plants**, e.g. engineer support in plant design (planning), implementation and commissioning.
2. **Support in plant management and engineering during operation**, e.g. condition monitoring, diagnosis, maintenance and asset management.
3. **Integration and interoperability of different heterogeneous systems,** e.g. enterprise resource planning systems, or parameterization tools for field devices.

Today a lot of these engineering and integration tasks are done manually with high effort and costs. There is a strong need in the industry for extensive support of these tasks by additional engineering functionality of the automation system. However, the listed challenges result in strong requirements on flexibility and adaptability of the software during the whole life cycle [8]. And, for the automation of engineering and integration tasks also more autonomy in the software is needed. As explained in [6], existing automation system software concepts with static architectures and functionality are not capable to meet these requirements.

The agent-oriented paradigm is a promising new approach for systems that are complex, distributed and changeable. It is a reasonable alternative to contemporary approaches in software engineering [9]. But not much work has been done yet to investigate how agent-oriented approaches could help on dealing with the imbalance of existing automation system structures compared to the new engineering challenges. This paper analyses the problem domain and presents a agent-oriented concept that brings a substantial new approach for the engineering and integration challenges within existing automation software.

This paper is structured as follows. In Section 2 the classical way of engineering automation systems in plants together with its problems is introduced. In Section 3 modern component-based approaches are investigated. The agent-based engineering approach is presented in Section 4. It shows the use and the advantages of agent concepts for engineering automation systems.

2   Engineering of Industrial Automation Systems

In this paper the term *engineering* is used with regards to automation systems in industrial plants. According to [10], engineering is defined as

"...all tasks and activities, that are carried out for the purpose of planning, installation, commissioning, operation and maintenance of technical plants."

This definition emphasizes that engineering not only concerns the functional aspects of automation software, but spans over the whole life cycle of a plant. Fig. 1 depicts example engineering activities during the plant life cycle. Several engineering areas participate in the engineering process of the automation planning project, like process planning, plant structure planning, electrical planning, or control software design. They regard different aspects of the automation system. In each engineering area particular aspects of the entities (devices) are parameterized and the entity is integrated in the automation system in different ways. For instance in the process planning mechanical assembly of devices and material flows are determined while in the electrical planning the electrical connections of devices are established.

The most important characteristic of the classical engineering process is the strong orientation to the different participating engineering areas. Their separated activities - each representing a specific view on the plant - are done by engineering experts who use their expert's tools (CAD/CAE-systems), create a view-specific partial model of the plant and generate specific data output. The sum of all view-specific data represents the plant documentation. Although the tools and data are separated it is obvious that the various engineering activities are not independent of each other, but have a lot of interrelations as all views regard the same real plant.

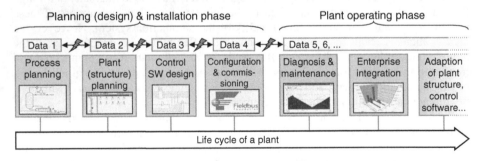

Fig. 1. Engineering activities during the life cycle of a plant (see also [11])

The isolated data storage and individual proprietary semantics of the view-specific tools cause a missing transferability (overall usability) of the created engineering data between the different tools. During the plant planning phase often changes have to be made in the automation planning project. Configurations of a particular entity, of a large number of entities or even a whole model may change frequently. As the view-specific activities have a lot of interrelations and dependencies, manual multiple data entry is necessary. For example, if changes in a process planning model occur, the control software has also to be adapted. The manual multiple entry and adaptation of data causes the strong problem of inconsistent data (usually manual naming conventions are used to reduce this problem). Also an extensive support of engineering processes (like problem solving processes and workflow between engineering areas) is not possible. Another effect of the separated planning tools and data is the missing availability of planning data for engineering activities during the operation of the plant like diagnosis, maintenance, asset management, integration of enterprise systems (like ERP or MIS), asset optimization amongst others.

Today the separation of views and tools of the different engineering areas do not match the requirements for effective engineering. Instead an integrated consideration of all engineering activities as well as the activities during plant operating phase is necessary (see also [11]). Modern engineering approaches try to address the problems of data and process integration as explained in the following Section.

3   Modern Engineering Approaches with Technological Components

The goal of modern engineering approaches is to increase the productivity of the engineering activities by supporting of the engineering process in three points:

- Automation of task sequences during the engineering process
- Integration and transferability of engineering data
- Reuse of engineering solutions (automation planning projects or parts of them)

New approaches for the development of automation systems have to consider the fact that the automation system itself hardly can be changed [6]. Alternative solutions have to support existing system architectures and legacy systems to a large extend. To solve this problem, automation software companies developed modern approaches for the engineering of automation systems based on component-based ideas.

Starting point of modern engineering approaches are the different engineering views on a plant. For the integration of the engineering data, similarities between the different views can be identified: the link between all individual views on the plant is the real existing device within the plant with its various aspects for the automation of the plant. All participating engineers view their respective aspects of the device. Some aspects concern the device itself like mechanical / electrical characteristics, electrical / process connections and control software. Other aspects concern the actual position and tasks of the device within the automation system like device configuration, wiring diagrams and operating graphs.

The basic idea of the approach is to combine all different views in a single entity and thus to modularize the engineering data analogous to the real entities in the plant (physical decomposition, see [2]). The entities are called "technological components" [7] (other notions are e.g. "planning objects"). They represent a kind of data container, where the several engineering aspects are integrated and associated. Based on this component approach for the integration of engineering data the different views, their interrelations and the engineering processes as well as workflow can be supported. Fig. 2 illustrates the idea of data integration into technological components.

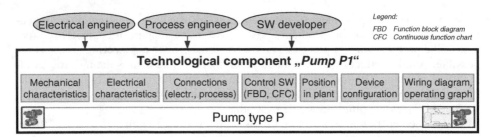

Fig. 2. Integration of engineering data with technological components

The technological components are the starting point for a higher-level engineering view on the plant's automation system. They represent a hierarchical structuring of the plant from an abstract technological perspective (e.g. mechanical assembly, location). Technological components represent mechanical or process elements (valve, pump), electronic elements (switch, contactor), automation hardware (PLC, I/O-card) or even automation software [7]. In the example in Fig. 3 on the right a project is designed with a boiler, consisting of a valve and a pump. Attached to the technological components are their particular views and the views they are part of. The example shows the boiler's operating graph and the function block diagram of the pump.

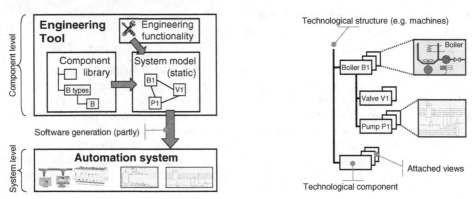

Fig. 3. Engineering with technological components: principle (left) and example (right)

Fig. 3 on the left shows the principle of a engineering with technological components. It represents a higher abstraction level of engineering on a component-based level. The engineering process for a particular automation project now is done by the creation of a system model of the automation system by instantiation, composition and parameterization of predefined 'empty' technological components from a library. Different technological structures (e.g. the mechanical assembly view) can be created and combined to an overall structure, whereas in every view different connections are established. For example in a control diagram the same elements are connected in another way than in a wiring diagram or in a operating graph.

This concept generally advances the engineering process in three main points:

1. Integration of engineering data in a high-level technological view with associated aspects: basis for integrated workflow and the reuse of solutions – of predefined library components as well as of created model (parts).
2. Support of engineering processes by creation of system model by component selection, instantiation, composition and parameterization.
3. Technology independent reuse by abstraction of the created system model from the target automation system technology (e.g. Siemens S7), partly generation of automation system software possible (depends on tool).

Examples of tools are Innotec Comos PT, ABB Industrial IT, Intergraph SmartPlant, Eplan PPE. They offer extensive engineering functionality (see Fig. 3) to support the various facets of the engineering process. They provide methods and functions to meet the prevailing challenges and problems, the engineer has to cope when designing a plant's automation system in a component-based way. Examples are:

- **Management of components' dependencies.** There are a lot of different types of complex associations between components, e.g. type-instance associations (library and planning project), associations and inheritance in technological hierarchy, or connections (like motor and wires). Associations depend on particular views. When changes are made in the model, conflicts have to be recognized and solved.
- **Model consistency.** E.g. ensuring data consistency between particular views.
- **Mass data changes.** E.g. when a parameter of a certain valve type has to be changed in a large number of valves. This requires support for search, selection of components and propagation of changes. Here also conflicts have to be recognized.
- **Reuse of engineering solutions.** Reuse addresses a wide range of problems, e.g. in what way reuse is possible (project internal or between projects), granularity of reusable solutions, intelligent management of components' dependencies, data reuse vs. know-how reuse (design decisions and patterns).
- **Support for different users and access rights**
- **Configuration management and deviation management**
- **Diagnosis of engineering errors**

The next Section discusses the constraints of modern engineering tools regarding theses challenges. An agent-oriented view leads to a basically improved approach.

4   Applying Agents for Plant Engineering

The merits of modern component-based engineering approaches result from the idea to create an abstract model of the automation system. The engineering process itself is a transformation process of the engineer's understanding about the automation system into a model of the system. In the depicted component-based approach this model is a *static* image of the automation system. The components are solely data containers for the engineering data (what from parts of the automation software can be generated). The transformation process is characterized by the specific challenges discussed in Section 3. Component-based engineering tools try to meet these challenges by supporting the transformation process by providing a set of engineering functionality. As the problem domain of automation systems and therefore the engineering process itself is quite multifaceted and complex, the functionality the tools have to provide is also extensive and complex (e.g. an "intelligent" copy-paste functionality for managing the dependencies when reusing model parts). It is arguable, if along with new challenges on the engineering process this functionality can be maintained.

A basically different approach in supporting the engineering process is to proceed decisions and handling of engineering functionality in the place where the most information on the current situation (position, tasks, associations, dependencies) of a particular entity in the model is available: within the entity itself. Therefore a concept is needed that provides more than static data containers.

The agent-oriented paradigm is a software paradigm that especially emphasizes the localization of knowledge and decision. In our understanding of agent-oriented software engineering, the concept of an agent is an *"encapsulated (software) entity with a defined objective. An agent tries to reach it's objective with autonomous actions and in doing so it can interact with it's environment and other agents, while keeping a persistent state.*[1]*"* Based on the agent concept a solution for the support of the engineering process can be developed, where the entities themselves perform the engineering functionality actively. Seeking this solution, the first step is analyzing the engineering of automation systems from an agent-oriented view.

4.1   Agent-Oriented Analysis of the Engineering Process

Agent-oriented analysis is the abstraction of a problem by means of agent concepts. In Section 2 the problem of engineering automation systems in plants was described in general. The main engineering activities, processes and goals can be regarded independently from a particular automation planning project. We can analyze these activities from an agent-oriented point of view. To this end, the concept of role analysis can be applied. In role analysis, the notion of a role focuses on the position and responsibilities of an entity within an overall structure or system [13]. Roles result from tasks a particular entity has to fulfill within the system, in order to provide the system's overall functionality. Applying this concept to the problem of engineering automation systems, both the challenges in the engineering process as well as the characteristics of the industrial automation systems domain that influence these challenges[2] have to be regarded. In the description in Section 2 we can identify that nearly all engineering tasks have an association to some kind of real existing entity within the plant. Each entity is integrated in the plant in different ways, where different engineering activities have to be accomplished. Focussing on the entities within the plant we can identify roles that e.g. a particular device obtains during the engineering process. Table 1 shows an overview of these roles.

The result of the agent-oriented analysis based on roles is an agent-oriented meta model of the engineering process. The overview in Table 1 shows the most important characteristic: the predominantly active elements in the engineering process are the

---

[1]   This definition adapts those of Jennings & Wooldridge (see [9;12]). The author strongly agrees with their definition, but additionally wants to stress the fact that the notion of an agent has to be seen not only in the sense of an implemented computer system, but as a comprehensive concept for thinking about and designing software.

[2]   The meaning of roles in the context of automation systems is discussed in [6].

Table 1. Roles of entities in the engineering process

Role	Explanation	Activities (examples)
Representation of particular view (multiple occurrence)	Reflects the different participating engineering areas. All activities are view-specific, but depend on settings in other views.	• Acquire view-specific data • Accomplish engineering sequences • Manage view-specific associations to other entities • Ensure consistency to other views
Instantiation, configuration	The entity's functionality has to be customized when it is instantiated for a planning project.	• Support selection of desired entity and functionality • Support setting of parameters • Adapt or reconcile parameters
Integration (composition)	On integrating an entity in the system, it is assembled in a particular place[3] in a particular environment.	• Establish associations to other existing entities (view-specific) • Consider existing rules / constraints
Access rights management	Manage data access of different user types.	• Provide / deny read and write access to engineering data
Configuration management	Entities or models have different configurations.	• Handle several configurations • Recognize configuration conflicts
Commission, monitoring, maintenance	Part of engineering processes during plant operating phase (see sect. 5).	• Manage deviation between model and automation system • Condition monitoring of an entity
Superordinate responsibilities	Roles that are spanning over several or all entities.	• Manage devices search data • Inspect model for engineering errors

planned entities in the plant. In every engineering activity one or more entities are concerned and obtain one or more roles. Obtaining a role the entities handle data and accomplish activities. These planned entities are the same abstract elements as the technological components used as data-containers in the component-based engineering approach. On one hand, this shows that both approaches are reasonable ones for the plant engineering process. On the other hand, the component-based approach falls short in separating engineering data (within technological components) and engineering functionality (provided by the tool). However, engineering with technological components is familiar to the engineer's way of thinking [7] and in most cases it is transparent to the user how a certain functionality in a tool is achieved. Therefore a combination of both approaches could bring the most value.

---

[3] The term "place" depends on the current view, it means either physically in mechanical assembly views or logically in other views.

4.2   Agent-Based Plant Engineering Approach

In the agent-oriented meta model of the engineering process based on role analysis the entities in the automation system are aware of their position and tasks. The conceptual model of technological components encapsulates all engineering data belonging to an entity. The combination of both enables an entity to handle actively all necessary engineering functionality. Fig. 4 on the left metaphorically shows the consolidation of this meta model with the conceptual model of technological components: the agent representing an entity within the plant is integrated in the technological component. The agent-oriented meta model can be implemented as an agent-based component library, providing both predefined engineering data and functionality. The agent represented as a technological component can - based on its roles - actively support the engineering process using the knowledge of its current position, data and dependencies in the planning project. Therefore the term of agent-based engineering in the context of this paper means **engineering based on agents**.

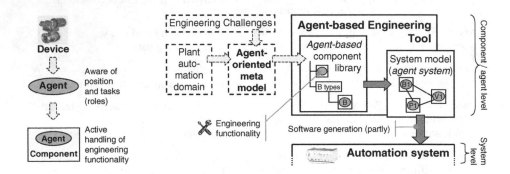

Fig. 4. Agent-based plant engineering: metaphor (left) and principle (right)

In designing the automation system with the agent-based component library the same engineering process is performed with selection, instantiation, integration and parameterization of the familiar components. However, in doing so now an agent system is build (Fig. 4 on the right). The whole engineering process is based on an agent-system which is transparent to the engineer. Metaphorically speaking the created agent system is a "living" system model, that takes care of itself.

Fig. 5 shows the roles and associations within an agent-based engineering environment. When a component is selected from the component library and instantiated in the system model (the planning project), a type-instance association is established between the two involved agents. Thereby a flexible handling of the various dependencies, e.g. the reconciliation of changes between library component and instances (delta generation) is realized. In the case of a previous individually changed instance later inheriting changes from the library component, inevitable conflicts can be recognized and handled immediately. When the component is integrated in the planning project, connections are established between agents, that can also be handled actively in the course of the engineering process. Integrating the component in different views then addresses different roles and their respective representations, associations and restrictions. Engineering process support now can also be done by the management of requirements concerning particular "places" in the model. In Fig. 5 a requirement restricts the operating temperature for the Motor in the place of M1. It is represented by an agent. When the library component is integrated in this place, the two agents have to co-ordinate this requirement and in case the instantiated motor does not meet it, the user can be automatically informed.

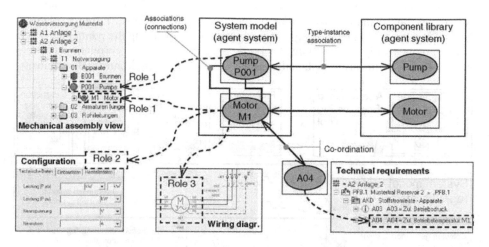

Fig. 5. Agent based plant engineering: roles and associations

The merits of the agent-based engineering approach are active support in instantiating and integrating components, management of components' dependencies, active propagation of changes and recognition of possible conflicts as well as engineering errors. Active management of dependencies also fundamentally improves the reuse of models or model parts. It represents a step towards the reuse of engineering know-how (like design decisions and patterns) instead of reuse of data. In the next Section the further possibilities of the approach are estimated.

4.3   Plant Integration with the Agent-Based System Model

In the agent-based engineering process a system model is created as an instantiated agent-system. It actively supports the engineering process and thus meets the first of the tree challenges mentioned in Section 1: *Faster development and modification of automation systems*. But moreover the model has further possibilities. It also absorbs the engineering knowledge about the plant like positions, tasks, associations and dependencies. And it is a standalone application, a kind of parallel high-level process control system. This high-level system with "active components" that are aware of their position and tasks contains the essential engineering knowledge to be the basis for meeting the remaining two engineering challenges discussed in sect. 1: *support in plant management and engineering during operation* and *integration of different heterogeneous systems in the environment of the automation system*. The active components (alias agents) can be used to acquire necessary information from the automation system, using the technical possibilities of existing interfaces and to coordinate all of the information flows to connected systems. And in some cases it is even possible to intervene in the running automation system.

For example an agent representing a pump *P1* in the model could be assigned the goal to observe the physical pump. It can address the pump via the automation system's interfaces [3] and collect the diagnosis status signals. Moreover, by the maintenance system the agent could be given the goal to analyze the status signals and if required generate a maintenance order in the associated enterprise resource planning system. It even could guide or support the mechanic in repairing the pump and if necessary automatically re-configure the pump. Fig. 6 shows the correlation between system model, engineering tool, automation system and the environmental systems.

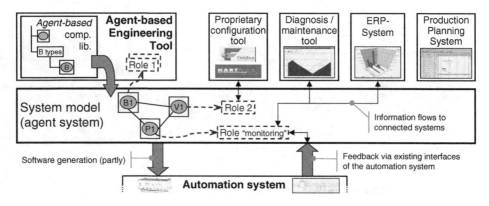

Fig. 6. Plant integration with an agent-based system model

All necessary infrastructure for the system model to fulfill its engineering tasks during plant operation is provided by the *Agent Plant Integration Framework*. It provides infrastructure like access to the automation systems interfaces. External systems can be encapsulated by agent adapters and data semantics of inhomogeneous systems can be mapped within the framework. In designing the system model of the plant the framework is tailored for the real automation system. Its infrastructure combined with the agent-based system model provides the basis for all engineering tasks during operation like monitoring, supervision, diagnosis, maintenance, simulation, quality analysis as well as integration of legacy and proprietary configuration tools, enterprise & business administration systems and electronic plant documentation.

5   Conclusion

The challenges on plant automation systems require improved support of engineering and integration tasks by the automation system itself. The classical fragmentation of the engineering process into separated views and view-specific tools leads to missing transferability of data, high engineering and integration effort in both plant design and plant operation phase, and to less reusable solutions. New component-based approaches integrate the specific views and data in a higher-level technological image of the system. However, they fall short due to the facts of separating engineering data from functionality and the created system model remaining a static data model.

In this paper the idea of combining the component-based higher-level system model with an agent-oriented meta model of the engineering process was presented. It leads to the approach of agent-based engineering, where the engineering functionality is accomplished by the components themselves. Thereby a better and more flexible support of processes is possible. And, the essential engineering knowledge now is absorbed by the created system model as it is an agent-system. This knowledge can be used as the basis for all engineering tasks during the life cycle of a plant. The Agent Plant Integration Framework therefore provides all necessary infrastructure.

The presented approach employs the merits of agent concepts like autonomous acting, flexible interactions and goal-orientation to extensively support the engineering of automation systems in plants and the integration of heterogeneous systems in the environment of the automation system. Refinement and realization of this approach is subject to work in progress. Working points are the agent-oriented engineering model, design of the framework, "agentification" of legacy component-based engineering models and establishing technical communication to the automation system, like data access for automatic adaptation of the model to changes in the plant.

References

1. Lauber, R.; Göhner, P.: Prozessautomatisierung I, 3. Edition, Springer-Verlag Berlin, 1999
2. Shen, W. and Norrie, D.H.: Agent-Based Systems for Intelligent Manufacturing: A State-of-the-Art Survey. Knowledge and Information Systems, 1(2), 1999, p. 129–156
3. Barata, J.; Camarinha-Matos, L.; et.al.: Integrated and Distributed Manufacturing, a Multi-agent Perspective, 3. Workshop on European Scientific and Industrial Collaboration, 2001
4. Leitão, P.; Barata, J.; Camarinha-Matos, L.; and Boissier, R.: Trends in Agile and Co-operative Manufacturing. Proceedings of Low Cost Automation Symposium, 2001
5. Parunak, H.V.D.: Practical and industrial applications of agent-based systems. Environmental Research Institute of Michigan (ERIM), 1998
6. Wagner, T.: An agent-oriented approach to industrial automation systems. In: Kowalczyk et. al. (Eds.), Agent Technologies, Infrastructures, Tools and Applications for E-services 2002, Lecture Notes in Artificial Intelligence Nr. 2592, Springer-Verlag, 2003, p. 314–328
7. Löwen, U.: Informationstechnologie als Enabler für effizientes Anlagenengineering. Lecture: Methods of Software Engineering, Institute of Automation and Software engineering, 2002
8. Albrecht, H.; Meyer, D.: Ein Metamodell für den operativen Betrieb automatisierungs- und prozessleittechnischer Komponenten. at – Automatisierungstechnik, Heft 50, 3/2002
9. Jennings, N.R.: On agent-based software engineering. Artificial Intelligence 117, 2000
10. Simon., R.: Gerätemodell zur Feldinstrumentierung von verteilten Automatisierungs-systemen. at – Automatisierungstechnik, Heft 10, 2002
11. Rauprich, G.; et. al.: PLT-CAE - Integration in gewerkeübergreifendes Engineering und Plant-Maintainance, atp - Automatisierungstechnische Praxis 44 (Heft 2), 2002
12. Jennings, N.R.; Sycara, K.; Wooldridge, M.: A Roadmap of Agent Research and Development. Autonomous Agents and Multi-Agent Systems, 1, 1998, p. 275–306
13. Kendall, E.: Role Modeling for Agent System Analysis, Design, and Implementation. First Internat. Symposium on Agent Systems and Applications (ASA'99), Palm Springs, 1999

SimMarket: Multiagent-Based Customer Simulation and Decision Support for Category Management

Arndt Schwaiger and Björn Stahmer

DFKI GmbH
Stuhlsatzenhausweg 3
66123 Saarbrücken
{Arndt.Schwaiger, Bjoern.Stahmer }@dfki.de

Abstract. A key to an optimal assortment of goods and pricing of individual items in a store is the knowledge about potential customer's behaviour. In this paper we present the simulation of individual customers based on a *multiagent system* which models the important elements and external influences as single agents. An agent can be member of several agent groups which are represented as *holons*. We model each individual customer as an agent which behaves according the customer's individual preferences. These preferences are extracted from real world data, such as customer cards, sales data and interviews. The customer's shopping behaviour is represented in *behaviour networks* (Bayesian nets) which are stored in the customer agents' knowledge bases. The behaviour of a representative group of customers induces the overall sales figures, which support decisions what to sell at which price. The presented concepts are based on ideas of Joachim Hertel from DACOS and Jörg Siekmann from the DFKI. They are implemented as a prototype, which provides, after further evaluation, the basis for a new and final system to be used by retailers.

1 Introduction

Increasing globalisation helps international retail chains to gain more and more market share and more pressure is put onto local competitors. This is especially true for supermarkets and drugstores which have to develop new strategies to remain competitive. An essential part of the competitive position is the optimization of assortments and prices. This is often done by Category Managers, who are making the decisions concerning product prices, promotions, placement and assortment of goods which are crucial for the success or failure of an individual store.

In the daily decision making process there are many different alternatives and combinations from which the person in charge has to map out an optimal strategy. The biggest problem is the enormous amount of alternatives and the complexity of internal relationships and external influences, such as competitor's prices and promotions, market trends, the economic situation and weather conditions. An average supermarket sells several thousand different items which could be selected out of up to half a million of products. These numbers alone illustrate the "combinatorial explosion" of possible combinations quickly exceeding human capabilities. In addition, most of the changes concerning a single item, such as price increase or reduction are

M. Schillo et al. (Eds.): MATES 2003, LNAI 2831, pp. 74–84, 2003.

likely to interfere with the sales of other items. The decision processes are usually supported by a computer but the support is mostly limited to the provision of information about current market figures and the generation of some sales forecast which are unsuitable for "*what-if*"-scenarios.

A number of approaches have been considered, e.g. regress analysis [14] in economics, which provides means for a more accurate forecast. More recent approaches in computer science include the use of neural networks [14, 13]. Yet, all these approaches have significant disadvantages: regress analysis provides us with acceptable quantitative results; however, it allows for just a few factors to be included in the analysis and can only treat linear dependencies. Neural networks can cope with a much higher number of influencing factors and while single-layered networks can only model linear dependencies, a multi-layer neural network can even model nonlinear dependencies. The problem with neural networks is their fast rise in complexity which renders them unsuitable when augmenting the number of factors. As shown in [1] the possible existence of local minima and the large dimensional degree of the weights makes it increasingly difficult to train large multi-layer networks. Furthermore, even a small neural network becomes a black box in the sense that it takes an input and returns an output without providing the user with any insight on how the various factors correlate.

But more important is the fact that both approaches simply predict future values out of past experience without a deeper understanding of how the individual factors correlate. To sum up these approaches can support the decision making process only up to a certain extent resulting in suboptimal solutions to be optimized by man.

A fully satisfactory approach to this problem must be able to model and simulate the individual customer's behaviour as a reaction to both internal and external influences. Given perfect information on the individual behaviour of a customer we could then predict the overall behaviour of a group by considering the sum of the predictions for all individuals. For a large group it would even suffice to consider a representative subgroup to determine the likely overall reactions to influences like promotions or changes in price or location. The SimMarket approach does just that. It simulates a representative set of individual behaviours by modelling each individual customer through an individual software agent. Note that the behaviour is determined from real world data by using special learning algorithms to extract the relevant information where "real world" refers to data gathered by a store on its human customers. The agent architecture uses also known models from psychology and economics. It models the relevant entities and external factors of a supermarket in order to create a test scenario, where the agents react to the scenario according to their individual behaviour patterns. As these patterns are derived from the actual behaviour of individual human customers the system is capable of predicting realistic results. The data collection has been arranged by DACOS and is done in a partnership with three modern German retailers (tegut, dm-Markt and Globus) to ensure the desired level of realism. For example, the (anonymised) data contain information about customer card usage, sales, distribution, detailed information about individual products or promotions. We can furthermore include the experience of the responsible assortment and pricing managers in the system to guarantee realistic evaluation and testing of the system.

Current research on agent based customer modelling and simulation includes the following: *Consumat* by W. Jager [2] and the *SIMSEG* project [3] of the Vienna University of Economics and Business Administration as they share some conceptual approaches with SimMarket. The Consumat model is an agent-based implementation of psychological meta-models based on a number of customer behaviour relevant theories which unfortunately uses an abstract representation of the actual act of purchasing due to which it is not suited for practical use.

The SIMSEG project is a simulation environment for the analysis of market partitioning and strategies for positioning based on an abstract model which has to be designed manually. Its primary aim is to determine the results of corporate image chance with respect to the shopping behaviour on a larger level.

The area of user modelling which has a long history at DFKI [8], is closely related to the area of customer modelling. Multiagent based user modelling provides a rich basis of concepts for representing patterns of human behaviour in agents. Schaefer [9] successfully uses dynamic Bayesian networks [10]to model users of dialog systems and to personalise the application flow.

2 SimMarket Architecture

The aim of the SimMarket project is to develop a realistic representation of a single store or supermarket including the goods and customers to be modelled as agents.

We use a *holonic* multiagent system (MAS) which supports agent groupings as *holons* so that each individual agent can be a member of different agent groups. A *holon* is an agent that represents a group of agents whereas each group member keeps its individuality [4]. In addition the MAS is connected to a *data warehouse*[1] which stores real data from the related supermarket.

Fig. 1 shows the current architecture where each element is modelled as an agent. The whole supermarket is also represented by a *supermarket agent* which provides detailed information about the specific store, such as assortment of goods, item prices and promotions, shelf layouts, sales data, costs and so on.

The *customer agents* model the individual customers and their personal shopping behaviour. The system is able to represent each customer individually as well as an arbitrary number of (possibly not disjoint) customer groups and subgroups. The largest group of customers, the group of all customers, is represented by a *meta customer agent*.

Similarly all items are represented as *item agents* which are grouped into predefined commodity groups modelled by *commodity group agents*. In addition, items can be dynamically classified in order to generate item groups such as private brand items, all items which are lower than n Euros and so on. The group of all items is represented by the *meta item agent*.

The architecture of the MAS supports also *competitor agents* which model relevant competitors. These agents provide information about the competitor's prices, promotions and strategies. They may have links to common customers and items.

In forthcoming versions we want to add *manufacturer agents* which mainly provide information about the current range of products, their prices and promotions as well as details about forthcoming products.

---

[1] „A Data Warehouse is a subject-oriented, integrated, non-volatile, and time variant collection of data in support of managements decisions. " – Bill Inmon (1996)

Important external effects and influences e.g. current season, economic situation and weather conditions are represented by *environment agents*. These are information agents which collect and administrate the relevant data from external services or the internet. They generate simple forecasts or (if provided with insufficient data) request more detailed prognosis from external services (such as e.g. the daily weather forecast).

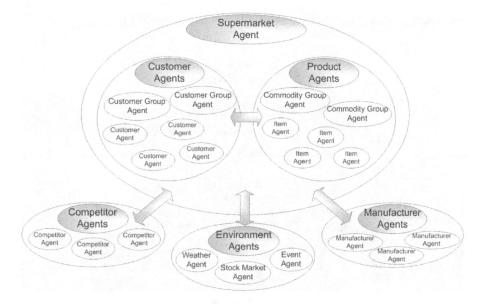

Fig. 1. The Holonic Multiagent Architecture of SimMarket

3   Customer Agent Architecture

The predictions of the shopping behaviour and preferences of customers are represented in the *customer agents*. Any individual customer that is known to the supermarket through empirical surveys, the use of customer cards, electronic payment or direct contact is represented as an individual customer agent.

Fig. 2 shows the model of a customer agent which administrates the knowledge and information about a related customer and his behaviour. The knowledge consists of a *personal profile* (information about age, income, gender, domicile etc.) and a special model of the customer's individual buying preferences.

We consider the customer's behaviour as an interaction of many different factors e.g. characteristics, addictions, needs and environmental influences. These factors may correlate or even contradict each other. For example, it is interesting whether the quality sensitivity outweighs the price sensitivity for a certain offer or not, i.e. whether a very low price can "persuade" a customer to purchase a low grade product or not.

Metaphorically speaking the characteristics of a customer compete for the greatest influence on the customer's decision. For this reason it is important to consider the customer's characteristics and factors themselves as *feature agents*. Each feature agent represents a single factor of the customer's behaviour, such as price and promotion consciousness or brand loyalty. Collectively, these agents form a multiagent system of their own, the *society of feature agents*. From this point of view the customer's (shopping) behaviour is the result of the interaction of its feature agents, a view which conforms with Marvin Minsky's "society of mind" [4].

Fig. 2. The Customer Agent Architecture including the *Society of Feature Agents*

3.1 Customer Agent Groups

According to the literature, the classification of a customer can be based on a variety of criteria or similarities, e.g. there are many different concepts and models of customer groups developed in marketing [12] and psychology, such as the "Sinus-Milieus" from Sinus Sociovision [6] or the "Euro-Socio-Styles" from CCA/Europanel [7].

In order to support complex groupings of customers in our system, each customer agent can be a member of one or more customer agent groups (see Fig. 3), which are represented as holonic agents. Thus, we are able to simulate a certain group of customers either by simulating all related individual group members (higher accuracy) or by simulating the average group behaviour (higher computational efficiency) depending on situation at hand.

Customer groups can be built beforehand or dynamically at runtime where the criteria can vary, for examples similarities concerning the personal profile (same age, gender or domicile etc.) or patterns of shopping (similar baskets of goods, same product interests, similar price consciousness etc.) or a combination (Fig. 3).

Evaluating the actual distribution of customers over *typical* customer groups by comparing the shopping data of individual customers to *typical* shopping baskets is our next goal. This will allow for a detailed ratio analysis of the customer groups of a supermarket and thereby to fine-tune the weighing of the group based simulation results.

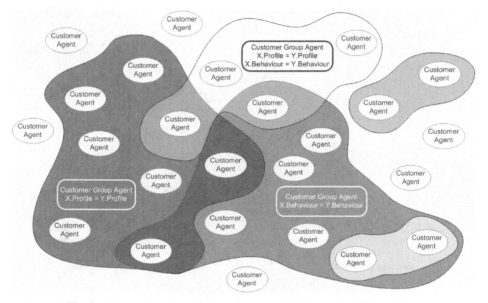

Fig. 3. Holonic Grouping of Customer Agents Concerning Different Criteria

3.2 Behaviour Networks

The empirical data, i.e. the characteristics of individual customer shopping behaviour, was primarily extracted from customer cards data, questionnaires and from general marketing knowledge. It is represented in behaviour networks, i.e. Bayesian nets. The quality of the customer simulation and prognosis depends mainly on how exact and realistic these characteristics and thus the shopping behaviour of individual customers can be modelled.

Our approach is based on a rule system where customer data is encoded in a set of rules which are associated with conditional probabilities. The rules are stored in a specific network structure - the behaviour network - to represent the dependencies between them. Bayesian networks are an example of such a network formalism. Currently, we model the behaviour of a customer by generating a specific Bayesian network for each relevant commodity group. We extract these networks by data mining patterns of behaviour from individual customer data (see Fig. 4). As a source for modelling the networks, we use anonymous customer cards and sales slip data of the retail company Globus.

In addition, we integrate the individual dependencies of single customers of external influences, e.g. weather, economic situation or seasons into the behaviour networks.

In later versions we will encode the customer's attitudes and habits in a matrix of feature agents. Every feature agent contains - as part of his knowledge base - a specific feature network which simulates the characteristics of a customer with respect to this feature.

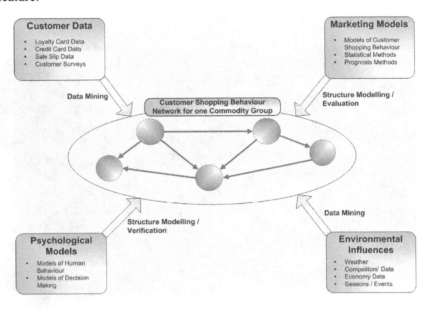

Fig. 4. Generation of the Customers' Behaviour Networks

Fig. 5 shows the user interface of the *SimMarket Customer Manager,* presenting a simple example of a Bayesian network which models the behaviour of a customer concerning a specific commodity group "Brötchen", i.e. bread roll. In this example, we are interested in the customer's price consciousness and his favoured shopping dates. On this account we create a behaviour network with the following nodes representing the price consciousness: "low-priced units", "mid-priced units", "high-priced units" and "value", i.e. how many low-priced, mid-priced and high-priced units the customer is expected to buy depending on the shopping date which in turn is modeled by the nodes "month", "part of month" and "weekday".

The customer's precise individual dependencies are data mined from his real shopping data and can be used for simulation. Therefore the date nodes have to be set accordingly to the desired date. Then the propagation algorithm [11] of the Bayesian network infers the effects on the dependent nodes. The result is summed up as expected values of the numbers of units which the customer is expected to purchase. E.

g. he buys 1 low-priced and 5 high-priced products of the related commodity group on the first Friday in June.

Similarly, it is possible to model more characteristics of the customer's personal behaviour to improve the simulation quality. In a later version each feature agent will contain at least one behaviour network for the related feature. The dependencies between the different characteristics are modeled by negotiation of the feature agents.

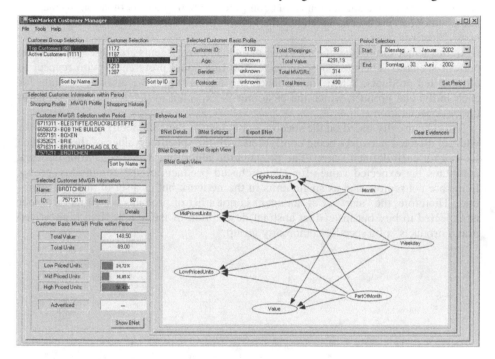

Fig. 5. The SimMarket System with a simple Bayesian Network

4   Agent-Based Simulation of Customer Behaviour

The decision about assortment, prices and promotions is based on assumptions concerning *future external influence factors* as well as the *current situation* and the result is a set of *internal changes* and *promotions* likely to lead to the company's business objectives.

Finding optimal sets of changes and promotions is the main challenge of the SimMarket project. The problem is that the company's primary objectives can vary between e.g. profit maximisation, cost reduction and increasing the number of customers.

Fig. 6 illustrates the simulation process of SimMarket at the level of a supermarket, i.e. regarding all possible decisions of a specific store.

First, a possible future scenario for the store is defined in accordance with the current situation on the basis of predicted external influences and planned internal changes. Based on this scenario a prediction about the possible impact of planned changes is generated by agent-based simulation. From the result the most important key figures are computed to indicate the degree to which the defined business objectives will be accomplished. To allow comparison and evaluation of the different scenarios more than one simulation run is computed. Finally the combination of changes and promotions is chosen, which has the highest probability to fulfil the defined business objectives.

In the actual simulation, the customer agents and item agents are presented with the current scenario. Their response indicates the individual preferences with respect to all affected products. When "questioned" the agents return the amount of units for each individual product, which the customer is expected to purchase in the scenario under consideration.

This is currently based on the specific behaviour of the commodity group networks with all affected networks being configured with the specified values of the influence factors for each defined action. The propagation algorithm of the behaviour network computes the expected values for all purchased products of the commodity group. Items are not represented as single units in the network but as a set of abstract attributes. Therefore, the "answer" of an agent is not a list of products which its customer is expected to buy but instead an abstract description of them, e.g. "five high-priced brand products" of a specific commodity group.

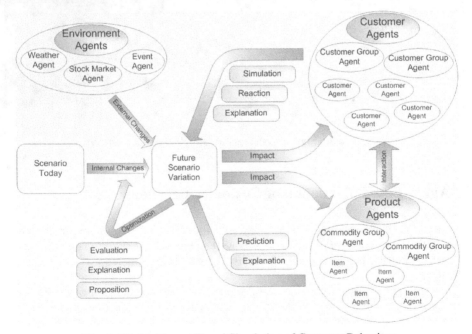

Fig. 6. The Multiagent-Based Simulation of Customer Behaviour

In later versions the simulation will comprise several steps. Initially, all relevant item agents give a description of their items in the form of an attribute list containing e.g. price category, placing, quality and promotions. These attributes are then matched with those of the feature agents and the feature agents are confronted with these item descriptions. The relevant feature agents react internally with quantified acceptance or rejection and the feature agents then "negotiate" the overall reaction of the customer agent with respect to the relevant commodity group. Again the result is a list of item descriptions which the customer is expected to buy. The list of attributes can be mapped to specific items. Based on this the expected amount of units sold per product is computed. A quantified prognosis about the behaviour of all customers is obtained by summing up the expectations.

Using this approach it is also possible to integrate *virtual customers* into the simulation, representing typical customer groups instead of individual customers e.g. young families, students or senior citizen. The quantitative distribution of these prototypes of customer groups is determined by an analysis of sales slip data or questionnaires and is then used for the simulation.

The use of behaviour networks serves also an explanatory purpose as it allows a new kind of evaluation: besides computing scenario rankings and key figures it is also possible to give detailed verbal and graphical explanations for the simulation results.

For example a direct connection between increasing the price of a product and loss of customers to a discounter may to be due to the extreme price sensitivity of a certain group and this is what the system reveals.

A selective simulation of customer groups is possible since the customer groups are modelled as holons and the system explicitly forecasts the effects on specific customers and/or customer groups. Thus, a simulation is highly scaleable as the system can optionally simulate all, only some or just the individual customers.

5 Conclusion and Outlook

SimMarket is a MAS-based approach which models a real supermarket with all items, customers and relevant external influences, where the holon-paradigm supports arbitrary dynamic agent groupings.

A model based on a combination of a top-down (predefined general agent structure) as well as a bottom-up (individual behaviour and agent groupings based on real data) approach is presented. The extraction of individual shopping behaviour of single customers from the sales records of supermarkets and its representation as behavioural networks in the knowledge bases is the core of SimMarket. It is the basis for simulation of customer behaviour (regarding assortment, price and promotion changes) and supports the assortment and pricing manager in his decision making process.

Future research will improve the model of the customer agents by enhancing the society of feature agents. By defining adequate measurements of similarity, customers are divided into groups and represented as holons. The simulation results will be empirically evaluated in comparison to realistic sales data of the past to predict the effects on the future.

References

1. Russell, S., and Norvig, P.: *Artificial Intelligence: A Modern Approach*. Second Edition. Prentice Hall, 2003.
2. Jager, W.: *Modelling Consumer Behaviour*. Rijksuniversiteit Groningen, Dissertation June 2000.
3. Buchta, C., and Mazanec, J.: SIMSEG/ACM – A Simulation Environment for Artificial Consumer Markets. Working Paper Nr. 79, May 2001.
4. Fischer, K., Schillo, M., and Siekmann, J. (In print): Holonic Multiagent Systems: The Foundation for the Organization of Multiagent Systems. Proceedings of the First International Conference on Applications of Holonic and Multiagent Systems (HoloMAS'03).
5. Minsky, M.: The Society of Mind. Simon and Schuster (Touchstone), 1986.
6. Sinus Sociovision, Paris, France, www.sociovision.com.
7. Europanel, London, UK, www.europanel.com.
8. A. Jameson. *Systems That Adapt to Their Users*. Tutorial presented at IJCAI 2001, www.dfki.de/~jameson.
9. R. Schaefer. Benutzermodellierung mit dynamischen Bayes'schen Netzen als Grundlage adaptiver Dialogsysteme. Dissertation, University of Saarland, 1998.
10. Judea Pearl. Probabilistic Reasoning in Intelligent Systems. Morgan Kaufmann Publishers INC. 1988.
11. R. E. Neapolitan. *Probabilistic Reasoning in Expert Systems: Theory and Algorithms*. A Wiley-Interscience Publication. John Wiley & Sons, Inc., New York. 1998.
12. W. Kroeber-Riel, P. Weinberg. *Konsumentenverhalten*. 7. Aufl., (Vahlen) München 1999.
13. Hean-Lee Poh, Jingtao Yao, Teo Jasic. Neural Networks for the Analysis and Forecasting of Advertising and Promotion Impact. Intelligent Systems in Accounting, Finance and Management, Vol. 7, No. 4, 1998.
14. Frank M. Thiesing. *Analyse und Prognose von Zeitreihen mit Neuronalen Netzen*. Dissertation, Mai 1998.

A Multi-agent Approach to the Design of an E-medicine System

Jiang Tian and Huaglory Tianfield

School of Computing and Mathematical Sciences
Glasgow Caledonian University
70 Cowcaddens Road, Glasgow, G4 0BA, UK
{j.tian, h.tianfield}@gcal.ac.uk

Abstract. E-medicine covers the whole range of medical process and service. Multi-agent approach is suitable for the development of e-medicine systems. In this paper, firstly the requirements of e-medicine are analysed, and a taxonomy is proposed for e-medicine systems. Secondly multi-agent approach is introduced for developing e-medicine systems, and the design of agents and the design of multi-agent structure are presented for e-medicine systems. Finally a case study is presented on a telemedicine for diabetes to illustrate the development of e-medicine systems.

Keywords: E-medicine; telemedicine; multi-agent

1 Introduction

With the progress of information technology e-medicine has become popular in the last decade and numerous variants of e-medicine have appeared such as e-diagnosis, e-pharmaceutics, e-healthcare, telemedicine, telehealth, etc.

E-medicine entered as a part of the routine clinical as early as in 1990s [1]. E-medicine delivers healthcare by integrating the information, communication and human-machine interface technologies with health and medical technologies [2]. E-medicine relies upon the technology enabler to realise the vision for health [2] and its advantage is to deliver healthcare across geographic, temporal, social, and cultural barriers [3].

E-medicine has wide applications, from diagnostics (such as teleradiology), treatment, through telesurgery or telementoring where a specialist surgeon can guide a beginner [4]. The applications of e-medicine can be classified as four areas [2], i.e., (1) lifetime health and medicine, (2) personalized health information, (3) teleconsultation and (4) continuing medical education. Moreover, e-medicine also has great impacts upon the traditional healthcare system. The national/provincial/regional health systems, health regulation, clinical programs, health institutions/organisations, and so on will be affected by e-medicine systems [3].

New technologies and methods must be explored to release the full potential of e-medicine. Multi-agent system approach has been widely used in the development of large complex systems. Agents have the autonomy and social ability, and multi-agent

M. Schillo et al. (Eds.): MATES 2003, LNAI 2831, pp. 85–94, 2003.

system is inherently multi-threaded for control [5]. Therefore, multi-agent approach is very effective for tackling the complexity of e-medicine systems and suitable for the development of e-medicine systems.

2 Requirements and Taxonomy of E-medicine Systems

Medicine has four basic functions. Firstly, disease prevention—focuses on epidemical disease prevention, deadly diseases prevention (such as cardiovascular disease and AIDS), and emergent prevention (such as SARS Virus). Secondly, disease diagnosis—focuses on interview based diagnosis, instrument based diagnosis and collective diagnosis. Thirdly, disease treatment—focuses on clinic, prescription, medicine, surgery operation, emergent treatment and hearth care. Fourthly, health consultation—focuses on grouped consultation (such as pregnant consultation, children health consultation), individual consultation and health knowledge.

Accordingly requirements of e-medicine systems can be divided as functional and non-functional requirements. The functional requirements of e-medicine systems include providing distant medical service (such as telemedicine, e-healthcare and teleconsultation) and clinical practice (such as telesurgery, telementoring and training patient), establishing medical database (such as computer-based patient records) and exchanging medical information (such as physicians' education and sharing the medical experience or research).

The non-functional requirements of e-medicine systems include security and privacy (such as protecting patients' privacy and encrypting medical records), efficiency, convenience and reusability. Medical information security and privacy are very important. How to protect the system security and the privacy of patients becomes the focus with the wide use of e-medicine, because more and more data for patient treatment are exchanged through national networks or Internet [4]. For example, privacy can prevent disease or delay disease's offset [4]. E-medicine has to face the purposeful violations of privacy and the accuracy of medical knowledge for patient's benefit while it tries to provide more and more medical service on line. Moreover, medical information is dynamic because of the complexity of symptom. For example, fever is usually the typical symptom of cold, but it also is the one of symptoms of SARS Virus.

E-medicine is the digitalisation of medical process and service. It is a broad term and can include telehealth, telemedicine and other healthcare related activities, such as health education, administration, and training [1]. A taxonomy can be proposed for e-medicine as follows.

E-pharmaceutics focuses on the standard and evaluation of the functions of pharmaceutics, especially the biomedicine.

Telemedicine is the use of communications technology in the provision of healthcare. Telemedicine system aims at providing medical service over a wide area, especially remote rural areas, and sharing the existing medical experience and technique based on telecommunication and information technology.

E-healthcare is one of the clinical activities that focuses on the health knowledge and evaluation of health status. Information and communications technologies enable the interaction between professionals and patients and the mediation of clinical data across time and space [6]. E-healthcare has two models of t, i.e., asynchronous (store-and-forward)—that is non "real time", e.g., digital recording, processing and storage of images and data; and synchronous (interactive)—that is "real time", e.g., videoconferencing system, with parallel transmission of clinical data [6].

E-diagnosis focuses on analysis and judgement of patients' status in term of the medical information. Decision support provides the physician with medical knowledge that is pertinent to the care of the patient [4].

E-consultation focuses on the provision on consultation and delivery of health knowledge for individual patients.

E-clinic focuses on the clinical diagnosis and treatment, and acquires the practical information of the patients.

Computer-based patient record (CPR) is the collection of electronic data about a patient's healthcare. Data entry and form of CPR are various. The data may be inputted by keyboard, dictation and transcription, voice recognition and interpretation, light pen, touch screen, hand-held computerized notepad, and other means [4]. CPR provides data presentation, storage, and access to the clinical decision maker (usually a physician or nurse). CPR may present data to the physician as text, tables, graphs, sound, images, full-motion video, and signals [4]. Moreover, CPR can provide the knowledge with proper context, i.e., specific data and information about the patient's identification and conditions [4].

3 Multi-agent Approach to the Design of E-medicine Systems

Multi-agent approach is effective for tackling the complexity of e-medicine systems because of the properties of agents and multi-agent system.

An agent is a computer system that is capable of independent action on behalf of user or owner [5]. An autonomous agent has the following properties [7].

Autonomy—an agent encapsulates some state of its environment and makes decision about what to do based on this state;

Reactivity—an agent perceives its environment and responds to changes that occur in the environment;

Pro-activeness—an agent can exhibit goal-directed behaviour by taking the initiatives to satisfy the given design objectives; and

Social ability—an agent interacts with other agents via an agent communication language and engages in social activities in order to achieve goals or cooperate.

A multi-agent system is a system that consists of a number of agents, which interact with each other, typically by exchanging messages through some computer network infrastructure [5]. A multi-agent system is a dynamic society made up of a great number of "intelligent agents" [8], so it is an intelligent society.

The multi-agent approach to system development consists of four steps [5], i.e.,

- Identification of the agent' roles
- Identification of the responsibilities and services for the roles
- Determination of the goal and plan to achieve the goals
- Determination the belief structure of the system

These four steps can be grouped as two stages, i.e., design of agent and design of agent society (structure) [9].

3.1 Design of Agents

The task in the design of agents is to identify the roles of all agents and their responsibilities and services in e-medicine systems. This can be elaborated as follows.

Interface agent provides guidance to an e-medicine system. Personal agent is one type of interface agents, which provides the user with a graphical interface to the multi-agent system and initiates a search or shows the results of a query to the user.

Broker agent is an agent that knows about all capabilities of the multi-agent system. Through the broker agent the user can communicate with agents or perform a general search among all agents.

Doctor agent maintains the schedule and appointment of a given doctor, and is aware of the doctor's times for visiting patients.

Administration agent implements the medical administration such as the assignment of task and the cooperation between departments and agents.

Controller agent controls the whole e-medicine systems and mediates the conflicts among the agents.

Department agent has the knowledge of a certain medical department and manages the medical affair in the department.

Monitoring agent, diagnosis agent, therapy agent, surgery agent, consultation agent, training agent and record agent carry out the functions of monitoring, diagnosis, therapy, surgery, consultation, training patient and medical record in a department, respectively. For example, training agent provides patients with instructions such as how to take medicine and how to take daily care.

Database wrapper agent is an agent that controls the access to a database that contains the medical records of patients. All the communications between database wrapper agent, patient agent and doctor agent are encrypted.

Education agent introduces the newest medical technologies and pharmaceutics, and provides e-learning for physicians or even for other agents in the e-medicine systems.

Decision support agent integrates various knowledge and provides diagnosis agent with effective decision approaches.

3.2 Design of Multi-agent Society (Structure)

Design of multi-agent society focuses on the establishment of the architecture of the multi-agent system and the interactions between the agents.

Multi-agent system has three architecture, i.e., deliberative, reactive and hybrid [7]. In e-medicine systems, the multi-agent system architecture tends to be hybrid. Different multi-agent systems are responsible for different specialist medical services of medical departments such as urology and cardiology.

A multi-agent system is a dynamic system and is similar to a society. On the one hand, the multi-agent system interacts with its external systems. On the other hand, within the multi-agent system agents interact with one another. The interactions consist of internal communication and external communication, ciphered or non-ciphered [10]. So the interaction model in multi-agent system is divided into external model and internal model [9]. The internal interactions of e-medicine systems are those not only between agents within one department, but also between different departments. The external interactions of e-medicine systems are those with other systems such as medical instrument, psychology, medical university and institute, etc. Agent in the multi-agent society of e-medicine systems are grouped control, implementation and interface, as shown in Fig. 1. The internal communication is among the control, interface and implementation group, and the external communication is with the environment through the interface part. The kernel of multi-agent society is the implementation group where various implemental agents cooperate to fulfil the requirements from control group or patients.

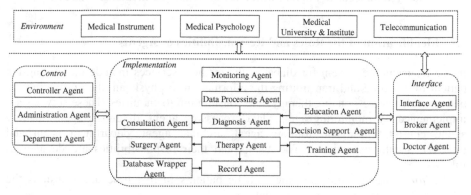

Fig. 1. The multi-agent society of e-medicine systems

4   A Case Study—Telemedicine for Diabetes

To illustrate multi-agent approach to the development of e-medicine systems, a case study of telemedicine for diabetes is presented below.

Diabetes is a chronic disease with a sustained elevated blood glucose level. The symptom of diabetes is that the metabolism can not work properly because of the reduction of insulin secretion [11]. The diabetic patients need to be injected with exogenous insulin to regulate blood glucose metabolism. Moreover, patients have to perform a daily strict self-monitoring of blood glucose level, such as measuring it before every injection and recording it on diaries, together with the amount of insulin injected and the information about diet and life style [12]. Using telemedicine system to manage this healthcare process can give diabetic patients real-time monitoring and immediate therapy. Telemedicine system for diabetic patients has been studied since early 1980s [11].

4.1 Requirement Analysis of Telemedicine for Diabetes

The telemedicine system must provide following services for diabetic patients on a daily basis.

- Visiting the patients and providing individual therapy.
- Monitoring the patients in real time and processing the monitored data immediately.
- Diagnosing the patients in term of the monitored data and making a proper therapy for the diabetic patients.
- Training the diabetic patient to monitor themselves and educating the physicians to update their skills.
- Establishing the patients' database the entry of which is ciphered.
- Providing the diabetic patients with consultation.
- The system needs to interact with other systems in e-medicine systems.

4.2 Identification of the Roles and Responsibilities of Agents

In the telemedicine system for diabetes, the medical services include monitoring the patient in real time and transmitting the information to physician, then providing the patient with a corresponding therapy, and consultation to enquiries. These services are implemented by monitoring agent, data processing agent, diagnosis agent, therapy agent, consultation agent, training agent, archival agent, department agent and interface agent, respectively. The agents and their responsibilities are detailed as follows.

Monitoring agent—monitors the diabetic patients in real time and transmits the monitored data to data processing agent.

Data processing agent—makes statistic and integrates the monitored data.

Diagnosis agent—analyses the situation and makes an accurate judgment for the patient.

Therapy agent—determines a proper therapy method.

Consultation agent—provides consultation to the enquiry of patients and contacts with diagnosis agent.

Decision support agent—provides decision support and cooperation for diagnosis agent.

Training agent—trains patients about how to take medicine and how to care himself. It implements the method of therapy agent.

Archival agent—edits and archives the patient record and therapy methods, and updates the database of the individual patients. Moreover, it integrates with the medical database and encrypts the important database.

Department agent—implements the control of the telemedicine system.

Interface agent—provides search service and information service.

4.3 Identification of the Goal and Plan to Implement

This telemedicine service is implemented by diabetes department in a hospital. The telemedicine system must not only provide the diabetic patient with immediate medical services through distant monitoring, diagnosis, therapy and consultation, but also integrate with other e-medicine systems for the functions of education, training, management, security and database.

How to achieve the goal by the multi-agent system? The multi-agent system consist of three groups, i.e. interface, implementation and control. In the implement group, there are many agents to individually and orderly carry out different responsibilities. The proposed architecture of multi-agent system is depicted in Fig. 2.

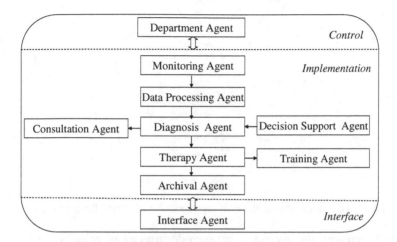

Fig. 2. The architecture of the multi-agent system of telemedicine

In the multi-agent system, the control group assigns the work and mediates the conflicts between agents. The interface group keeps the link with patients and other e-medicine systems. The implementation group implements the monitoring, diagnosis, therapy, consultation and archival functions to achieve the goals.

4.4 Determination of the Belief Structure

This is to determine the information requirement for each plan and goal in the interactions between agents [5]. In the multi-agent system, the external interactions focus on the integration with other e-medicine systems and its environment, while the internal interactions focus on the cooperation between agents to realize the telemedicine process, as shown in Fig. 3, where the bi-directional arrow represents the interactions.

In Fig. 3, the bigger dashed ellipse indicates the range of telemedicine while the smaller dashed ellipse indicates the range of the implementation group of the telemedicine system. So arrow 1 and 2 indicate that the telemedicine system interacts with its environment and other e-medicine systems, respectively. And arrow 3 and 4 indicate that the implementation group interacts with the control group and interface group in the telemedicine system, respectively.

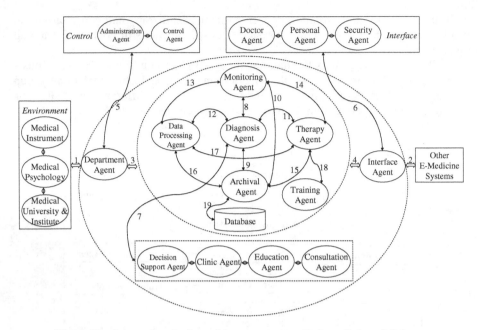

Fig. 3. The interactions in the multi-agent system of telemedicine of diabetes

Arrow 5 represents the interaction between department agent and the control group in e-medicine such as administration and control agent, while arrow 6 represents the interaction between interface agent and the interface of e-medicine systems such as doctor agent, personal agent and security agent. In the implementation group, diagnosis agent plays an important role. Because diagnosis is a complex process, diagnosis agent not only interacts with other agents in the implementation group, but also integrates with decision agent, clinic agent, education agent and consultation agent, as show by arrow 7.

Arrow 8-17 represents the internal interactions between agents in implementation group of the telemedicine system, respectively, which can be described by a matrix, as shown in Table 1.

Moreover, training agent implements the method of therapy agent, as shown by arrow 18, and archival agent directly interacts with the database, as shown by arrow 19.

The interactions in the matrix are explained in a symmetrical order as follows.

Entry <1, 2> represents monitoring agent transmits the monitored data to data processing agent. And entry <2, 1> represents data processing agent may require monitoring agent to provide other related data.

Entry <1, 3> represents monitoring agent may transmit the monitored data to diagnosis agent if required. And entry <3, 1> represents diagnosis agent may require monitoring agent to further monitor the patient's activities and symptom.

Entry <1, 4> represents monitoring agent may transmit the monitored data to therapy agent if required. And entry <4, 1> represents therapy agent may emphasise further monitoring the patient's improvement after making the treatment.

Table 1. The matrix of interaction of the telemedicine system for diabetes

	Monitoring Agent	Data Processing Agent	Diagnosis Agent	Therapy Agent	Archival Agent
Monitoring Agent		1, 2	1, 3	1, 4	1, 5
Data Processing Agent	2, 1		2, 3	2, 4	2, 5
Diagnosis Agent	3, 1	3, 2		3, 4	3, 5
Therapy Agent	4, 1	4, 2	4, 3		4, 5
Archival Agent	5, 1	5, 2	5, 3	5, 4	

Entry <1, 5> represents monitoring agent may transmit the monitored data to archival agent if it needs the further data. And entry <5, 1> represents monitoring agent acknowledges the requirement from archival agent.

Entry <2, 3> represents data processing agent will transmit the summarised data to diagnosis agent, such as graph, table and related medical historical records. And entry <3, 2> represents diagnosis agent may require data processing agent to reprocess the data if it does not feel the summarised data are sufficient.

Entry <2, 4> represents data processing agent may transmit the summarised data to therapy agent if required. And entry <4, 2> represents therapy agent may require data processing agent to reprocess the data for further information.

Entry <2, 5> represents data processing agent may transmit the summarised data to archival agent if required. And entry <5, 2> represents archival agent may provide more data for the data integration required by data processing agent.

Entry <3, 4> represents diagnosis agent will report the conclusion of the diagnosis, implying the treatment, to therapy agent. And entry <4, 3> represents therapy agent may require diagnosis agent to diagnose again or require the integration with other agents such as decision support agent.

Entry <3, 5> represents diagnosis agent may search the related medical history record of the patient through archival agent. And entry <5, 3> represents archival agent will require diagnosis agent to archive the diagnosis conclusion.

Entry <4, 5> represents therapy agent may require archival agent related records. And entry <5, 4> represents archival agent will require therapy agent to archive the therapeutic data.

5 Conclusion

Multi-agent system can not only integrate the medical knowledge and clinical experience and make decision support, but also adapt the system rapidly to the change in environment. So multi-agent approach can effectively tackle the complexity of e-medicine systems.

References

1. B. H. Stamm and D. A. Perednia. Evaluating psychosocial aspects of telemedicine and telehealth systems. Professional Psychology: Research and Practice, Vol. 31, No. 2, 2000, pp. 184–189.
2. A. B. Suleiman. The untapped potential of telehealth. International Journal of Medical Informatics, Issue 61, 2001, pp. 103–112.
3. P. A. Jennett, and K. Andruchuk. Telehealth: 'real life' implementation issues. Computer Methods and Programms in Biomedicine, Issue 64, 2001, pp. 169–174.
4. L. G. Kun. Telehealth and the global health network in the 21st century. From homecare to public health informatics. Computer Methods and Programms in Biomedicine, Issue 64, 2001, pp. 155–167.
5. M. Wooldridge. An Introduction to MultiAgent Systems. John Wiley & Sons Ltd, 2002.
6. T. Williams, C. May, F. Mair, M. Mort and L. Gask. Normative models of health technology assessment and the social production of evidence about telehealth care. Health Policy, Volume 64, Issue 1, 2003, pp.39–54.
7. M. K. Lim and Z. Zhang. Iterative multi-agent bidding and co-ordination based on genetic algorithm. Proceeding of 3rd International Symposium on Multi-Agent Systems, Large Complex Systems, and E-Businesses, Erfurt, 7-10 October 2002, pp. 682–689.
8. A. Garro and L. Palopoli. An XML-Agent System for e-learning and skill management. Proceeding of 3rd International Symposium on Multi-Agent Systems, Large Complex Systems, and E-Businesses, Erfurt, 7-10 October 2002, pp.636–647.
9. M. Pankowska and H. Sroka. Business process reengineering and software agent development. Proceeding of 3rd International Symposium on Multi-Agent Systems, Large Complex Systems, and E-Businesses, Erfurt, 7-10 October 2002, pp.608–620.
10. A. Moreno and D. Isern. A first step towards providing health-care agent-based services to mobile users. Proceedings of the 1st International Joint Conference on Autonomous Agents and Multiagent Systems, Part 2, Bologna, July 2002, pp. 589–590.
11. O. Orlov and A. Grigoriev. Space technologies in routine telemedicine practice: commercial approach. Acta Astronautia, Vol. 51, No. 1-9, 2002, pp 295–300.
12. M. Y. Sung, M. S. Kim, E. J. Kim, J. H. Yoo and M. W. Sung. CoMed: a real-time collaborative medicine system. International Journal of Medical Informatics, Issue 57, 2000, pp 117–126.

Implementing Heterogeneous Agents in Dynamic Environments, a Case Study in RoboCupRescue

Jafar Habibi, Mazda Ahmadi, Ali Nouri, Mayssam Sayyadian, and
Mayssam M. Nevisi

Department of Computer Engineering,
Sharif University of Technology, Tehran, Iran
habibi@sharif.edu
(m_ahmadi,nouri,sayadian,mayssam)@ce.sharif.edu

Abstract. Design and construction of multi-agent systems is a challenging but an intriguing problem. It is because of the intrinsic distribution of the intelligent components. In such environments the interaction and communication between the constituent parts extends the complexity since appropriate coordination methods need to be designated and employed. In this paper a successful experiment in designing and implementing such an environment is presented [1]. The test bed for this research is the rescue simulation environment. The architecture of the implemented heterogeneous agents takes advantage of various algorithms. These algorithms make the agents act intelligently by themselves albeit they happen to act quite in coordination with each other. The implemented algorithms for the sake of cooperation between the heterogeneous agents enhance the overall pay off of the system. The autonomy of the agents is guaranteed by means of some methods such as reinforcement learning, decision trees and some sort of heuristic functions. In order to settle the agents in coordination with each other and make them act cooperatively, some other methods have been applied. Among these methods, combinatorial auctions, coalition formation, function approximation for evaluating the value of cooperation, and some probabilistic and heuristic methods can be named.

1 Introduction

Nowadays design and construction of multi-agent system infrastructures is a challenging but an interesting problem. Designing systems for soccer player robots[5], computer-aided design of a generic robot controller for a multi- robot system[9], design and implementation of automated highway systems[2], and the hot topic of trading agents[8] are a few examples of the works in this field. In this paper we will present our experiment in the design and implementation of a complex environment of multi heterogeneous agents, so that it can be used for further similar activities.

---

[1] The implemented agents won the first place award in RoboCup Rescue Simulation league in Fukuoka, Japan, 2002.

M. Schillo et al. (Eds.): MATES 2003, LNAI 2831, pp. 95–104, 2003.

The engaged test bed is the rescue simulation environment. This test bed is basically designed for the goal of disaster mitigation of an earthquake. Three kinds of completely different agents are aimed to minimize the overall damage to the city. Such agents have various abilities and hence different responsibilities such as extinguishing burning buildings, rescuing injured civilians, etc. Also they are supposed to come across a mutual agreement so that their cooperation and coordination would enhance their collaborative efforts and this adds to their complexity. Two aspects of a multi-agent system with intelligence are eligible to note. The first one is the intelligence of each agent - the micro level issue. The other one is considered with the system as a whole and it is the agents' coordination and cooperation to reach desired goals. In the implemented system both issues are considered and emphasized. It means that although each agent tries to perform his assigned tasks as perfect as possible, he tries to act so that the overall system benefits. In other words the agents are not selfish.

This paper is organized as follows: After introduction we present some general explanation of the rescue simulation environment as our test bed. In section three the fire brigade algorithms are presented. In section four the topics related to police agents are discussed. In section five ambulance team algorithms are presented. Inter-agent communication methods and related subjects are discussed in section six. In section seven a comparison of experimental results is presented and we come to conclusion in that section.

2   Overview of RobocupRescue Simulation

RoboCup Rescue Simulation is one of the competitions in RoboCup. The main aim of RoboCup Rescue Simulation is simulating a disaster situation in a city. There is a kernel simulating the city and some simulators simulating the disaster conditions[4,6]. The parts that we have developed are the agents. The agents are:

- Fire Brigades
- Ambulance Teams
- Police Forces
- Head Quarters

The main goal of the agents is to rescue more civilians[4]. Although ambulances are responsible for rescuing civilians, but polices will clear the roads so that ambulances and fire brigades can move in the city. Fire brigades have to extinguish fires to reduce the amount of damage (the less fire, the more alive civilians).

3   Fire Brigade Agents

In this environment, the fire brigades are responsible for controlling the spread of fire in the city, and extinguishing as many buildings as possible. For this purpose, each agent takes advantage of his visual perception and identifies the buildings on fire. For each burning building the agent autonomously tries to estimate how dangerous that building would be and how much it threatens its neighbors. After this phase, the fire brigades need to act upon the world's situation in a unified approach to increase their coordination. The most obvious approach in this phase is finding the most important buildings on fire and extinguishing them. So, the way agents calculate a building's priority plays an important role in this phase.

A proposed workflow for a fire brigade is depicted in figure 1. As the figure suggests, the workflow contains four phases, namely: perception, analysis, decision making, and implementation. This means that the agent first receives raw information about the environment. Then by means of communication with other agents, his experiments and his experiences, the agent uses this information to gain some kind of knowledge that would be useful in the decision making phase. Then the agent's world model is investigated to find appropriate targets. The most useful and the best estimated targets are selected in this decision making process. In the last phase the agent implements the desired actions according to the target he has chosen.

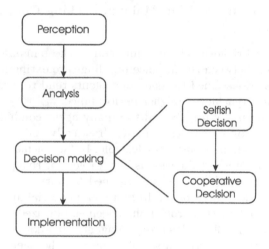

Fig. 1. Agent's workflow

The decision making section is the most important phase in the agent's workflow in each cycle. The fire brigade agents use a two layered architecture for this phase. In the first stage, the agents decide independently. They do not care the state of other agents and they selfishly choose some targets for their own. In the next stage, the agents try to both actively coordinate with other fire brigades and also communicate with other types of agents. In this way the overall rescue integrity is guaranteed and this collaboration enriches the result and the overall performance of the system. One of the advantages of this architecture is the independence of the two layers. This enables implementation and evaluation of different algorithm in each layer.

3.1   Preliminary Decision Making Based on Agents' Selfishness

The implemented agents estimate the buildings' priorities in an individual manner and without considering the existence of other agents. The buildings are sorted afterward based on their priorities and a few of the most critical ones are selected from the many available. The values according which the importance of buildings are calculated, mainly includes two types of criteria; The intrinsic value of a building, which is a measure of importance in the city independent of the situation of the disaster (e.g. geographical location of the building in the city) and the strategic importance which, on the other hand is dependant on the relative location of the buildings according to the distributed sites of burning buildings[2].

This list of candidate buildings is then fed to the next layer of decision making where the targets are assigned to the agents so that the cooperation and coordination between them is also guaranteed.

3.2   Improvement in Decision Making, Seeking Coordination, and Cooperation

While designing fire brigades, it is very important to keep in mind the significance of the coordination between them. Since buildings are extinguished much faster if multiple agents are assigned to them, our agents tend to form coalitions with each other in order to achieve a higher performance.

As there are too many targets and too many agent combinations, the number of possible coalition structures increases drastically and therefore brute force checking of all the combinations is not feasible. In fact, achieving an optimal solution with the help of approximation is inevitable. For this purpose, the agents are regarded as resources that will be assigned to burning buildings. This approach leads us to view the problem from a combinatorial auction perspective.

The combinatorial auction problem has been emphasized in research recently mostly in combinatorics[3]. In this problem agents are allowed to bid directly for bundles of resources. Suggesting a set of resources, the agents propose a value for them. Then the auctioneer is assumed to allocate resources to bidders so that the overall benefit of the system is maximized.

In the proposed system, the auctioneer is simulated so that the optimal resource allocation and coalition formation is achieved. In this system the buildings are assumed to play the role of bidders and agents are regarded as the extinguishing resources. So it can be assumed that buildings suggest values for a bundle of fire brigades. To evaluate each bid the followings are important:

- The importance of the building which is an indicator of its strategic and intrinsic importance.
- The amount of time it takes the proposed coalition to put out the building. This measure can be calculated by means of statistical and computational analysis.

---

[2] A group of connected burning buildings is called a site of fire

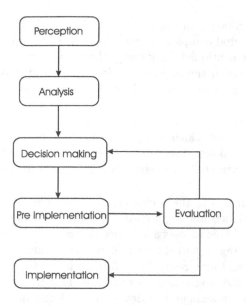

Fig. 2. Agent's workflow with feedback

The most complex part of the combinatorial auction is the winner determination algorithm for the auctioneer. As a matter of fact, the most difficult part of the combinatorial auction simulation is to find an optimal coalition structure among the many possible, so that the overall payoff of the system is maximized. Since the algorithms for this problem are NP, in this system the approximate algorithms developed by Edo Zurel have been exploited. This algorithm uses some heuristic functions to prune the search space very fast. Then it uses some greedy methods and by means of hill climbing it finds a very good coalition structure which is an approximate of the optimal solution[11]. This way by simulating a coalition formation via combinatorial auction for the fire brigades the inter-agent coordination is guaranteed in a satisfactory manner and it is very close to the optimal solution.

3.3   More Improvement in Decision Making

The mentioned agent workflow in figure 1 suffers a major drawback: In decision making phase the fire brigades try to select the best possible coalition structures and as to collaboratively extinguish the target buildings. As a matter of fact these coalition structures are formed in the implementation phase. The performance of the system is tightly related to the successful implementation of these coalition formations. According to this workflow, no feedback is given to the decision making phase so it is not too surprising if a selected coalition structure can not be formed in the next phase. This can be as a result of some problem such as path planning. Hence all the agents that are supposed to form that coalition are failed in their mission. Also it must be noted that the feasibility of path planning can not be regarded as a factor in the decision making. It is because path planning is a time consuming and complex activity. In this system to leverage the impact of this problem the mentioned workflow is changed in two steps.

The first change is in the implementation phase and it is in path planning. The implemented algorithm in path planning uses the same raw data that have been extracted for decision making in the analysis phase. Hence, without direct invocation of the path planning algorithm in decision making, it can not be guaranteed that a target which will fail to reach in path planning will not be selected in decision making. Also the selected paths using this method are more reliable than those extracted by means of classic algorithms and other proposed methods.

The second change is in the architecture of the agent's workflow. Although the strategies mentioned above play an important role in increasing the confidence of finding reachable targets and hence decreasing the possibility of loosing cycles, but still loosing a working cycle could be a huge burden over the system's performance and may result in malfunctioning of agents. Therefore some changes have been made to the agent's workflow. This change is in form of adding a feedback from the implementation layer to the decision making layer (see fig. 2). This way after selecting a target, it would be routed and the result would be evaluated. If the extracted path was applicable, then the decision would be implemented. Otherwise the selected building would be removed from candidate buildings and the agent would re-decide. According to the experiments, since the buildings are spread all over the city, usually in the 300 working cycle of the agents, only the agents needed to re-decide more than three times for 5-10 cycles. Also they managed to find a well suited target by two times of re-decision.

4   Police Force Agents

In Rescue Simulation, the police forces are supposed to clear roads. Trying to clear more roads is not the optimum action. Polices have to select the most important roads. Importance of a road is defined as how many times other agents will pass through this road in the following cycles. Although the exact value of this measure is not computable before the simulation, the probable value is computed. For this purpose, roads are prioritized according to two types of parameters, dependant to the system state, and independent of the current state of the system.

Static value of roads: It is obvious that some roads like those around the city are less important than the central roads. To estimate this kind of importance, it is assumed the roads that are subject to use more frequently are more important. We compute this value in this way:

1. The city is saved in form of graph so that the nodes are the graph's vertexes and the roads are the edges.
2. Taking advantage of Floyd's shortest path, all shortest paths between all pairwise nodes are computed and saved.

3. For each edge (road), the number of occurrence of that road in shortest paths are counted.
4. The static value of each road is equal to the number of occurrence of this road in all the shortest paths. This way the road that is more reliable to appear in a selected path is more important.

Dynamic value for roads: At first all dynamic road values are equal to one. During the simulation if an agents requests for clearing a road, its priority is multiplied by ten. The roads around the burning buildings are also multiplied by two. As time passes this dynamic value for each road is decreased.

Total roads values: It is computed as the road's dynamic value times its static value.

This roads values are considered when the police has decided what to do according to his state in the disaster. In order to improve the police forces' in decision making, reinforcement learning has been used. In this method each agent has three actions as follows:

- Stay in his area: When this action is chosen, the police stays in his area and walks around the area he is currently in.
- Help other agents: Selection of this action means the police will be leaving his current area so as to clear a specific road to help another agent achieve his goal
- Change the area of responsibility

Q-Learning[10] has been used for this learning. In latter version of Arian's police forces an algorithm based on function approximation has been used. More details could be found in [1].

5   Ambulance Teams

Ambulance team agents rescue injured civilians. They obtain information of civilians by means of communication, and gathering auditory and visual information. In order to determine whether to go to rescue a civilian or move around to find an injured civilian, a QLearning method has been used.

6   Inter-agent Communication

In the inter-agent communication model, each agent can communicate with its homogeneous agents as well as its center. In the implemented communication system there are two kind of messages:

- Informative messages: These are the messages which are aimed for informing the agents. For example police forces inform ambulance teams of the injured civilian positions.
- Imperative messages: These messages are requests for help. For example fire brigades ask police forces to clear a specific road.

One of the challenges each agent faces is determining what to do among his own decisions according to his intelligence and the requests received from other agents. Design and implementation of a useful method for selecting the best messages to evaluate was of the most important challenges the implemented agents had to face. In the suggested algorithm, each agent sets a priority in the message that is dependent on the following factors :

- Goal's importance: the more important the goal of the sender, the more important is his message.
- The importance of the request in reaching the agent's goal.
- The importance of other possible actions the agent can do if not considering his request.

Each agent with his internal algorithm finds a priority for his decision and comparing this priority with the priority of the messages decides what to do.

Since the way the agents' priorities may be different from each other, and from the priorities set in the messages, the agents use a function approximation method[7] so that in case of failure, the way they set priorities would change.

6.1   Message Evaluation

In our communication system every agent who asks for help, sets a priority in that message. This priority indicates the importance of the situation and how accurate the information is.

One of the problems in communication is to derive a value for the message. we derived an equation for evaluating the message, that is:

$$V_i(t) = f(t) * P(i)/succ(t-1)$$

In the above equation $V_i(t)$ indicates the value of i'th message in each time period and of course each agent has its own queue of messages and has its own $V_i(t)$. $f(t)$ is a coefficient which is related to time and so makes $V_i(t)$ related to time. $f(t)$ is what we are aiming to learn and has a constant value at initial state. By learning $f(t)$ we can say that $V_i(t)$ is learned. $P(i)$ indicates the priority that the message has. $succ(t-1)$ is the measure of the success of the agent in last time period. If this value of $f(t)$ is less than a threshold we will accept the message and do what the message has told us to do, if not, we will ignore that message.

We use and incremental function approximation method for learning the value of $f(t)$. In our function approximation method we use an initial value for $f(t)$ and in each cycle we update the $f(t)$ function. The way we update this function has an explicit relation with the agent abilities and the environment of the problem. Further information and more detailed discussion on the above method and the formula can be found in [1] .

Table 1. Result of RoboCup2002 final game

Team Name	Result
Arian	90.46
YowAI2002	87.85

Table 2. Result of RoboCup2002 semi-final game

Team Name	Environment 1	Environment 2	Environment 3	Environment 4
Arian	68.58	75.77	85.94	53.49
NITRescue	22.56	66.56	54.61	88.15

7   Experimental Results and Conclusion

The implemented agents has participated in the RoboCup Rescue Simulation league in the RoboCup competitions. For the Seattle-2001 competitions, the Arian team succeeded to won the silver medal. In the Fukuoka-2002 competitions, the Arian team managed to become the world champion of the league. Undoubtedly achieving such positions, specially the golden medal in 2002 competitions were the result of the methods and algorithms that we discussed in this paper.

The way participating teams are evaluated against each other, is based on the number of dead civilians, and the number of burned buildings. In the table 1,2 a comparison of Arian score and other final and semi-final teams's scores is reflected [3]. It must be mentioned in the competitions the cooperation and coordination between Arian agents were very dominant.

References

1. Mazda Ahmadi, Mayssam Sayyadian, Jafar Habibi, A Learning Method for Evaluating Messages in Multi Agent Systems, Proceedings of the Agent Communication Languages (ACL2002) , Italy, Bolognia
2. A. Deshpande, D. N. Godbole, A. G. and P. Varaiya, "Design and Evaluation Tools for Automated Highway Systems", Hybrid Systems pp. 138-148, 1995.
3. Luke Hunsberger, Barbara J. Grosz, A Combinatorial Auction for Collaborative Planning, Proceedings of the Fourth International Conference on Multi-Agent Systems (ICMAS-2000), pages 151–158, 2000
4. H. Kitano, S. Tadokor, H. Noda, I Matsubara, T. Takhasi, A. Shinjou, and S. Shimada. Robocup-rescue: Search and rescue for large scale disasters as a domain for multi-agent research. In Proc. of the IEEE Conference on Systems, Men, and Cybernetics, 1999.
5. I. Noda and P. Stone, "The RoboCup Soccer Server and CMUnited Clients: Implemented Infrastructure for MAS Research" Journal of Autonomous Agents and Multi-Agent Systems, Kluwer Academic Publisher, 2002.
6. "http://www.robocup.org"
7. Van Roy, B., Learning and Value Function Approximation in Complex Decision Processes, Ph.D. Thesis, Massachusetts Institute of Technology, May 1998. 30

---

[3] This score is computed based on how much the agents have reduced the city damage.

8. T. Sandholm and V. Lesser, "Issues in Automated Negotiation and Electronic Commerce: Extending the Contract Net Framework", Proceedings of the First International Conference on Multi-Agent Systems (ICMAS'95), The MIT Press: Cambridge, MA, USA, San Francisco, CA, USA, pp. 328–335, 1995.

9. D. Simon, B. Espiau, E. Castillo and K. Kapellos, "Computer-aided design of a generic robot controller handling reactivity and real-time control issues", RR-1801, 1995.

10. Christopher J. Watkins and Peter Dayan. Q-learning. Machine Learning, 8:279–292, 1992.

11. Edo Zurel, Noam Nisan, An Efficient Approximate Allocation Algorithm for Combinatorial Auctions, Proceedings of ACM Conference on Electronic Commerce (EC-2001), 2001

Model for Simultaneous Actions in Situated Multi-agent Systems

Danny Weyns and Tom Holvoet

AgentWise, DistriNet, Department of Computer Science,
K.U.Leuven, B-3001 Heverlee, Belgium
{danny.weyns,tom.holvoet}@cs.kuleuven.ac.be

Abstract. The main focus of multi-agent research so far has been on concepts and techniques to analyze and specify multi-agent systems. Much less attention has been devoted to the implementation of the concepts and techniques. This paper intends to bridge the gap between the mere concept of simultaneous actions and its implementation. Simultaneous actions are actions that are executed by different agents at the same time. We study simultaneous actions in the context of situated multi-agent systems where agents and objects have an explicit position in the environment. To clarify the concept of simultaneous actions, first we propose a classification for simultaneous actions and illustrate each type with examples. Then we present a generic model for simultaneous actions that is independent of the applied agent architecture. Support for simultaneous actions involves two aspects: first it must enable agents to act together and second, it must ensure that the outcome of a combination of simultaneously performed actions is in accordance with the domain that is modeled. In the model, acting together is established through synchronization, while the domain requirements are ensured through reification of actions and subsequently combining the simultaneously performed actions in accordance with the valid laws. We used the model to implement the Packet–World with centralized as well as with regional synchronization. In the paper we illustrate the model for both approaches and discuss the implications for the complexity of implementation, the autonomy of agents and the scalability of the multi-agent system.

1 Introduction

Interaction is a central issue of multi-agent systems (MAS). An interaction occurs whenever two or more agents come into contact with each other. The focus of this paper is on interactions in *situated MASs*. In particular we focus on infrastructure to support the implementation of *simultaneous actions*, i.e. actions performed by different agents at the same time.

Situated Multi-Agent Systems. In situated MASs, agents as well as objects have an explicit position in the environment. Situatedness reflects the local relationships between agents and objects. Through its situatedness, a situated agent is placed in a local context that he is able to perceive and in which he can

M. Schillo et al. (Eds.): MATES 2003, LNAI 2831, pp. 105–118, 2003.

act. The model for simultaneous actions we discuss in this paper is independent of the applied architecture of the agents in the MAS.

Model for Action. For actions, we use a model that is based on the theory of influences and reactions to influences, proposed by J. Ferber [4]. Roughly spoken, this theory separates what an agent wants to perform from what actually happens. Agents produce influences into the environment and subsequently the environment reacts by combining the influences to deduce a new state of the world from them. The reification of actions as influences enables the environment to combine simultaneously performed activity in the MAS. Based on this theory, J. Ferber and J.P. Müller developed a model for action with centralized synchronization that is described in [5]. In [13], we extended this model for regional synchronization.

Support for Simultaneous Actions. Simultaneous actions are actions that conceptually happens at the same time, but physically are executed separated in time, e.g. on a single or sequential processor system. Support for simultaneous actions involves two aspects: first such support must enable agents to act together and second, support must ensure that the outcome of a combination of simultaneously performed actions is in accordance with the domain that is modeled.

Outline of the Paper. To clarify what simultaneous actions are, we first propose a classification for simultaneous actions and illustrate each type with examples. Then, in section 3, we present a generic model for simultaneous actions in situated MASs. This model functionally describes how simultaneous actions can be treated towards implementation. Section 4 illustrates the model for centralized and regional synchronization and discuss the implications for both approaches with respect to the complexity of implementation, the autonomy of agents and the scalability of the MAS. Finally, in section 5 we conclude and look at future work.

2   Simultaneous Actions

In this section we elaborate on simultaneous actions. First we present a classification for simultaneous actions and then we illustrate each type of simultaneous actions with examples in the Packet-World.

2.1   Classification of Simultaneous Actions

In the literature, several researchers distinguish between different kinds of simultaneously performed actions. Some examples: Allen and Ferguson [1] differentiate between 'actions that interfere with each other' and 'actions with additional synergistic effects'. Boutilier and Brafman [2] distinguish 'concurrent actions with a positive or negative interacting effect'. Griffiths, Luck and d'Iverno [6] introduce the notions of a 'joint action that a group of agents perform together' and 'concurrent actions, i.e. a set of actions performed at the same time'. These latter

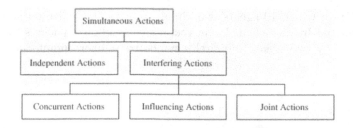

Fig. 1. Classification of Simultaneous Actions.

notions are build upon the concepts of 'strong and weak parallelism' described by Kinny [8].

We propose a classification for actions that happen at the same time as depicted in Fig. 1. We use the common name of *simultaneous actions* as general designation for actions that happen together. Further, we make a distinction between two kinds of simultaneous actions: *independent actions* and *interfering actions*. Independent actions are actions that do not interfere with one another. Interfering actions on the other hand, bring two or more agents directly in contact with each other. Depending on the nature of these interactions, we distinguish between *concurrent actions, influencing actions* and *joint actions*. Concurrent actions are of a conflicting nature. The result is typically non-deterministic, e.g. one arbitrary agent of the set of involved agents succeeds in his action while the other agents fail. Influencing actions are actions that positively or negatively affect each other. For this kind of interaction the outcome of the simultaneous actions is the resultant of the individual actions. Joint actions are actions that must be executed together in order to produce a successful joint result. In joint actions agents typically play complementary roles in a compound interaction.

This classification for simultaneous actions takes the viewpoint of the observer of the actions. An observer interprets the interactions as a whole and distinguish types on the basis of the possible outcomes of the interactions. Whether or not the individual agents intend to, or are aware of their participation in the interaction is independent of the classification.

2.2   Examples of Simultaneous Actions

Before we illustrate the different types of simultaneous actions, we first introduce the the example case: the Packet–World.

The Packet–World. The Packet–World[1] consists of a number of different colored packets that are scattered over a rectangular grid. Agents that live in this virtual world have to collect these packets and bring them to their corresponding colored destination. The left part of Fig. 2 shows an example of a Packet–World

---

[1] The Packet–World is based on an exercise proposed by Huhns and Stephens in [7] as a research topic to investigate the principles of sociality in MASs.

with size 10 in which 10 agents live. Small squares symbolize packets that can
be manipulated by one agent, larger rectangles symbolize packets that must be
manipulated by two agents and circles symbolize delivery points.

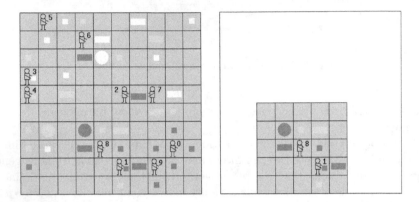

Fig. 2. The Packet–World.

In the Packet–World agents can interact with the environment in a number
of ways. An agent can make a step to one of the free neighbor fields around him.
If an agent is not carrying any packet, he can pick up a small packet from one
of his neighbor fields. An agent can put down a small packet he carries at one of
the free neighbor fields around him, or of course at the delivering point of that
particular packet. In addition, we allow agents to transfer small packets directly
to one another. During such a transfer, the agent that carries the packet passes
it to the receiver, while the receiver simultaneously accepts the packet. Agents
can also push small packets to a neighboring square. A push only succeeds when
there is no obstacle on the destination square of the pushed packet. In case two
agents simultaneously push the same packet, the packet moves according to the
resultant of both actions. Contrary to small packets, to pick up a large packet
two agents have to lift up the packet together, each of them on one short side of
the packet. Agents that carry a large packet can only move together in the same
direction. Large packets too can be put down at any free field or at the delivering
point of the packet. However, to put down a large packet, both agents have to
release the packet simultaneously. Finally, when there is no sensible action for
an agent to perform, he may wait for a while and do nothing.

Besides acting into the environment, agents can also send messages to each
other. Conversations between agents follow a specific protocol. Examples are: a
request for information followed by an answer or a refusal; a request to set up
a form of cooperation followed by an acceptance to cooperate and later on a
notification of the end of the cooperation, or a refusal to cooperate.

It is important to notice that each agent of the Packet–World has only a
limited view on the world. The view–size of the world expresses how far, i.e. how

many squares, an agent can 'see' around him. The right part of Fig. 2 illustrates the limited view of agent 8, in this example the view–size is 2.

We monitor the Packet–World via a number of counters that measure the efficiency of the agents in performing their job. There are counters to measure the energy invested by the agents, the message transfer between the agents and the number of conflicts that happens between two agents. The overall performance can be calculated as a weighted sum of this counters. For more details about the Packet-World we refer to [11].

2.3   Examples

Now we illustrate the different types of simultaneous actions in the Packet–World.

An example of *independent actions* are two neighboring agents that make a step to a different location. When in the depicted situation agent 3 decides to step in the direction NE[2] while agent 4 simultaneously decides to step SE, both these actions can happen independent of one another.

An example of *concurrent actions* are two agents that simultaneously try to pick the same small object. Which of the involved agents gets the packet is not determined. When for example in the situation of Fig. 2 agent 5 picks up the packet positioned E to him while agent 6 simultaneously picks up the same packet, one randomly selected agent of the two gets the packet while the other misses it.

When two agents in the Packet–World push the same object at the same time then these are *influencing actions*. If for example in Fig. 2, agent 9 pushes the packet N to him while agent 0 pushes the same packet at the same time, the packet will move on to the square NW to its depicted position. Whether or not this resulting movement is profitable for the individual agents depends on their possible intentions. But in case two agents push the same packet at the same time in opposite directions both will be frustrated since the result of such interaction is that the packet will not move at all.

Finally, in the Packet–World different kinds of *joint actions* are possible. A first example in Fig. 2 is agent 1 who passes the small packet he carries to agent 8. As stated above, such transfer only succeeds when the involved agents act together, i.e. agent 1 has to pass the packet while agent 8 simultaneously has to accept the packet. Another example of joint actions are agents 2 and 7 who make a step with the large packet they carry. Such a step only succeeds when both agents step in the same direction, in the situation of Fig. 2 for example, in the direction SW toward the destination of the packet they carry.

---

[2] We denote each neighboring field of a field with the first capital letter(s) of the direction from the field to that neighboring field.

3   A Generic Model for Simultaneous Actions

In this section first we give a high level description of the model for simultaneous actions. Subsequently we discuss each layer and the flow between layers in detail. At the end, we reflect on issues with respect to the implementation of the model.

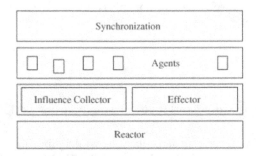

Fig. 3. High level model for simultaneous actions.

3.1   High Level Description of the Model

Fig. 3 gives a graphical description of the model. As stated in section 1, support for simultaneous actions must: (1) enable agents to act together and (2) ensure that the outcome of a combination of simultaneously performed actions is in accordance with the domain that is modeled. Different layers in the model take care of these requirements. At the top we have the *synchronization layer* that accounts for the first requirement: enabling agents to act together. This layer is responsible for composing sets of synchronized agents, i.e. sets of agents that act together. The second layer contains the *agents* of the MAS. The two lowest layers are responsible for the second requirement to support simultaneous actions: combining simultaneously performed actions in accordance with the domain laws. The third layer has a double functionality spread over two components. First this layer contains the *collector* which is responsible for collecting influences and composing sets of influences for simultaneously acting agents. The second component is the *effector* that must ensure that the consequences of the activity of the agents are realized, keeping the state of the environment up to date and bringing the effects of their actions to the agents. The fourth, bottom layer contains the *reactor*. It is the reactor's responsibility to calculate the effects of the influences of simultaneously acting agents according to the actual state of the environment and the laws of the modeled MAS.

3.2   Layers and the Flow between Layers

A detailed overview of the model for simultaneous actions is depicted in Fig. 4. To explain the different layers of the model and the flow amongst the layers, we follow one action cycle for a particular agent, say A_i. Note that since the model of Fig. 4 is a generic model, several aspects remain abstract. Concrete interpretations of these aspects are discussed in the next section.

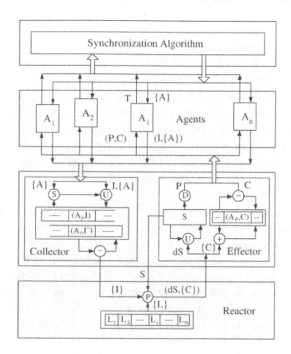

Fig. 4. Detailed model for simultaneous actions.

The cycle starts when agent A_i of the agent layer triggers the synchronization layer to compose a new set of synchronized agents. This request is denoted as T. Depending on the synchronization algorithm implemented by the synchronization layer, T may just be a signal, possibly containing the identity of agent A_i or it may contain more required information, e.g. the set of visible agents of A_i at that moment. As soon as the synchronization algorithm completes, the synchronization layer sends the set of synchronized agents, denoted as $\{A\}$, to agent A_i. Now the agent starts decision making, resulting in the selection of an action. This action is sent as an influence, together with the set of synchronized agents to the environment, denoted as $(I, \{A\})$.

It is the influence collector who collects such tuples. The collector maintains sets of *pending influences*, each set representing the influences produced by one group of simultaneously acting agents. Each element of a set is a tuple (A, I), where A represents an agent and I is the influence produced by A. However, as long as A has not yet produced its influence, I is registered as I^0 denoting that the influence is expected to be produced soon. Based on the set of synchronized agents passed by agent A_i, the collector first searches for a set of pending influences that corresponds to the agents in set $\{A\}$. This functionality is represented as the encircled S in the model. A set matches if at least one of the agents of $\{A\}$ belongs to the set. If the collector found such a set he updates it, based on the $(I, \{A\})$ tuple. If no set is found, a new set is composed with $(I, \{A\})$ and added to the repository of sets of pending influences. The update of a set of pending influences with the $(I, \{A\})$ tuple is denoted as the encircled U. For each agent of $\{A\}$ that does not belong to the selected set of pending influences, U adds a new entry in the set, initialized as (A, I^0). Other members are left untouched. Finally, U updates the entry of the invoking agent with its actual influence, thus for invoking agent A_i the entry (A_i, I^0) is update to (A_i, I_i), with I_i the influence of the tuple $(I, \{A\})$ invoked by A_i.

As soon as the collector detects that a set of pending influences is completed, he passes the set of corresponding influences, denoted by $\{I\}$, to the reactor. A set of pending influences is completed if all agents of the set have produced their influences, i.e. no tuple in the set contains an initial I^0. Together with passing the set of influences, the collector removes the corresponding set of pending influences from its repository.

In the reactor the set of influences $\{I\}$ is composed with a set of applicable laws, denoted as $\{L\}$, given the current state of the environment denoted as S. This composition is represented by the encircled P. P results in a tuple $(dS, \{C\})$, whereof dS denotes the state changes in the environment, while $\{C\}$ denotes the set of consumptions. A consumption is an element from the environment reserved for a particular agent. When an agent 'consumes' a consumption, the consumed element can be absorbed by the agent (e.g. food that is turned into energy) or the agent may simply hold the element (e.g. a packet he has picked up in the Packet–World).

The reactor passes the tuple $(dS, \{C\})$ to the effector. With dS, the effector updates the environmental state. This update is represented by the encircled U. Furthermore, the effector adds the set of consumptions $\{C\}$ it has received from the reactor to the repository of *pending consumptions* it maintains. Pending consumptions are consumptions that have not yet been picked up by the agents. A pending consumption is a tuple (A, C) whereof C is a consumption intended for agent A.

Subsequently agent A_i can perceive the updated environment and consume the results of its previous action, denoted as (P, C). Since agents have only a limited view on the world, P is only a segment of S. The demarcation of S is represented as the encircled D. Finally, the agent triggers the synchronization layer to produce the next set of synchronized agents for him, starting a new action cycle.

It is important to notice that from the point of view of the agents, the model for simultaneous actions offers *implicit* support for simultaneous actions. Whether the agents are aware of the possible simultaneity of their actions is unimportant for the model. To put it another way, this model *enables* simultaneous actions in situated MASs, however the model does not offer support for the agents to decide about *what* actions they should perform simultaneously. Some agents may follow complex negotiation protocols to agree about the kind of simultaneous actions they perform, other may simply act based on local perception.

3.3 Issues with Respect to the Implementation of the Model

The layered model presented in the previous section is a generic, conceptual model for simultaneous actions that abstracts from concerns such as scheduling, distribution or fault-tolerance. This model is suitable to guide an implementation of simultaneous actions, e.g. with a framework [9], or even with language technology [10]. As such the reader should be aware that the model only gives a conceptual view on support for the implementation of simultaneous actions. While for example, conceptually the collector layer is accessible for all agents in the MAS, physically the collector layer may be distributed over different hosts and contains one collector for each location where the MAS is deployed. When distribution is required, it should be implemented as a separate concern using available middleware support.

4 Centralized versus Regional Synchronization

In this section we illustrate the generic model for simultaneous actions for two concrete synchronization approaches: centralized and regional synchronization. Since our focus is on infrastructure for simultaneous actions, we do not go into details of the synchronization algorithms. The interested reader is referred to the references in the text.

4.1 Centralized Synchronization

With centralized synchronization, all agents act at one global pace. Synchronization is regulated by one central synchronizer. An example of centralized synchronization is discussed in [3]. Fig. 5 depicts the model for simultaneous actions applied for centralized synchronization. The major advantage of centralized synchronization is simplicity. The synchronization layer contains a collection to store synchronization requests T. Each entry is reserved for a particular agent of the MAS. Initially all entries are set to the initial state, i.e. (A, T^0) for each agent A in the MAS. When an agent A_i sends a request T to synchronize, the synchronizer replaces the corresponding entry to (A_i, T). When all agents have sent their request, the synchronizer triggers the agents to act by means of sending them the complete set of synchronized agents. Simultaneously, the collection for synchronization requests is re-initialized. This functionality is represented in the model as the encircled R.

Subsequently, the agents send their influences to the collector. For centralized synchronization the repository of influences is a simple data structure, containing one entry for each agent of the MAS. A start each entry is initialized to (A, I^0). When an agent sends his influence to the collector, the corresponding entry is updated with the passed influence. Only when all agents have sent their influences, the collector passes the complete set of influences $\{I\}$ to the reactor and re-initializes the influence repository. This functionally of the collector is represented as R in Fig. 5.

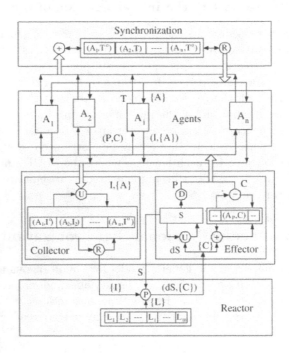

Fig. 5. Model for simultaneous actions with centralized synchronization.

Then the reactor handles the influences and passes the state changes and consumptions to the effector. This latter updates the state of the environment, composes a new set of consumptions and makes them available for the agents. When the agents start a new cycle they perceive the new local state of the environment, and consume the available consumptions from the effector.

Evaluation. The implementation of simultaneous actions with centralized synchronization is rather straightforward. The synchronization layer and influence collector have a simple structure. However, with respect to the acting pace, the autonomy of the agents is a serious problem. Centralized synchronization implies centralized control. All agents act at one global pace, and that ignores the opportunity costs of agents waiting while other agents spend time for decision making. Especially for MASs populated with heterogeneous agents this can be a serious disadvantage. For scalability we have to weigh the cost for collecting influences against the cost of reacting to influences and this in relation to the number of agents in the MAS. With centralized synchronization no search is needed to find the right set of pending influences. However, since the influences for all agents are passed together to the reactor, and since each influence can possibly interfere with any other influence in the set, the complexity to calculate the reaction of the influences is $O(n^2)$ for a MAS with n agents. Therefore we have to conclude that centralized synchronization scores poorly for scalability of the MAS.

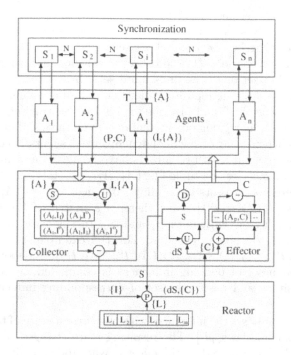

Fig. 6. Model for simultaneous actions with regional synchronization.

4.2   Regional Synchronization

With regional synchronization agents themselves take care of their synchronization. Each agent of the MAS is equipped with a personal synchronizer. Before acting, each agent triggers his synchronizer to synchronize with the agents within his perceptual range. The result of the synchronization process is the formation of independent groups of synchronized agents. The composition of these groups depends on the actual locality of the agents. When agents enter or leave each others perceptual range, the composition of synchronized groups dynamically changes at the same time. For a detailed description of regional synchronization, we refer to [12]. Fig. 6 depicts the model for simultaneous actions applied for regional synchronization. The synchronization layer with regional synchronization is populated with synchronizers S, each synchronizer connected to an agent. Before an agent A_i acts, he sends a request T to his synchronizer S_i to establishing synchronization with his neighboring colleagues. To do so, T must contain the set of agents visible to A_i. A_i deduces this set from his last perception P. Then S_i starts synchronization by requesting the set of visible agents to

synchronize. Synchronization messages are represented by N. Only when negotiation is concluded and a mutual agreement is reached with the synchronized
agents, S_i informs his agent A_i to proceed, sending him the set of synchronized
agents $\{A\}$.

Then the agent decides about his next action and sends an influence, together with the set of synchronized agents to the collector. Based on this latter
set, the collector searches for a matching set of pending influences. Now there
are three possible scenario's: (1) the collector can not find a matching set, (2)
he finds one such a set or (3) he finds more sets. In case he did not found any
set he adds a new set to the repository of sets of pending influences according to
$(I, \{A\})$. For the case he found just one set he updates this set. We explain the
third scenario (with more then one matching set) by means of an example. Such
scenario occurs when a set of regional synchronized agents is composed of different subsets whereof at least two subsets have no agents in common[3]. Suppose
that the collector receives the tuple $(I_1, \{A_1, A_{11}, A_6, A_9\})$ sent by A_1. Further,
we suppose there are two sets of pending influences, $S_1 = \{(A_7, I_7), (A_{11}, I^0)\}$
and $S_2 = \{(A_9, I_9), (A_{14}, I^0)\}$. Now there is a match of the set of synchronized agents sent by A_1 with both S_1 and S_2. In this case the collector combines all the sets to one resulting set. For the example, the resulting set is
$\{(A_7, I_7), (A_{11}, I^0), (A_9, I_9), (A_{14}, I^0), (A_6, I^0), (A_1, I_1)\}$. As soon as the collector detects that a set of pending influences is completed, he removes this set
from the repository and passes the set of corresponding influences $\{I\}$ to the
reactor.

The reactor composes the influences with the current state of the environment
S and the applicable laws $\{L\}$. The resulting state changes dS and the set of
consumptions $\{C\}$ are passed to the effector who updates with them the state
of the environment and the repository of pending consumptions. Subsequently
the agent can perceive the updated state and consume its consumption to start
a new action cycle.

Evaluation. The implementation of simultaneous actions with regional synchronization is more complicated than with centralized synchronization. The
synchronization layer must implement a non–trivial synchronization algorithm
to set up regional synchronization, for details see [12]. Further, the influence
collector must provide a dynamic data structure for sets of pending influences.
This structure must be maintained in a consistent manner, including possible
merges of sets as the one discussed in the example above. Contrary to centralized synchronization, the approach with regional synchronization guarantees
much better autonomy for the agents. Since agents only synchronize with their
direct neighbors (these are exactly the candidates for simultaneous actions), the
pace at which they are able to act only depends on this set of synchronized
agents. The price that is paid for this gain is the communication overhead to
establish regional synchronization. [12] reports simulation results that compares

---

[3] For regional synchronization each agent establishes synchronization with only the
agents visible to him, so when not all agents of a set of regional synchronized agents
see each other, each agent only passes a subset of synchronized agents to the collector.

the pros and cons. Collecting influences is clearly more expensive for the regional synchronization approach. Selecting matching sets of pending influences requires a search through the repository of the collector. In addition, if more then one set is found these sets have to be merged into one compound set. On the other hand, the cost to calculate reaction is much lower than for centralized synchronization. Since only sets of influences on a per region basis are passed to the reactor, the cost for calculating reaction only depends on the size of such sets. Therefore, regional synchronization scales much better then centralized synchronization. Agents that have no colleagues to synchronize with can act asynchronously, while the calculation of the reaction for a group of synchronized agents only depends on the size of the group. This makes the complexity to react to the influences $O(n * r)$ for a MAS populated with n agents that synchronize in clusters with an average size r. As explained in section 4.1, the complexity of the reaction to the influences for centralized synchronization is $O(n^2)$.

Contrary to centralized synchronization where all agents simply act together, with regional synchronization, the possibility for acting together is established as a *natural consequence* of the situatedness of the agents. In other words, agents that are in each others neighborhood are able to perform simultaneous actions. Such support for simultaneous actions can be implemented in a meta–layer, where synchronizers are meta–agents that act on behalf of their associated agents to establish synchronization at the beginning of each action cycle.

5   Conclusion and Future Work

The objective of this paper was to present a model that can bridge the gap between the concept of simultaneous actions and its implementation. To bring order in the range of simultaneous actions we first proposed a classification. This classification takes the viewpoint of the observer, i.e. it distinguishes between different kinds of simultaneous actions based on the way how such actions interfere with one another. To underpin the different types of simultaneous actions, we illustrated each of them with examples in the Packet–World.

Then we presented a generic model for simultaneous actions in situated MASs. This model is independent of the applied agent architecture. The model functionally describes how simultaneous actions in situated MASs can be treated towards implementation. The model is composed of four layers. The top layer is responsible for composing sets of synchronized agents, i.e. agents that act together. The second layer contains the agents in the MAS. The third layer contains the collector who is responsible for composing sets of influences for simultaneous acting agents and the effector that keeps the state of the environment up to date and brings the effects of their actions to the agents. The fourth and final layer contains the reactor that is responsible for calculating the effects of the influences of simultaneous acting agents according to the actual state of the environment and the laws of the modeled MAS.

In the final section we illustrated the model for simultaneous actions for centralized and regional synchronization. The approach with centralized synchronization is the easiest to implement, however the price is poor autonomy for the agents and bad scalability of the MAS. With regional synchronization the implementation is more complex, but this approach results in better autonomy of the agents and better scalability with respect to the number of agents in the MAS.

As a proof of concept, we have implemented the model for simultaneous actions in the Packet–World. We applied the model for centralized and regional synchronization. The interested reader is referred to [11]. The next step is to integrate the experiences with simultaneous actions from the Packet–World into a generic framework for situated MASs. Our goal is then to develop a language to program situated MASs that can be executed on top of this framework. Such a language can extend an existing programming language with different constructs that capture key concepts for situated MASs such as simultaneous actions.

References

1. J. F. ALLEN AND G. FERGUSON, *Actions and Events in Interval Temporal Logic*, Journal of Logic and Computation, Special Issue on Actions and Processes, 1994.
2. C. BOUTILIER AND R. I. BRAFMAN, *Partial–Order Planning with Concurrent Interacting Actions*, Journal of Artificial Research 14, 4-2001.
3. J. FERBER, *Multi-Agent Systems, An Introduction to Distributed Artificial Intelligence*, Addison-Wesley, ISBN 0-201-36048-9, Great Britain, 1999.
4. J. FERBER, *Un modele de l'action pour les systemes multi-agents*, Journees sur les systemes multi-agents et l'intelligence artificielle distribue, Voiron, 1994.
5. J. FERBER, AND J.P. MÜLLER, *Influences and Reaction: a Model of Situated Multiagent Systems*, Proceedings of ICMAS'96, AAAI Press, Nara, Japan, 1996.
6. N. GRIFFITHS, M. LUCK AND M. D'IVERNO, *Cooperative Plan Annotation through Trust*, Workshop Notes of UKMAS'02, Eds. P. McBurney, M. Wooldridge, UK Workshop on Multi-agent Systems, Liverpool, 2002.
7. M. N. HUHNS AND L. M. STEPHENS, *Multi-Agent Systems and Societies of Agents*, G. Weiss ed., Multi-agent Systems, MIT press, 1999.
8. D. KINNY, M .LJUNDBERG, A. RAO ET AL., *Planning with Team activity*, MAA-MAW'92, LNCS 830, S. Martino al Cimino, Italy, 1992.
9. M. E. MARKIEWICZ, C. J. P. LUCENA, *Object Oriented Framework Development*, ACM Press, 2001. See: http://www.acm.org/crossroads/xrds7-4/frameworks.html
10. B. ROBBEN, *Language Technology and Metalevel Architectures for Distributed Objects*, Ph.D, K.U.Leuven, Belgium, ISBN 90-5682-194-6, 1999.
11. D. WEYNS AND T. HOLVOET, *The Packet-World as a Case to Investigate Sociality in Multi-agent Systems*, Demo presented at AAMAS 2002, Bologna, Italy, 2002. For information see: www.cs.kuleuven.ac.be/~danny/aamas02demo.html.
12. D. WEYNS AND T. HOLVOET, *Regional Synchronization for Simultaneous Actions in Situated Multi-Agent Systems*, CEEMAS 2003, LNAI 2691 pp. 497–511, Prague, Czech Republic, 2003.
13. D. WEYNS AND T. HOLVOET, *A Model for Situated Multi-Agent Systems with Regional Synchronization*, CE/AMAS, Balkema Publishers, ISBN 90-5809-622-X vol. I, 2th chapter, Madeira, Portugal, 2003.

Handling Sequences of Belief Change in a Multi-agent Context

Laurent Perrussel

IRIT – Université Toulouse 1, Manufacture des Tabacs
21, allée de Brienne
F-31042 Toulouse Cedex – France
Laurent.Perrussel@univ-tlse1.fr

Abstract. This paper focuses on the features of belief change in a multi-agent context. Agents have to consider information received from the other agents and the ability of how to change beliefs after receiving a message is a prerequisite for many multi-agents problems. The agents are embedded in an environment where they are communicating and they have to prevent potential internal conflicts in their beliefs. We study the belief change operators in that context. Our approach is to consider that agents' belief state is a set of pairs ⟨belief, origin of the belief⟩ combined with a preference relation over the agents embedded in the multi-agent system. The belief revision procedure for handling received messages is a syntactic approach which aims at selecting the minimal subsets of the belief base in conflict with the received information and, according to the reliability of the sources of the conflicting beliefs, removing the less reliable beliefs in order to handle the received message. The proposed belief change operators ensure that an agent makes as few changes as possible but also handle iterated belief changes by preserving the order on the beliefs.

1 Introduction

It is quite common to characterize intelligent agents in cognitive terms such as the well known belief, desire intention mental attitudes [16]. In that context, belief change is a key problem for agents. In a multi-agent system, agents communicate with each other in order to solve a problem such as building a plan or negotiating a price. When a first agent communicates with a second agent, the first one intends to change the mental state of the second one.

In this paper we focus on how an agent should change its beliefs when it receives new information from the other agents, i.e. how its beliefs should look like after interpreting the received message [15]. We focus here on multi agent systems that exchange messages about a world that do not change. In that context, belief change has to be considered as belief revision. In order to know if an agent has to adopt the received messages, it considers the reliability of the sender. Next, in order to define what beliefs should be dropped to get a new consistent belief base, it drops the beliefs issued from the less reliable agents.

M. Schillo et al. (Eds.): MATES 2003, LNAI 2831, pp. 119–130, 2003.

This criterion is not enough for specifying what beliefs should be dropped since agents may believe statements issued from agents which could be equally reliable. Thus, a second criterion is introduced in order to uniquely define what beliefs the agent should drop. We show that our belief change operators respect most of the AGM postulates.

In our proposal, when the sender of the message is not enough reliable, the receiver agent do not drop the message, it keeps it. As the communicated statement becomes consistent with the current beliefs of the receiver agent after some change actions, this agent will integrate this piece of information in its current belief set. This approach enables agents to consider as much as possible of the received messages. At the same time, agents maintain a set of statements that should not be believed: these statements, called disbeliefs, are justified by messages describing what should not be believed.

The account of belief change we advocate here handles iterated belief change. This is a key feature when we consider autonomous agents, they should be able to take into account a sequence of messages and thus a sequence of belief change actions.

The paper is organized as follows: Section 2 briefly reviews the AGM approach. Section 3 presents the formal definitions for describing an agent's belief state, messages and reliability level of beliefs. In section 4 and 5, we present constructive definitions for the change functions. Section 6 presents the related works and section 7 concludes the paper.

2 Preliminaries

The AGM postulates [1] describe how the beliefs of an agent should change according to the main following principles: minimal change and syntax-independence. Let K be a belief set, i.e. a set of propositional formulas, such that K is closed under logical consequence. K_ϕ^+ is the deductive closure of $K \cup \{\varphi\}$ and it represents the *expansion* of K by φ. K_φ^* represents the *revision* of K by φ. Let $K_\perp$ be the inconsistent belief set. According to [9], a revision function should satisfy the following postulates:

(R1) K_φ^* is a belief set.
(R2) $\varphi \in K_\varphi^*$.
(R3) $K_\varphi^* \subseteq K_\varphi^+$.
(R4) If $\varphi \notin K$ then $K_\varphi^+ \subseteq K_\varphi^*$.
(R5) $K_\varphi^* = K_\perp$ iff $\vdash \neg\varphi$.
(R6) If $\vdash \varphi \leftrightarrow \psi$ then $K_\varphi^* = K_\psi^*$.
(R7) $K_{\varphi \wedge \psi}^* \subseteq (K_\varphi^*)_\psi^+$.
(R8) If $\neg\psi \notin K_\varphi^*$ then $(K_\varphi^*)_\psi^+ \subseteq K_{\varphi \wedge \psi}^*$.

And the postulates for the contraction function, K_ϕ^- are:

(C1) K_ϕ^- is a belief set.

(C2) $K_\phi^- \subseteq K$.

(C3) If $\phi \notin K$ then $K_\phi^- = K$.

(C4) If $\nvdash \phi$, then $\phi \notin K_\phi^-$.

(C5) If $\phi \in K$, then $K \subseteq (K_\phi^-)\phi^+$.

(C6) If $\vdash \phi \leftrightarrow \psi$ then $K_\phi^- = K_\psi^-$;

(C7) $K_\phi^- \cap K_\psi^- \subseteq K_{\phi \wedge \psi}^-$;

(C8) If $\phi \notin K_{\phi \wedge \psi}^-$ then $K_{\phi \wedge \psi}^- \subseteq K_\phi^-$.

3 Agent Beliefs

We assume that beliefs are expressed in a propositional language $\mathcal{L}$. Changes in a belief set are caused by communication only. We assume throughout the paper that the external world is *static*; handling changes caused by "physical" actions would require the integration of belief update to our formalism, which we leave for further work. Thus, we are considering cases such as diagnosis. We assume that messages are sent point-to-point. In order to identify the sender of messages we introduce a set of agent id: let $A = \{a_1 \cdots a_n\}$ be this set.

3.1 Describing Messages

In our context, an agent may send two kinds of messages to the other agents: an agent a informs an agent b that ϕ holds or an agent a informs an agent b that ϕ does not hold. These messages may occur after a request sending by b to a and asking if ϕ holds or not. In more formal terms, we get:

Definition 1 (Message). *A message M is defined as a tuple of receiver r, sender s, content ϕ, status st. The receiver and the sender are agent ids, the content is an $\mathcal{L}$-formula and the status is one of the two possible status: $\{\texttt{Hold}, \texttt{NotHold}\}$. Self addressed messages are not allowed, i.e. $M = \langle r, s, \phi, st \rangle$ s.t. $s \neq r$ and $\phi \nvdash \bot$. Let $\mathcal{M}$ be the set of all possible messages.*

Remarks $\texttt{NotHold}\phi$ is not equivalent to $\texttt{Hold}\neg\phi$. We do not consider how agents acquire information. The agents interact with the others: they send and receive messages. At each moment the agents may receive a message and they will change their epistemic state.

Definition 2 (Sequence of messages). *A sequence of messages σ is a function which associates moments in time and messages. Moments in time are represented by the set of integers: $\sigma : \mathbb{N} \to \mathcal{M}$*

3.2 Describing Agent Beliefs

The key idea is to represent the "belief state" of an agent as three sets:

- a set of labelled statements representing the current beliefs, i.e. statements are indexing with their corresponding message number (their origins);
- a set of potential beliefs: messages received by the agent which could not be handled since they are in conflict with its current beliefs. Since the current beliefs change with respect to the received messages, some potential beliefs will be consistent with the new current beliefs and thus will be considered as current beliefs in future states.
- a set of "disbeliefs" representing statements that should not be believed by the agent. The set of disbeliefs changes with respect to the flow of messages about statements that do not hold.

To represent beliefs of an agent, we define a signed belief as a pair ⟨statement, origin of the statement⟩ (the received message):

Definition 3 (Signed belief). *A signed belief is a pair $\langle \phi, i \rangle$ where ϕ is a $\mathcal{L}$-formula and $i \in \mathbb{N}$ s.t. $(\exists r, s, st)(\sigma(i) = \langle r, s, \phi, st \rangle)$. Let $\mathcal{S}$ be the set of signed beliefs and Let $\mathcal{SB} = 2^{\mathcal{S}}$ be the set of all sets of signed beliefs.*

Example 1. Let a_1 and a_2 be two agents and a message $\sigma(1) = \langle a_1, a_2, \neg \varphi, \text{Hold} \rangle$. The pair $\langle \neg \varphi, 1 \rangle$ is the associated signed belief.

Based on the set of signed beliefs, we can define what statements could be inferred by an agent:

Definition 4 (Beliefs set and beliefs base). *Let Bel be a function which maps a signed beliefs set s to a set of $\mathcal{L}$-formulas: $Bel(s) = \{\psi | \bigwedge_{\langle \phi, i \rangle \in s} \phi \vdash \psi\}$. $Bel(s)$ represents the* beliefs set *associated to a set s of signed beliefs. Let Base be a function which maps a signed beliefs set s to a set s of $\mathcal{L}$-formulas: $Base(s) = \bigcup_{\langle \phi, i \rangle \in s} \{\phi\}$. $Base(s)$ is the* beliefs base *associated to s.*

Example 2. Let $s = \{\langle \neg \varphi, 1 \rangle, \langle \neg \varphi \to \varphi', 2 \rangle\}$ be a signed beliefs set. The beliefs set associated to s is: $Bel(s) = Cn(\{\neg \varphi, \neg \varphi \to \varphi', \varphi'\})$ where Cn is the deductive closure operation; and the beliefs base is equal to $Base(s) = \{\neg \varphi, \neg \varphi \to \varphi'\}$.

From a set of signed beliefs, we consider the minimal subsets entailing a specific conclusion. Let ϕ be a formula and s a set of signed beliefs. Let *support* be a function returning the set of minimal subsets of s entailing ϕ.

$$support(s, \phi) = \{s' | s' \subseteq s, Bel(s') \vdash \phi \text{ and } \forall s'' \subset s'(s'' \nvdash \phi)\}$$

In order to describe what is believed by an agent, we introduce the notion of epistemic state. An epistemic state describes what is "currently" believed by the agent, what could be potentially believed and what should not be believed. Let us stress that our definition of epistemic states should not be confused with the epistemic states defined by [4,11].

Definition 5 (Epistemic state). *An epistemic state is a structure:* $\langle CB, PB, DB \rangle$ *where $CB \in \mathcal{SB}$, $PB \in \mathcal{SB}$ and $DB \in \mathcal{SB}$. The first one represents the current belief of the agent, the second one represents potential belief and the third one represents disbeliefs such that:*

- $CB \in \mathcal{SB}$, $\forall \langle \phi, i \rangle \in CB$ s.t. $\sigma(i) = \langle r, s, \phi, \mathtt{Hold} \rangle$ and $Bel(CB) \nvdash \perp$;
- $(\forall \langle \phi, i \rangle \in PB)(Bel(CB) \wedge \phi \vdash \perp$ or $(\exists \langle \phi', i' \rangle \in DB)(Bel(CB) \wedge \phi \vdash \phi'))$;
- $(\forall \langle \phi, i \rangle \in DB)(\sigma(i) = \langle r, s, \phi, \mathtt{NotHold} \rangle$ and $Bel(CB) \nvdash \phi)$.

According to this definition, (i) potential beliefs are signed beliefs in conflict with the current beliefs and (ii) the belief set associated to the current beliefs do not entail any of the disbeliefs.

Example 3. Let $E = \langle \{ \langle \neg \varphi, 1 \rangle, \langle \neg \varphi \rightarrow \varphi', 2 \rangle \}, \{ \langle \neg \varphi', 3 \rangle, \langle \neg \varphi' \rightarrow \varphi'', 5 \rangle \}, \{ \langle \varphi'', 4 \rangle \} \rangle$ be an epistemic state; i.e. $CB = \{ \{ \langle \neg \varphi, 1 \rangle, \langle \neg \varphi \rightarrow \varphi', 2 \rangle \} \}$, $PB = \{ \{ \langle \neg \varphi', 3 \rangle, \langle \neg \varphi' \rightarrow \varphi'', 5 \rangle \} \}$ and $DB = \{ \{ \langle \varphi'', 4 \rangle \} \}$. The signed belief $\langle \neg \varphi', 3 \rangle$ belongs to PB since $\neg \varphi'$ contradicts $Bel(CB)$. The signed belief $\langle \neg \varphi' \rightarrow \varphi'', 3 \rangle$ also belongs to PB because if it were a member of CB then the disbelief $\langle \varphi'', 4 \rangle$ would have been violated. Thus this epistemic is well-defined.

In order to define to what set of signed beliefs should belong a signed belief, the agents consider a procedure for changing their epistemic states.

4   Epistemic State Change

In order to handle the messages that agents exchange, each of them needs a specific procedure for handling belief change. The common base of each procedure is an order over the set of agents $\leqslant$: each agent considers their own most reliable sources. Agents that could not be distinguished are considered in an equal way (and thus entailing a total preorder). Since $\leqslant$ is a total preorder, A may be partitioned in $\leqslant$-equivalence classes of equally reliable agents. These classes are themselves totally ordered. The second element is a criterion defining how potential beliefs issued from equally reliable agents should be considered. In this paper we focus on two possible criteria: NEW (priority to the newest messages) and OLD (priority to the oldest ones). In order words, this criterion combined with $\leqslant$ induces a linear order over the messages received by an agent. Let us mention that there is no meta-criterion for selecting the priority criterion. In fact, any kind of criterion that can be combined with $\leqslant$ so that it induces a linear order over the messages is valid.

Definition 6 (Agent revision program). *Let p be an agent revision program defined as a structure: $\langle \leqslant, choice \rangle$. $\leqslant$ is a total preorder over A and choice is a constant belonging $\{ \mathtt{NEW}, \mathtt{OLD} \}$. Let $\mathcal{P}$ be the set of agent revision programs.*

Writing $a < b$ means that b is a strictly better source than a: $a \leqslant b$ but $b \nleqslant a$; writing $a = b$ means that b is equal to the source a: $a \leqslant b$ and $b \leqslant a$. According to their current epistemic state and their revision program, the agents change their epistemic states as they interact with the other agents. Notice that reliabiliy of agents defined by the revision program is static. We leave for further work this problem: how to rchange the *choice* constant and the pre-order?

4.1   Qualifying Beliefs

Each belief of an agent a issued from the set of current beliefs mat be compared to the other signed beliefs according to the order $\leqslant$. This order is refined by considering the constant *choice*.

Definition 7 ($\prec$). *Let p be an agent revision program of an agent r. Let $a = \langle \phi, i \rangle$ and $b = \langle \psi, j \rangle$ be two signed beliefs s.t. $\sigma(i) = \langle r, s, \phi, st \rangle$ and $\sigma(j) = \langle r, s', \psi, st' \rangle$. $a \prec b$ iff:*

- *if $s < s'$ or*
- *if $s = s'$ and $i <_{\mathbb{N}} j$ and choice is defined in p as* OLD;
- *if $s = s'$ and $i >_{\mathbb{N}} j$ and choice is defined in p as* NEW.

Let us notice that $\prec$ is a linear order

5   The Change Functions

In this section, we describe the three kinds of belief change: expansion, revision and contraction. Let us consider a set of agents A where their initial epistemic states is empty: $(\forall a \in A) E_a^0 = \langle \emptyset, \emptyset, \emptyset \rangle$, a set of revision programs $prog : A \to \mathcal{P}$ and a sequence of messages σ. Messages received by the agents entail a revision or contraction action of their epistemic state. Now we describe the three kinds of belief change: expansion, revision and contraction. Let us consider a set of agents A where their initial epistemic states is empty: $(\forall a \in A) E_a^0 = \langle \emptyset, \emptyset, \emptyset \rangle$, a set of revision programs $\mathcal{P}$ and a sequence of messages σ. Messages received by the agents entail a revision or a contraction action of their epistemic states. Let $n \in \mathbb{N}$ and $\sigma(n) = \langle r, s, \phi, status \rangle$ be a message. Suppose $E_r^n = \langle CB, PB, DB \rangle$ be the epistemic state of the agent r at n. The epistemic state of r is recursively defined accordingly to p, its revision program, for any message received by r at $n' < n$. Since one message is sending at n, only one agent changes its epistemic state.

Definition 8. *Let A be a set of agents, E_a^n be the epistemic states of every agent a and $\sigma(n) = \langle r, s, \phi, status \rangle$ be a message.*

$$E_a^{n+1} = \begin{cases} (E_a^n) & \text{if } a \neq r \\ (E_a^n)^*_{\langle \phi, n \rangle} & \text{if } status = \text{Hold and } a = r \\ (E_a^n)^-_{\langle \phi, n \rangle} & \text{if } status = \text{NotHold and } a = r \end{cases}$$

Expansion are not directly caused, however we introduce this change action since AGM postulates used it.

5.1   Expansion

Let $sb = \langle \phi, i \rangle$ s.t. $\sigma(i) = \langle a, s, \phi, \text{Hold} \rangle$ and E the epistemic state of the agent a. Classically, expansion are based on the deductive closure of the belief set:

$$E_{sb}^+ = \langle CB^+, PB^+, DB^+ \rangle = \langle CB \cup \{sb\}, PB, DB \rangle$$

Let K' be the current belief set associated to E_{sb}^+. By definition $K' = Bel(CB) \cup \{\phi\}$ and thus our expansion operator follows the AGM postulates for this operator [9].

5.2   Revision

Agents are autonomous: for each message they receive, they use their own revision program in order to prevent inconsistencies in their beliefs. In other words, the selection mechanism that select signed beliefs to be remove must not be specific to a belief state but must be appropriate for handling multiple belief change. Thus, the agent revision program is able to handle iterated belief change [4,11]. In order to handle this, agents have to determine what beliefs should be dropped. Here we are considering beliefs in their syntactic form, i.e. the messages, and thus revision will be based on this approach [8,13,3]. The procedure for revising epistemic states is based on the safe revision function [2]

Let n be a moment, $M = \sigma(n) = \langle r, s, \phi, st \rangle$ be a message such that $st = \texttt{Hold}$, and $E^n = \langle CB, PB, DB \rangle$ be the epistemic state of the agent r at the moment n. The epistemic state is recursively defined accordingly to $prog(r)$ for any message received at a moment $m < n$ by r.
In a first stage, the current belief set has to be revised with respect to the set of disbeliefs. Next, in a second stage all the potential beliefs consistent with the new current belief set will be added to the new current belief set and removed from the set of potential beliefs. Finally, the disbeliefs that must be no longer considered are removed.

First stage: revising CB. Here, we use the degree of each conflicting belief defined by the total preorder $\leqslant$. First, we consider the set of minimal subsets of $\mathcal{L}$-statements Γ issued from CB entailing $\neg\phi$: $\Gamma = support(CB, \neg\phi)$. In a second stage we remove the less credible signed belief associated to each minimal subset $\gamma \in \Gamma$. The order $\prec$ ensures us that there exists a unique minimal element in γ $(min(\gamma))$. In order to define what beliefs have to be be dropped, we employ a complete pre-order with maximal elements on the entire set Γ [13]. We say that a set γ_1 is preferred to a set γ_2, $\gamma_2 \ll \gamma_1$, if the maximal element of γ_1 is preferred to the maximal element of γ_2; γ_1 is equally preferred to γ_2, $\gamma_2 = \gamma_1$, if the maximal element of γ_1 is equal to the maximal element of γ_2. Note that such maximal elements of γ always exist. Let esr be a safe revision function based on $\ll$.

We remove minimal elements in every set γ, one by one, in an iterative way. Let $CB^0 = CB$, $\Gamma^0 = \Gamma$ and $min(\Gamma^0)$ the set of minimal elements of Γ^0 with respect to $\ll$. Let a be the signed belief being the minimal element belonging to the union of the elements of $min(\Gamma^0)$ (w.r.t. $\prec$). The revision function, esr, for revising the current signed beliefs set removes the least preferred element to each minimal subset entailing $\neg\phi$.

Definition 9 (*esr*). *The revision of the current signed beliefs of an epistemic state E by a signed belief $sb = \langle \phi, n \rangle$, s.t. $\sigma(n) = \langle r, s, \phi, \texttt{Hold} \rangle$ is defined as $esr(E, sb) = CB^{|\Gamma|} \cup \{sb\}$ where $|\Gamma|$ represents the number of elements of Γ and such that:*

- *let $a = \langle \psi, i \rangle$ s.t.:*
  1. *$\exists \gamma \in \min(\Gamma^i)$ s.t. $a \in \gamma$,*
  2. *$\forall \gamma \in \min(\Gamma^i), \nexists \langle \psi', i' \rangle \in \gamma$ s.t. $\langle \psi', i' \rangle \prec \langle \psi, i \rangle$.*
- *$CB^{i+1} = CB^i - \{a\}$ and*
- *$\Gamma^{i+1} = \Gamma^i - \{\gamma | \gamma \in \min(\Gamma^i) \text{ and } a \in \gamma\}$.*

Theorem 1. *Let r be an agent, p be its agent revision program, $E^n = \langle CB, PB, DB \rangle$ its epistemic state and a message $\sigma(n) = \langle r, s, \phi, \texttt{Hold} \rangle$. The revision function esr determined by E^n and p satisfies postulates (R1) through (R5), (R7) and (R8) when $esr(E^n, \langle \phi, n \rangle) = CB^{|\Gamma|} \cup \{\langle \phi, n \rangle\}$.*

(R6) is not satisfied since *esr* is a syntax-based function[1].

Second stage: adding/removing potential beliefs and disbeliefs. After revising its current set of signed beliefs, the agent has to consider all the potential beliefs. These beliefs must not entail (i) an inconsistency in the current beliefs and (ii) any of the disbeliefs. For this, we consider the most preferred potential beliefs.

Definition 10 (Π and Δ). *The set Π of potential beliefs to add to the new current belief set and the set Δ of potential disbeliefs that have to be considered as disbeliefs are defined as follows:*

- *$PB^0 = PB$, $\Pi^0 = \emptyset$, $\Delta^0 = \emptyset$;*
- *let $m = \langle \psi, j \rangle = max(PB^i)$ with respect to $\prec$ defined over the set PB^i;*
- *if $\sigma(j) = \langle r, s', \psi, \texttt{Hold} \rangle$ (i.e. the status is Hold) and*
  1. *the belief set $Bel(esr(E, sb) \cup \Pi^i \cup \{m\}) \nvdash \bot$;*
  2. *$\forall \langle \psi', j' \rangle \in DB \cup \Delta^i$ if $\forall \gamma \subseteq esr(E, sb) \cup \Pi^i \cup \{m\}$ s.t. $\bigwedge_{\langle \psi'', l \rangle \in \gamma} \psi'' \vdash \psi'$, γ is minimal for ϕ' and $m \in \gamma$ then $\{\langle \psi', j' \rangle\} \ll \gamma$.*
  then $\Pi^{i+1} = \Pi^i \cup \{m\}$ and $\Delta^{i+1} = \Delta^i$;
- *if $\sigma(j) = \langle r, s', \psi, \texttt{NotHold} \rangle$ and $Bel(esr(E, sb) \cup \Pi^i) \nvdash \psi$ then $\Delta^{i+1} = \Delta^i \cup \{m\}$ and $\Pi^{i+1} = \Pi^i$;*
- *$PB^{i+1} = PB^i - \{m\}$.*

The sets Π, Δ are equal to $\Pi^{|PB|}$ and $\Delta^{|PB|}$.

The sets Π and Δ are removed from the potential beliefs. Finally, the disbeliefs that should be no longer considered have to be removed from DB and transferred into PB. Let $\bar{\Delta}$ be the set of this disbeliefs:

$$\bar{\Delta} = \{\langle \psi, j \rangle | \sigma(j) = \langle r, s', \psi, \texttt{NotHold} \rangle \text{ and } Bel(esr(E, \langle \phi, n \rangle) \cup \Pi) \vdash \psi$$
$$\text{and } (\exists \gamma \in support(esr(E, \langle \phi, n \rangle, \psi)) \langle \psi, j \rangle \prec min(\gamma)\}$$

---

[1] Postulates are reformulated w.r.t. our definitions; for instance (R1): $esr(E^n, \langle \phi, n \rangle)$ is a set of signed beliefs (i.e. $Bel(esr(E^n, \langle \phi, n \rangle))$ is a belief set).

When we revise the epistemic state of the agent, $E^*_{\langle\phi,n\rangle} = \langle CB^*, PB^*, DB^* \rangle$, we distinguish two cases: the degree of ϕ, i.e. s is lower than the highest degree of a conflicting belief of r and the case where the sending agent has to be trusted. If the resulting set $CB^{|\Gamma|} \cup \{sb\}$ (cf. definition 9) entails that a disbelief ψ holds where the degree of this disbelief is better than the degree of the new belief then the revision is canceled. The revision action is also canceled when ϕ is weaker than the minimal statement supporting $\neg\phi$.

Definition 11 (*). *Let $E^*_{\langle\phi,n\rangle} = \langle CB^*, PB^*, DB^* \rangle$ be the epistemic state of the agent r at the moment $n + 1$:*

- *if $(\exists \langle\psi, k\rangle \in DB$ s.t. $esr(E, \langle\phi, n\rangle) \vdash \psi$ and $\langle\phi, n\rangle \prec \langle\psi, k\rangle)$ or $(Bel(CB) \vdash \neg\phi$ and $\exists\gamma \in support(CB, \neg\phi)$ s.t. $\langle\phi, n\rangle \prec min(\gamma))$ then $E^*_{\langle\phi,n\rangle} = \langle CB, PB \cup \{\langle\phi, n\rangle\}, DB \rangle$*
- *else $E^*_{\langle\phi,n\rangle} = \langle esr(E, \langle\phi, n\rangle) \cup \Pi, PB - \Pi - \Delta \cup \bar{\Delta}, DB \cup \Delta - \bar{\Delta} \rangle$*

5.3   Contraction

In this section, we briefly describe the contraction operator $-$. This action is very close to the revision operator $*$. The contraction operator is also a two stage operator: at first the current beliefs are contracted if the sender of the message is reliable and secondly, the potential beliefs that are consistent with the resulted current beliefs are added to them.

Let n be a moment, $M = \sigma(n) = \langle r, s, \phi, st \rangle$ be a message such that $st = \mathtt{NotHold}$, and $E^n = \langle CB, PB, DB \rangle$ be the epistemic state of the agent r at the moment n.

First stage: contracting CB. The process for contracting the current beliefs is close to the process for revising CB. We characterize all the minimal subsets entailing the statement which have to be removed. Let $\Gamma = support(CB, \phi)$. Next, as for the function esr, we iteratively remove the less reliable beliefs from each set $\gamma \in \Gamma$. Definitions for $\ll$ and $min(\Gamma)$ are unchanged.

Definition 12 (esc). *The contraction of the current signed beliefs of an epistemic state E by a signed belief $sb = \langle\phi, n\rangle$ is defined as $esc(E, sb) = CB^{|\Gamma|}$ where $CB^{|\Gamma|}$ is defined as follows:*

- *Let $a = \langle\psi, i\rangle$ be a signed belief s.t.:*
  1. *$\exists\gamma \in min(\Gamma^i), a \in \gamma$,*
  2. *$\forall\gamma \in min(\Gamma^i), \nexists \langle\psi', i'\rangle \in \gamma$ s.t. $\langle\psi', i'\rangle \prec \langle\psi, i\rangle$.*
- *$CB^{i+1} = CB^i - \{a\}$;*
- *$\Gamma^{i+1} = \Gamma^i - min(\Gamma^i)$;*

Theorem 2. *Let r be an agent, p be its agent revision program, $E^n = \langle CB, PB, DB \rangle$ its epistemic state and a message $\sigma(n) = \langle r, s, \phi, st \rangle$. The contraction function esc determined by E^n and $\langle\phi, n\rangle$ satisfies postulates (C1) through (C5), (C7) and (C8) when $esc(E, \langle\phi, n\rangle) = CB^{|\Gamma|}$.*

(C6) is not satisfied since our approach is a syntax-based approach.

Second stage: adding/removing potential beliefs and disbeliefs. After contracting the current set of signed beliefs of the agent, the agent r has to consider all the potential beliefs since these beliefs may be consistent with the set $esc(E, s)$. Definitions for Π and Δ are unchanged (the set $\bar{\Delta}$ is not concerned by the contraction operation).

Definition 13 (-). *Let $E^-_{\langle\phi,n\rangle} = \langle CB^-, PB^-, DB^-\rangle$ be the epistemic state of the agent r at the moment $n+1$ s.t.:*

- *if $Bel(CB) \vdash \phi$ and $\exists\gamma \in support(CB, \phi)$ s.t. $\langle\phi, n\rangle \prec min(\gamma)$ then $E^-_{\langle\phi,n\rangle} = \langle CB, PB \cup \{\langle\phi, n\rangle\}, DB\rangle$*
- *else $E^-_{\langle\phi,n\rangle} = \langle esc(E, \langle\phi, n\rangle) \cup \Pi, PB - \Pi - \Delta, DB \cup \Delta \cup \{\langle\phi, n\rangle\}\rangle$*

Current beliefs which have been removed by the contraction function esc are adding to the potential beliefs and if the received message do not entail a contraction then it is considered as a "potential disbelief".

5.4   An Example

Let us consider three agents a_1, a_2, a_3. The revision program of the agent a_1 is: $prog(a_1) = \langle\{(a_1 < a_2, a_2 < a_3)\}, \texttt{OLD}\rangle$ and the initial state is $E^0_{a_1} = \langle\emptyset, \emptyset, \emptyset\rangle$. Let us consider the following sequence of 5 messages: 0, 1, 2, 3 and 4

$$\sigma = [\langle a_1, a_2, \phi, \texttt{Hold}\rangle, \langle a_1, a_3, \phi \rightarrow \psi, \texttt{Hold}\rangle,$$
$$\langle a_1, a_3, \psi, \texttt{Hold}\rangle, \langle a_1, a_3, \psi, \texttt{NotHold}\rangle, \langle a_1, a_2, \psi, \texttt{Hold}\rangle]$$

According to the revision program and the change operators, we get the following epistemic states for the agent a_1:

$$E^1 = \langle\{\langle\phi, 0\rangle\}, \emptyset, \emptyset\rangle$$
$$E^2 = \langle\{\langle\phi, 0\rangle, \langle\phi \rightarrow \psi, 1\rangle\}, \emptyset, \emptyset\rangle$$
$$E^3 = \langle\{\langle\phi, 0\rangle, \langle\phi \rightarrow \psi, 1\rangle, \langle\psi, 2\rangle\}, \emptyset, \emptyset\rangle$$
$$E^4 = \langle\{\langle\phi \rightarrow \psi, 1\rangle\}, \{\langle\phi, 0\rangle, \langle\psi, 2\rangle\}, \{\langle\psi, 3\rangle\}\rangle$$
$$E^5 = \langle\{\langle\phi \rightarrow \psi, 1\rangle\}, \{\langle\phi, 0\rangle, \langle\psi, 2\rangle, \langle\psi, 4\rangle\}, \{\langle\psi, 3\rangle\}\rangle$$

Messages 0, 1, 2 and 4 entail a revision operation while message 3 entails a contraction operation. Let us notice that the last message (a_2 informs a_1 that ψ holds) do not imply that ψ is believed by a_1. This is due to disbelief ψ which is stronger (since it has been send by a_3 and a_3 is better than a_2). The beliefs set associated to the current beliefs set of E^5 is $K = \{\alpha | \phi \rightarrow \psi \vdash \alpha\}$.

6   Related Works

Several works have already been done in the multi-agent revision area. A. Dragoni and P. Giorgini have presented a similar framework [5,6,7]. They proposed to consider belief revision in a multi-agent system by considering the origin of information. Based on the reliability of the incoming statements, agents can also reject new information. Agents can also reconsider all the previous messages and more specifically discarded beliefs can be reinstated. The main difference with our work is that they do not consider disbeliefs in an explicit way and thus they do not take into account contraction operations.

W. Liu and M.A. Williams propose in [12] a framework for handling belief revision. After distinguishing private and public knowledge, the authors describe a belief revision engine aiming at revising beliefs sharing by several agents. They propose this framework since agents should be able to consider common beliefs. We have made a different choice since we consider beliefs as private. However, our definition of beliefs can handle semi-public beliefs since every statement is qualified with its origin. Thus agents can "establish" some common beliefs. At the opposite, in [12], agents can only consider positive beliefs and they do not take into account at each stage the sequences of previously received messages. Concerning the iterated belief revision area, our work is loosely connected to [4] and [11] since we consider that a revision action may fail. Thus, the proposed postulates for qualifying iterated revision processes are not satisfied by our framework.

7   Conclusion

In this paper, we have presented belief change operators for handling iterated belief change. Our work focus on belief change when agents exchange information about a static world such as diagnosis. The first characteristic of our operators is to preserve an order over the beliefs. Because this information is retained, any agent may handle any sequence of messages. The second characteristic of our framework is to keep all the received messages and to reconsider them for taking care of what the agents should not believe and, according to their belief changes, how to reconsider previous messages (represented as potential beliefs).

Our approach does have some limitations. In this paper, we only look at cases where belief change concerns a static world. We only consider communication actions. If we consider more general actions, instead of beliefs changing only through messages, changes could result from sensing actions. In a short term, we would like to generalize our framework in order to handle these limitations, i.e. update rather than revision. Another direction of research for handling changes is to consider different policies for adopting/rejecting a message: effect of convergence, feed-back for getting a fine-grain reliability of information... In a more longer term, our aim is to enable agents to reason about their current beliefs and past beliefs so that they can initiate messages for acquiring new information. Another direction is to reconsider treatments of the semantics of the modal operators for describing beliefs in BDI models: a semantics based on the messages and epistemic states will be useful for describing not only beliefs and disbeliefs [14] but also beliefs change [10] and how agents may be aware about their beliefs and disbeliefs. We are currently investigating all these topics.

References

1. C. Alchourrón, P Gärdenfors, and D. Makinson. On the logic of theory change: Partial meet functions for contraction and revision. *Journal of Symbolic Logic*, 50:510–530, 1985.
2. C. Alchourrón and D. Makinson. The logic of theory change: safe contraction. *Studia Logica*, 44:405–422, 1985.
3. S. Benferhat, C. Cayrol, D. Dubois, J. Lang, and H. Prade. Inconsistency management and prioritized syntax-based entailment. In *Proc. of the 13th IJCAI*, pages 640–645, Chambery, France, 1993.
4. A. Darwiche and J. Pearl. On the logic of Iterated Belief Revision. *Artificial intelligence*, 89(1):1–29, 1997.
5. A. Dragoni. A model for belief revision in a multi-agent environment. In E. Werner and Y. Demazeau, editors, *Decentralized A. I. 3*. North Holland, Elsevier Science Publisher, 1992.
6. A. Dragoni and P. Giorgini. Belief revision through the belief-function formalism in a multi-agent environment. In J.P. Müller, M. Wooldridge, and N Jennings, editors, *Proceedings of the ECAI'96 Workshop on Agent Theories, Architectures, and Languages: Intelligent Agents III*, volume 1193, pages 103–116. Springer, 1997.
7. A. Dragoni and P. Giorgini. Revising beliefs received from multiple source. In M.A. Williams and H. Rott, editors, *Frontiers of Belief Revision, Applied Logic*. Kluwer, 1999.
8. R. Fagin, J. Ullman, and M. Vardi. On the semantics of Updates in Databases. In *Proceedings of the second ACM SIGACT-SIGMOD Symposium on Principles of Database Systems, Atlanta, Ga., USA*, pages 352–365, 1983.
9. P. Gärdenfors. *Knowledge in flux: Modeling the Dynamics of Epistemic States*. MIT Press, 1988.
10. L. Perrussel. A modal logic framework for describing belief revision. In M. Thielscher and M.A. Williams, editors, *Proceedings of the 4th International workshop on Nonmonotonic Reasonong, Action and Change (NRAC'01) - Seattle, USA, August 2001*, pages 58–63, 2001.
11. D. Lehmann. Belief revision, revised. In *Proceeding of the 14th International Joint Conference on Artificial Intelligence (IJCAI'95)*, pages 1534–1540, 1995.
12. W. Liu and M.A. Williams. A Framework for Multi-Agent Belief Revision, Part II: A Layered Model and Shared Knowledge Structure. *Link ping Electronic Articles in Computer and Information Science*, 5(21), 2000.
13. B. Nebel. Syntax-based approaches to belief revision. In P. Gärdenfors, editor, *Belief revision*, volume 29 of *Journal of Cambridge Tracts in Theoretical Computer Science*, pages 52–88. Cambridge University Press, 1992.
14. S. Parsons and P. Giorgini. On Using Degrees of Belief in BDI agents. In *Proceedings of the International Conference on Information Processing and Management of Uncertainty in Knowledge-Based Systems, Paris, July 1998*, 1998.
15. A. Rao. Dynamics of belief systems: A philosophical, logical, and ai perspective. Technical Report 02, Australian Artificial Intelligence Institute, Melbourne, Australia, 1989.
16. M. Wooldridge and N. R. Jennings. Intelligent agents: Theory and practice. *The Knowledge Engineering Review*, 10(2):115–152, 1995.

From the Specification of Multiagent Systems by Statecharts to Their Formal Analysis by Model Checking: Towards Safety-Critical Applications

Frieder Stolzenburg[1] and Toshiaki Arai[2]

[1] Hochschule Harz (University of Applied Studies and Research), Automation and Computer Sciences Department, Friedrichstr. 57–59, 38855 Wernigerode, GERMANY, `fstolzenburg@hs-harz.de`

[2] Information Technology Dept., Mitsubishi Nuclear Fuel Co.,Ltd, 622-1, Funaishikawa, Tokai-mura, Ibaraki 319-1197, JAPAN, `ara@mmc.co.jp`

Abstract. In order to design and implement multiagent systems, the specification method should be as expressive and comprehensive as possible. Statecharts, which are capable of describing dynamic systems and are widely accepted in the computer science community, are applied and investigated for this objective.

In this paper, multiagent systems are studied in the domain of robotic soccer, where the behavior of agents including collaboration is specified by means of UML statecharts [7,8]. This method is also applicable to industrial software applications. For example, a network application can be designed and specified by means of the same method (see [1]). The approach enables not only standardized design of multiagent systems, but also almost automatic translation of the specification into a running implementation.

As a natural extension of this methodology for designing multiagent systems, formal system analysis and verification should be possible, in order to investigate important system properties. In this paper, we will show how specifications of multiagent systems based on UML statecharts can be verified, by employing model checking techniques. Hence, the proposed specification technique can be used for both, automated multiagent system implementation and analysis.

Introduction

Multiagent systems are expected to be the foundation of robust, interconnected and highly advanced computing methods. This new technology is currently being applied to various fields such as electronic commerce, robotics, computer mediated collaboration, ubiquitous computing, and others.

In previous work, we investigated two domains of applications and discussed how the behaviors of multiagent systems are designed and specified by means of UML statecharts [1]. The advantage of this methodology is that both, researchers and engineers can design and develop software systems more rapidly, communication among team members becomes easier and more reliable, and the

M. Schillo et al. (Eds.): MATES 2003, LNAI 2831, pp. 131–143, 2003.

integration of relatively large software systems is equipped with features of multiagent systems, by means of a standardized specification technique. In addition, our formalism based on statecharts allows us the verification and formal analysis of multiagent systems [13].

We think that in the development of multiagent systems, standardized software design, which also makes software verification possible, is an important matter, such that more secure and reliable systems can be designed and implemented. In this paper, we introduce application domains in Sect. 1, and study how the behavior of agents can be specified by statecharts and analyzed by model checking technology.

We state our method with UML statecharts for the specification of multiagent systems in Sect. 2. There, we demonstrate how the behavior of state machines can be described by configurations and steps. After that, we show some examples of the specification of multiagent systems in Sect. 3.

Model checking is a very useful technique to verify behavioral properties of finite state systems with concurrency. In Sect. 4, we show how multiagent systems, specified by UML statecharts, can be formally analyzed by using model checking techniques. The rigorously formal specification of multiagent systems allows us to translate them into logical structures (Kripke structures), where verification of system properties by means of temporal logics, e.g. CTL, is possible. We end up with concluding remarks and remarks on related works in Sect. 5.

1   Example Applications

In this section, we introduce two applications, namely robotic soccer and a synchronous work flow manager in some detail. Although both applications are different at first glance, they can be described in a similar manner, using the same method for specification. We will describe these domains as multiagent systems in this section and continue in Sect. 3, where we also address the problem of specifying the interaction of several, possibly heterogeneous agents.

1.1   Robotic Soccer

In the RoboCup initiative, the soccer game is chosen as a central topic of research, aiming at innovations to be applied for socially significant problems and in industry. In order to perform actually a soccer game for a robot team, various technologies must be incorporated including design principles of autonomous agents. The RoboCup consists of several leagues with real robots in different sizes or virtual, i.e. simulated robots.

The RoboCup simulation league offers a software platform for research on the software aspects of RoboCup. And in our context, the software design aspect is the most important one. In the soccer domain, usually all agents have an identical internal structure except for the goal-keeper. Therefore, it is quite natural to state the behavior of the agents within one state machine.

1.2   Work Flow with Concurrent Actions

Concurrent actions often arise in industrial applications, that are connected to each other. In general, it is difficult to specify dynamically changing behaviors. In order to design, develop and test such applications, often complicated procedures are needed. But concurrently acting entities can be regarded as agents. And the interesting thing is that, also in this case, system specification is possible by means of the same method as for robotic soccer.

Let us introduce now the meeting organizer application—a case study chosen from typical industrial applications—as a testbed for the specification of multiagent systems with dynamic behavior and interrelationships. The *meeting organizer agent* and the *schedule manager agent* are deployed in this scenario. The meeting organizer agent provides the following functions: arranging appointments and notify meetings. On the other hand, the schedule manager agent holds all *user agents'* schedules.

Without explicit intervention of users, the meeting organizer agent shall be capable of arranging a meeting appointment, provided that each user's schedule manager agent keeps appropriate schedule data, i.e., the schedule manager agent gathers necessary data prior to the arrangement of the meeting organizer. It is assumed that many users can exploit the system via a local area network without direct connection. A user who initiates the arrangement is called organizer, by whom the desired meeting is specified to the system.

2   State Machines

Dynamic systems can be described appropriately as state machines. This also holds for the multiagent systems we have just introduced. Therefore, statecharts are used quite often for the specification of dynamic or procedural aspects of software systems, also in industrial applications. In order to provide a better understanding of statecharts, we give their formal definition in the following.

2.1   Basic Components

Statecharts are a part of UML [10] and a well accepted means to specify dynamic behavior of software systems. The main concepts for statecharts is a state, which corresponds to an activity or behavior of an agent. Hence, statecharts also may be used in the context of *behavior-based programming*. They can be described in a rigorously formal manner, allowing flexible specification, implementation and analysis of multiagent systems [13].

Definition 1. *The basic components of a* state machine *are the following four pairwise disjoint sets:*

S: *a finite set of states, which is partitioned into three disjoint sets:* S_{simple}, $S_{composite}$ *and* $S_{concurrent}$ — *called simple, composite and concurrent states, containing one designated* start state $s_0 \in S_{composite}$,

E: a finite set of events,

V: a set of variables, where each variable $v \in V$ has an associated domain $dom(v)$, and

A: a finite set of actions, which sometimes may be composed from a sequence of simpler actions.

In statecharts, states are connected via transitions, that are annotated with conditions and actions. They are represented as rectangles with round corners and can be structured hierarchically. Following the lines of [10], we define this structure as follows. Each composite state $s \in S_{composite}$ has one *initial state* $\alpha(s)$. Each state $s \in S$ except s_0 *belongs to* a state $\beta(s)$. $\beta(s)$ is defined for all $s \in S\backslash\{s_0\}$ and it must hold $\beta(s) \in S_{composite} \cup S_{concurrent}$. If $\beta(s) \in S_{concurrent}$, then $s \in S_{composite}$, i.e., a concurrent state is never directly contained in another concurrent state.

A *transition* is a relation between two states indicating that an agent in the first state will enter the second state and perform specific *actions* when a specified *event* occurs and the specified conditions—called *guards*—are satisfied in addition. Transitions are drawn as arrows labeled with an *annotation* of the form $e[g]/a$ where $e \in E$, $g \in G$ (the set of guards, first-order formulæ, including equations with variables in V), and $a \in A$. Since states may be simple, composite or concurrent, the behavior of agents or their state machines, respectively, cannot be described by sequences of simple states (as for plain finite state machines), but of configurations.

Example 1. The state machine in Fig. 1 sketches the overall behavior of robotic soccer agents. Some details are not shown, which is indicated by the *hidden decomposition icon* ∘–∘. The machine contains the simple states Init and GetBall, the composite states Behave, Defend, Marking, and Attack, and the concurrent states HandleBall and Communicate. Obviously, the start state is Behave, whose initial state is Init. The three states Init, Attack and Defend belong to the main (start) state Behave. Its initial state Init permits a transition annotated with KickOff/Kick(100%) (with empty guard that corresponds to True) to Attack, if the agent has a KickOff from the center point.

2.2   Configurations and Steps

How can the behavior of state machines be described? For this, we now introduce the concepts of configuration and step. Configurations reflect the state the multiagent system is in. If a new composite state s is entered, then also the initial substates contained in s are entered. For this, we introduce the notion *completion* of a configuration, defining it in operational terms. This is more natural than giving a declarative definition (of a completed configuration), because not always all composite state machines are in their initial substates.

Definition 2 (Configuration). *A configuration c is a rooted tree of states, where the root node is the topmost initial state of the overall state machine. A*

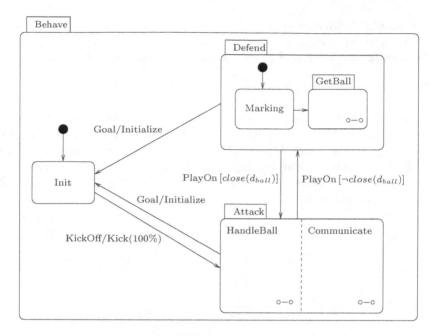

Fig. 1. State machine for the overall behavior.

configuration must be completed by applying the following procedure repeatedly as long as possible to leaf nodes:

1. *If there is a leaf node in c labeled with a composite state s, then $\alpha(s)$ is introduced as immediate successor of s.*
2. *If there is a leaf node in c labeled with a concurrent state s, then all (composite) states s' with $\beta(s') = s$ become successor nodes of s.*

In our context, state machines model the behavior of agents that act in their environment. The main effect of agents is that they interact with their environment. Therefore, state machines change the situation they are in, forming a trace, which is a sequence of situations. A *situation* σ is defined by mapping variables to values from given domains, characterizing the current world state, including the agent's configuration.

Agents perform steps from one configuration to another. For proper multi-agent systems, we also must take into account that several agents or different components of one and the same agent may perform steps at the same time concurrently. Therefore, one may distinguish between micro- and macro-steps as in [12,13].

Definition 3 (Micro-step). *A micro-step from one configuration c of a state machine to a configuration c' by means of a transition t from state s to state s' with annotation e[g]/a in the current situation—written $c \rightarrow_t c'$—is possible iff:*

1. *c contains a node labeled with s,*

2. c' *is identical with c except that s together with its subtree in c is replaced by the completion of s', and*
3. *the annotated event e and guard g hold in the actual situation.*

Fig. 2 shows some configurations of the state machine after several transitions. Since there is a transition from Init to Attack with annotation Kick-Off/Kick(100%) in the state machine, the step from the first to the second configuration shown in Fig. 2 is possible according to Def. 3. For this, the Init node is replaced by Attack. Since Attack is a concurrent state, the (composite) states HandleBall and Communicate belonging to Attack, become successor nodes of Attack. Again, these states have to be completed. This is indicated by triangles with the symbol o—o in it.

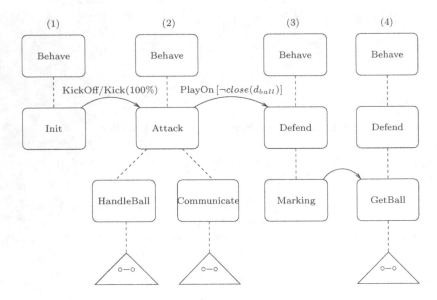

Fig. 2. Configuration after several transitions.

Definition 4 (Macro-step). *A macro-step from the configuration c to a configuration c' with given micro-steps is possible iff:*

1. *all micro-steps are possible in c,*
2. *all states $s_1, \ldots, s_l$ occur on different paths in the configuration tree c (i.e., all micro-steps are simultaneously applicable), and*
3. *c' is obtained by applying all given micro-steps to c.*

With macro-steps, we are able to model concurrent behavior. This is very important for the description of multiagent systems, since there we have several entities which interact concurrently. Concurrent states are the prerequisite for proper macro-steps, i.e., where several micro-steps are executed in parallel. In order to be able to formalize systems of multiple agents, we require the set of variables V to contain variables for the actual event e—we assume that only one event occurs at a time (discrete time model)—and the configuration c of the whole multiagent system. Several agents can act in parallel, where a concurrent state (called region) is employed for each agent (see Fig. 3).

Fig. 3. Generic statechart for a system of multiple agents.

3   Specification of Multiagent Systems

Let us now consider the specification of multiagent systems by examples. The first and the second example (Sect. 3.1) is taken from the organizer domain, while the other one (Sect. 3.2) is from the robotic soccer domain. We will use the latter example in order to demonstrate our procedure for analyzing multiagent systems (Sect. 4).

3.1   Dynamic Behavior of an Agent and Synchronization

The meeting organizer agent, as introduced in Sect. 1.2, requires several input data, e.g. the subject, participants, starting time and room for the meeting. These requirements are related to each other and may be constrained by several conditions. The function of the meeting organizer agent is based on these data, therefore the agent changes its behavior dynamically, which corresponds to a state transition in UML statecharts.

Example 2. The main function of the meeting organizer agent obviously is the arrangement of a meeting. Let us introduce now the Organizing state, which represents its main function, with its substates. As depicted in Fig. 4 (left), the Organizing state of the meeting organizer agent is that a user selects the participants of the desired meeting at first. Secondly, room and time for the meeting is decided. The meeting organizer agent is able to make transitions into two exclusive substates: ArrangeTimeFirst substate and ArrageRoomFirst substate. Thus, a user can select which rule has priority to the other, in order to determine the room and the time of the meeting.

Example 3. Concurrent actions often involve synchronization, so that they can satisfy certain constraints. This can be conveniently expressed by synch states of UML statecharts. The ArrangeTimeFirst substate in Fig. 4 (left) has two concurrent actions, i.e. substates and their actions: one of them checks common

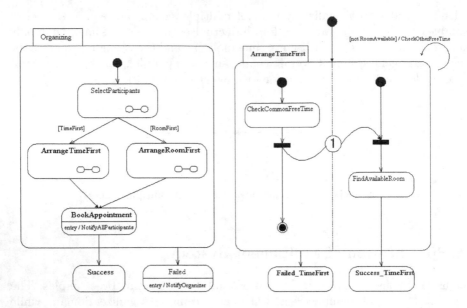

Fig. 4. State machine for Organizing substate and synchronized concurrent actions.

free time among the desired participants, and the other one tries to find an available room for the meeting at the time specified, see Fig. 4 (right). Here these two substates are mutually exclusive and concurrent. Moreover, the former procedure should be taken prior to the latter, and both substates need to be synchronized. If any room is available, the synch transition is fired, and the above procedure is taken again for a new combination of requirement data.

3.2   Obstacle Avoidance with Interrupts

Example 4. Let us consider now an example from the robotic soccer domain, describing the agent's behavior going to the ball. In principle, in this state the agent shall alternately turn its body towards the ball and go one step ahead. But if there is an obstacle in the way, then this procedure has to be interrupted, and the obstacle has to be avoided. The corresponding statechart is shown in Fig. 5. It makes use of a *history state*, shown as a circle with an H inside. Its semantics is that when returning into a state machine at a history state, then it is continued at the configuration that was valid when leaving it the last time.

This means, we have to memorize the actual configuration of the state machine with top state s containing the history state. For this, we introduce a variable h for each history state and each agent where $dom(h)$ is the set of all configurations of s restricted to H. For each transition in state s, the value of h has to be updated accordingly. In addition, when re-entering s, the state processing has to be continued with the stored configuration. Look at Fig. 5, where only the additional annotations for the treatment of the interrupt are shown (with abbreviated configuration names).

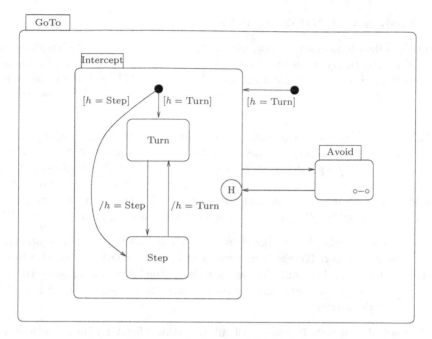

Fig. 5. Obstacle avoidance using history states.

Example 5. What are the different situations—given by assignments σ mapping each variable $v \in V$ into an element of its corresponding domain $dom(v)$—the agent may be in for this example? Situations change over time as an effect of actions the agents are performing. Since only the configuration c the agent is actually in and the history state h is interesting in this abstracted representation, we only have the following four different situations. Note that here we write configurations horizontally, in contrast to Fig. 2.

$$\sigma_1 : c = \text{Goto} \cdots \text{Intercept} \cdots \text{Turn}$$
$$\sigma_2 : c = \text{Goto} \cdots \text{Intercept} \cdots \text{Step}$$
$$\sigma_3 : c = \text{Goto} \cdots \text{Avoid} \ \wedge \ h = \text{Goto} \cdots \text{Intercept} \cdots \text{Turn}$$
$$\sigma_4 : c = \text{Goto} \cdots \text{Avoid} \ \wedge \ h = \text{Goto} \cdots \text{Intercept} \cdots \text{Step}$$

4   System Analysis by Model Checking

There are some properties of a system, that play a key role for the behavior of the system and its correctness. In multiagent systems, it is important to check system properties, e.g. whether from any state it is possible to reach a certain state, where a certain property must be satisfied. In industrial applications, especially for safety-critical applications, system behavior must be free from any failure.

4.1   Analysis with Kripke Structures

System specifications based on statecharts can be transformed into Kripke structures. This eventually allows us to reason over multiagent systems, by making use of temporal logics, e.g. Computation Tree Logic (CTL). For further information about Kripke structures and temporal logics, the reader is referred to [4].

Definition 5 (Kripke structure). *A Kripke structure consists of a finite set of states $\mathcal{S}$, a set $\mathcal{S}_0$ of initial states, a transition relation $R \subseteq \mathcal{S} \times \mathcal{S}$ that must be serial (i.e., for every state $s \in \mathcal{S}$ there is a state $s' \in \mathcal{S}$ with $R(s, s')$), and a function $L : \mathcal{S} \rightarrow 2^P$ that labels each state with the set of atomic propositions from the set P of all atomic propositions true in that state. In this context, an* atomic proposition *has the form $v = x$ with $v \in V$ and $x \in dom(v)$.*

Let us now describe, how a specification of a multiagent system by statecharts can be mapped into a Kripke structure, which yields the basis for the formal analysis of the original system. We can now define the following Kripke structure, which always exists for every given state machine. It is uniquely determined by the following definition:

1. The set of states $\mathcal{S}$ is the set of all valuations for V, which contains the actual system configuration c.
2. The set of initial states is a subset of all valuations which can be understood as situations σ satisfying the condition for the start situation, which is given by $c = s_0$, i.e., initially the state machine is in the (completed) start configuration.
3. The labeling function labels nodes with elements in Σ, the set of all situations.
4. Let $s, s' \in \mathcal{S}$, then $R(s, s')$ holds, if $L(s) \rightsquigarrow L(s')$, i.e., there is a macro-step leading from s to s' in effect. If, for some s, there is no s' such that $R(s, s')$, we add $R(s, s)$.

Example 6. Fig. 6 shows a Kripke structure modeling the state machine from Examples 4 and 5. One can see, that the agent steps and turns alternately (situations σ_1 and σ_2), unless it must do some obstacle avoidance (situations σ_3 and σ_4). Note that, since Fig. 5 in Sect. 3.2 is incomplete, the same is true for Fig. 6 in consequence.

4.2   Analyzing System Properties by Model Checking

Now we are ready for the formal verification of multiagent systems. By means of CTL, we are able to express safety-critical system properties. A transformation into Binary Decision Diagrams (BDDs) [4] can be done in order make formal analysis of the overall system as efficient as possible. For the sake of completeness, we introduce CTL briefly now. The syntax of CTL state (and path) formulæ is given by the following rules:

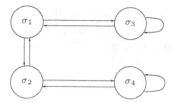

Fig. 6. Kripke structure for Example 5.

1. If p is an atomic proposition in P, then p is a state formula.
2. If f_0, f_1 and f_2 are state formulæ, then also $\neg f_0$, $f_1 \wedge f_2$ and $f_1 \vee f_2$.
3. If g is a path formula, then $\mathbf{E}\,g$ and $\mathbf{A}\,g$ are state formulæ.
4. If f_1 and f_2 are state formula, then $\mathbf{X}\,f_1$, $\mathbf{F}\,f_1$, $\mathbf{G}\,f_1$ and $f_1\,\mathbf{U}\,f_2$ are path formulæ.

The intended meaning of the temporal operators is as listed below. For more details, the reader again is referred to [4].

1. $\mathbf{E}$ ("for some computation path") denotes existential quantification.
2. $\mathbf{A}$ ("for all computation paths") denotes universal quantification.
3. $\mathbf{X}$ ("next time") requires that a property holds in the second state of the path.
4. $\mathbf{F}$ ("future") specifies that a property will hold at some state of the path.
5. $\mathbf{G}$ ("globally") specifies that a property holds at every state on the path.
6. $\mathbf{U}$ ("until") holds if there is a state on the path, where the second property holds, and on every preceding state on the path, the first property holds.

We can express planning tasks, but also more complex properties, e.g., that we can always achieve a certain goal. For instance, if we want to investigate whether we can reach a certain situation σ, i.e., there is a plan for achieving this goal (as in artificial intelligence planning [6]), then we just have to check $\mathbf{EF}\,\sigma$.

Example 7. We can now formulate temporal logic formulæ, checking e.g. that from any state it is possible to get to a state where obstacles are avoided, by the CTL formula $\mathbf{AG}(\mathbf{EF}\ c = \text{Goto}\cdots\text{Avoid})$. We can also express the fact that, by disregarding obstacle avoidance, the agent alternately steps and turns:

$$\mathbf{AG}\Big((\neg c = \text{Goto}\cdots\text{Avoid} \ \wedge \mathbf{AX}\neg\, c = \text{Goto}\cdots\text{Avoid}) \rightarrow$$
$$(c = \text{Goto}\cdots\text{Intercept}\cdots\text{Turn} \rightarrow \mathbf{AX}\,c = \text{Goto}\cdots\text{Intercept}\cdots\text{Step}) \wedge$$
$$(c = \text{Goto}\cdots\text{Intercept}\cdots\text{Step} \rightarrow \mathbf{AX}\,c = \text{Goto}\cdots\text{Intercept}\cdots\text{Turn})\Big)$$

5   Related Works and Conclusions

We have presented a method for the graphical specification of multiagent systems. This method is applicable to different domains: robotic soccer and industrial applications, e.g. a concurrent work flow manager, as stated in this paper.

This approach is advantageous, because multiagent systems are then specified by means of only one type of diagram, namely UML statecharts (see also [1]). By this, more strict specification is possible and design of various systems is facilitated using one unified method.

We also demonstrated that such multiagent systems specification can be formally verified by means of model checking. There exists related work in various disciplines, e.g. automation technology [5]. Furthermore, in [3] abstract state machines are proposed for the specification of software systems, that are related to UML state machines; but for verification, classical theorem proving techniques are proposed, which might be difficult in practice for complex applications.

There are several software engineering approaches for the design and specification of multiagent systems. *Agent UML* [11] makes use of several diagrams, e.g., sequence diagram, communication diagram and interaction overview diagram, which are useful to specify especially the interaction of agents. [9] also employs UML and focuses on requirements. This designing methodology covers a wide range of the development cycle. In contrast to these methods, the emphasis of our approach is laid on the dynamic behavior of multiagent systems using one diagram, namely UML statecharts. In order to facilitate formal analysis and verification methods, we restrict ourselves to only one type of diagram.

Gaia [14] is another methodology for agent-oriented analysis and design. The key concepts in Gaia are roles, which have associated with them responsibilities, permissions, activities and protocols. A role can be viewed as an abstract description of an entity's expected function. However, this approach is neither intended for graphical specification nor for formal analysis as in our approach.

[2] presents an approach for model checking multiagent systems. It also makes use of temporal logics, but there the multiagent system is given by a BDI architecture, whereas we specify agents with statecharts. We think this is an advantage, because this allows us a quite high-level design of multiagent systems. [2] exploits the intrinsic modularity existing in multiagent systems. But in our approach, the modular, hierarchical structure of statecharts does not cause any problems, too. Note that the extensive use of composite states only leads to list-like configurations, and hence there is no combinatorial explosion of states in the Kripke structure after translation.

In this respect concurrent states are more problematic, because they lead to branching configuration trees. But this is a problem inherent to every multiagent system specification, if several agents act in parallel. Therefore, further work shall concentrate on how combinatorial explosion can be avoided in this case. One idea is to exploit dependencies among concurrent states (expressible by synchronization states). In addition, further work shall address even more collaborative behavior and communication in multiagent systems, so that integration of various systems is enabled in a unified process, where expressive specification and verification techniques as introduced in this paper play an important role.

References

1. T. Arai and F. Stolzenburg. Multiagent systems specification by UML statecharts aiming at intelligent manufacturing. In *Proceedings of the 1st International Joint Conference on Autonomous Agents & Multi-Agent Systems*, pages 11–18, Bologna, Italy, 2002. ACM Press. Volume 1.
2. M. Benerecetti, F. Giunchiglia, and L. Serafini. Model checking multiagent systems. *Journal of Logic an Computation*, 8(3):401–423, 1998.
3. E. Börger and R. Stärk. *Abstract State Machines – A Method for High-Level System Design and Analysis.* Springer, Berlin, Heidelberg, New York, 2003.
4. E. M. Clarke, O. Grumberg, and D. Peled. *Model Checking.* MIT Press, Cambridge, MA, London, 1999.
5. T. Heverhagen. Verifikation von Funktionsbausteinadaptern durch Modelchecking. *Automatisierungstechnik*, 51(4):153–163, 2003.
6. H. J. Levesque, R. Reiter, Y. Lespérance, F. Lin, and R. B. Scherl. Golog: A logic programming language for dynamic domains. *Journal of Logic Programming*, 31:59–84, 1997.
7. J. Murray. Specifying agents with UML in robotic soccer. In *Proceedings of the 1st International Joint Conference on Autonomous Agents & Multi-Agent Systems*, pages 51–52, Bologna, Italy, 2002. ACM Press. Volume 1.
8. J. Murray, O. Obst, and F. Stolzenburg. Towards a logical approach for soccer agents engineering. In P. Stone, T. Balch, and G. Kraetzschmar, editors, *RoboCup 2000: Robot Soccer World Cup IV*, LNAI 2019, pages 199–208. Springer, Berlin, Heidelberg, New York, 2001.
9. J. Mylopoulos, M. Kolp, and J. Castro. UML for agent-oriented software development: The Tropos proposal. In M. Gogolla and C. Kobryn, editors, *Proceedings of the 4th International Conference on UML – The Unified Modeling Language, Modeling Languages, Concepts, and Tools*, LNCS 2185. Springer, Berlin, Heidelberg, New York, 2001.
10. Object Management Group, Inc. *OMG Unified Modeling Language Specification*, March 2003. Version 1.5.
11. J. Odell, H. V. D. Parunak, and B. Bauer. Extending UML for agents. In G. Wagner, Y. Lesperance, and E. Yu, editors, *Proceedings of the Agent-Oriented Information Systems Workshop (AOIS) at the 17th National Conference on Artificial Intelligence*, pages 3–17, 2000.
12. A. Pnueli and M. Shalev. What is in a step: On the semantics of statecharts. In T. Ito and A. R. Meyer, editors, *International Conference on Theoretical Aspects of Computer Software*, LNCS 526, pages 244–264, 1991. Springer, Berlin, Heidelberg, New York.
13. F. Stolzenburg. Reasoning about cognitive robotics systems. In R. Moratz and B. Nebel, editors, *Themenkolloquium Kognitive Robotik und Raumrepräsentation des DFG-Schwerpunktprogramms Raumkognition*, Hamburg, 2001.
14. M. Wooldridge, N. R. Jennings, and D. Kinny. The Gaia methodology for agent-oriented analysis and design. *Autonomous Agents and Multi-Agent Systems*, 3(3):285–312, 2000.

The SWAP Data and Metadata Model for Semantics-Based Peer-to-Peer Systems

Marc Ehrig[2], Peter Haase[2], Ronny Siebes[1], Steffen Staab[2],
Heiner Stuckenschmidt[1], Rudi Studer[2], and Christoph Tempich[2]

[1] Vrije Universiteit Amsterdam
{ronny, heiner}@cs.vu.nl
[2] Institute AIFB, University of Karlsruhe, D-76128 Karlsruhe
{ehrig,haase,staab,studer,tempich}@aifb.uni-karlsruhe.de

Abstract. Peer-to-Peer systems are a new paradigm for information sharing and some systems have successfully been deployed. It has been argued that current Peer-to-Peer systems suffer from the lack of semantics. The SWAP project (Semantic Web and Peer-to-Peer)[1] aims at overcoming this problem by combining the Peer-to-Peer paradigm with Semantic Web technologies. In this paper, we propose a data model for encoding semantic information that combines features of ontologies (concept hierarchies, relational structures) with a flexible description and rating model that allows us to handle heterogeneous and even contradictory views on the domain of interest. We discuss the role of this model in the SWAP environment and describe the model as well as its application.

1 Motivation

The essence of Peer-to-Peer (P2P) is that nodes in the network directly exploit resources present at other nodes of the network without intervention of any central server. The tremendous success of networks like Napster and Gnutella [1], and of highly visible industry initiatives such as Sun's JXTA [2] , as well as the Peer-to-Peer Working Group including HP, IBM and Intel, have shown that the P2P paradigm is a particularly powerful one when it comes to sharing files over the Internet without any central repository, without centralized administration, and with file delivery dedicated solely to user needs in a robust, scalable manner. At the same time, today's P2P solutions support only limited update, search and retrieval functionality, e.g. search in Napster is restricted to string matches involving just two fields: "artist" and "track". These flaws however make current P2P systems unsuitable for knowledge sharing purposes.

Metadata plays a central role in the effort of providing search techniques that go beyond string matching. Ontology-based metadata facilitates the access to domain knowledge. Furthermore, it enables the construction of semantic queries. Existing approaches of ontology-based information access almost always assume a setting where information providers share an ontology that is used to access the

---

[1] http://swap.semanticweb.org/

M. Schillo et al. (Eds.): MATES 2003, LNAI 2831, pp. 144–155, 2003.

information[3]. In a Peer-to-Peer setting, this assumption does not longer hold. We rather face the situation, where individual peers maintain their own view of the domain in terms of the organization of the local file system and other information sources. Enforcing the use of a global ontology in such a setting would mean to give up the benefits of the Peer-to-Peer approach mentioned above. Therefore, one has to find a way to deal with the existence of multiple, distributed and frequently changing views on the domain.

In this paper, we propose an RDF(S) [4] based metadata model that combines ontological structures with information needed to align, evolve and use these structures for query processing. In section 2, we explain the requirements for the metadata model that guided its development in more detail. Section 3 focuses on the SWAP environment in which the metadata model is used. The model itself is introduced in section 4. In section 5 we describe the methods for applying the metadata model. We conclude with a discussion of open problems.

2   Requirements

We will illustrate the requirements for the proposed system with a short scenario: Virtual organizations or large companies impose a complex situation, with respect to the number of domains, conceptualizations and documents in a peer-system for knowledge sharing. Typically their organizational units are distributed according to expertise or organizational tasks. Subsequently, a case study of a virtual organization in the tourism domain is used as real world example. The virtual organization comprises public authorities, hotels and event organizers. The public authorities require the number of guests visiting the country to plan for example public transport and waste management. Event organizers can customize their offerings according to the number of visitors and their age. Hotels can publish this information to attract more tourists. Today the exchange of this kind of information is time consuming, unpunctual and error prone, although it is often available in electronic form at every level. However, different organizations have diverse objectives and therefore use different conceptualizations of their domains. From a technical point of view, the different organizations can be seen as one or many independently operating nodes within a "knowledge" network. Nodes can join or disconnect from the network at any moment and can live or act independently of the behavior of other nodes in the system. A node may perform several tasks. Most important is that it acts as a peer in the network, so it can communicate with other nodes to achieve its goals. But apart from that it may act as an interface to interact with the human user of the network, or it may access knowledge sources to accomplish its tasks. One node may have one or more knowledge sources associated with it. These sources contain the information that a peer can make available to other peers. Examples are a user's filesystem and mail folders or a locally installed database.

A node must be designed to meet the following requirements that arise from the task of sharing information from the external sources with other peers:

- Multiple sources of information
- Mostly uniform treatment of internal and external sources
- Multiple views on available information
- Support for query answering and routing
- Distribution of information within the network

The metadata model we will introduce needs to reflect these requirements. We derive objectives for the metadata model with emphasis on information mediation:

Integration: Each piece of knowledge requires metadata about its origin. To retrieve external information, the metadata needs to capture information about where the piece of information was obtained from. This information will allow to identify a peer and locate resources in its repositories.

Information heterogeneity: As each peer uses its own local ontology, the distributed information is inherently heterogeneous. Mappings may be required, e.g. to overcome the heterogenous labelling of the same objects.

Information inconsistency: As information is added from a variety of peers, inconsistencies may occur in a local repository. Information needs to be assigned a confidence rating, such that the system will be able to handle heterogeneity and provide useful information. Similarly, a level of trust can be assigned to peers to model their reliability.

Security: Some information may be of private nature and should not be visible to other peers. Other information may be restricted to a specific set of peers. The metadata model needs to provide means to express these security policies.

Caching: Within Peer-to-Peer systems the availability of other peers is not always guaranteed. Moreover, some peers may have better connectivity, in terms of bandwidth, to the rest of the network than other peers. To improve network efficiency, caching of information can be useful. The caching mechanisms needs to be transparent to the user, but must be captured by the metadata model.

3   The SWAP Environment

The SWAP environment is a generic infrastructure which was designed to meet the requirements on a knowledge node. The proposed architecture is shown in figure 1. We will now briefly present the individual components.

Knowledge Sources: Peers may have local sources of information such as the local file system, e-mail directories or bookmark lists. These local information sources represent the peer's body of knowledge as well as its basic vocabulary. These sources of information are the place where a peer can physically store information (documents, web pages) to be shared on the network.

Knowledge Source Integrator: The Knowledge Source Integrator is responsible for the extraction and integration of internal and external knowledge sources into the Local Node Repository. This task comprises (1) means to access local knowledge sources and extract an RDF(S) representation of the stored knowledge, (2) the selection of the RDF statements to be integrated into the Local

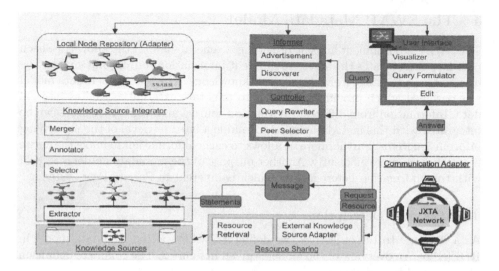

Fig. 1. Abstract Architecture of a SWAP Node

Node Repository, (3) the annotation of the statements with metadata, and (4) merging the statements into the ontology of the user. These processes, as described in 5.1, utilize the metadata model presented in section 4.1.

Local Node Repository: The Local Node Repository manages an integrated model of the knowledge that is available to the peer locally and remotely. The individual elements of the model are annotated according to the metadata model with their source and a ranking representing the peer's belief in their plausibility.

User Interface: The User Interface of the peer provides individual views on the information available in local sources as well as on information on the network. The views can be implemented using different visualization techniques (topic hierarchies, thematic maps, etc).

Informer: One of the main challenges in a Peer-to-Peer network is that peers initially don't know of each other. The informer provides mechanisms to discover or advertise knowledge pro-actively.

Controller: The Controller is the coordinating component which controls the process of distributing queries. It receives queries from the user interface and distributes them according to the content of the query. When the peer receives a query from another peer, it is tries to answer or forward it. The decision to which peers a query should be sent is made by the Peer Selector based on the knowledge about other peers. Answers received are finally passed back to the graphical interface and to the KnowledgeSource Integrator, which integrates selected content into the Local Node Repository.

Communication Adapter: This component is responsible for the network communication between peers. It serves as a transport layer for other parts of the system, for sending and forwarding queries. It hides and encapsulates all low-level communication details from the rest of the system.

4   The SWAP Metadata Model

The SWAP environment aims at providing a general view on the knowledge each
peer has. It facilitates the access to different information sources and enables the
user to take advantage from other peers' knowledge. Therefore a metadata model
was designed which provides semantics to annotate external as well as internal
data. Information from different information sources and from other peers can be
integrated with this metadata model to enable a later retrieval of the underlying
information items. Furthermore, it allows to cache information to make the entire
network work more efficiently. Another purpose of the metadata model is to deal
with the information heterogeneity which is inherent in Peer-to-Peer systems.

4.1   Detailed Description

As a response to the objectives, we define a SWAP specific metadata model in
RDF(S)[5]. An overview of the model is given in figure 2. The complete definition
of the model is available at:

`http://swap.semanticweb.org/2003/01/swap-peer#`

The model consists of two RDFS classes, namely the "Swabbi"-class and the
"Peer"-class. For these classes, several properties are defined to meet the objectives described above.

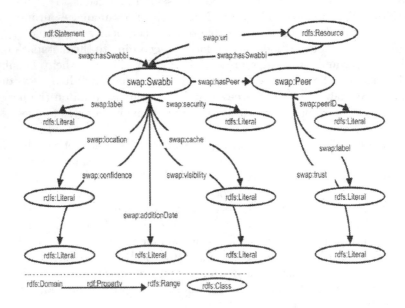

Fig. 2. The SWAP metadata model

Swabbi: Every piece of knowledge can be annoted with a "Swabbi"-object which contains meta-information. It has the following properties:

- *hasPeer:* This property is used to track which peer this "Swabbi"-object is associated with.
- *uri:* Each piece of information was originally created on one peer. To keep track of the origin of the information and to able to unambiguously address an object across the network, the primary URI is explicitly stored with the metadata.
- *location:* Whereas the URI identifies metadata resources within the ontology of the Local Node Repository, the location-attribute is an identifier to access the physical resource, e.g. a document e.g. file://c:/Projects/myfile.txt.
- *label:* The label stores how the specific information is called on the peer it originates from. The label-attribute is expressed in natural language. As one resource can have different names on different peers, this property is added to each "Swabbi"-object and not only to the original object.
- *confidence:* The confidence value indicates - on a scale from 0 to 1 - how reliable a specific statement is. A high confidence in a statement is expressed with high value, 1 meaning the peer is sure the statement is true, 0 meaning the statement is definitely false.
- *security:* Security issues and access rights are important in enterprizes. In the wide open Peer-to-Peer environment some access control is required to ensure proper usage of the information.
- *visibility:* Instead of completely removing objects, they can also be hidden, which can be achieved with this attribute.
- *additionDate:* This attribute keeps track of the date the related resource was added/updated to the Local Node Repository. This could be used to determine confidence; old information might become less reliable.
- *cache:* To increase the network efficiency caching of information will be necessary. The cached information is annotated with this property and set to the date of inclusion.

Peer: For every piece of knowledge we have to remember which peer it originated from. Therefore the Local Node Repository stores different information about each known peer. The information is grouped in the Peer object. The "Swabbi"-object links to the corresponding peer object.

- *peerID:* Each peer has a unique ID to be identified. For our purposes this will be the *JXTA UID*, as we use JXTA as our underlying communication infrastructure,
- *peerLabel:* This peer attribute stores the peer label, which is a human readable and understandable description of the peer in natural language.
- *peerTrust:* Some peers might be more reliable than others. This peer attribute is used to measure trust on a scale from 0 to 1, with 0 meaning having no trust at all and 1 the peer being very trust-worthy.

5   Applying the Metadata Model

In order to use the model described above for semantics-based information exchange, we have to provide a set of methods for constructing the repository according to the metadata model and to assess the knowledge that is stored therein. In the following, we describe methods that have been developed to (1) create and integrate repository content mostly automatically from local and remote information sources, and to (2) rate information in a repository based on the confidence we have in its reliability.

5.1   Knowledge Source Integration

The process of knowledge source integration comprises four subprocesses: This task comprises (1) extraction of an RDF(S) representation from the knowledge sources, (2) the selection of the statements to be included into the Local Node Repository, (3) the annotation of the statements with metadata, and (4) merging the statements into the user's knowledge model.

Extraction: As mentioned above, the SWAP-system provides an integrated model of different structures that exists locally on the peer itself and remotely on other peers in the network. These structures are file systems, emails, databases, ontologies and others. In order to include the different information sources, which have been selected by the user for sharing, into our model, we extract an RDF(S) representation from them. The following example shows a fragment of an extracted folder structure – a resource of type Folder with the label "Project" and the original location in the folder structure:

```
<rdf:RDF xmlns:rdf='http://www.w3.org/1999/02/22-rdf-syntax-ns#'
    xmlns:rdfs='http://www.w3.org/2000/01/rdf-schema#'
    xmlns:swapcommon="http://swap.semanticweb.org/2003/01/swap-common#"
    xmlns:swap="http://swap.semanticweb.org/2003/01/swap-peer#">
<swapcommon:Folder
        rdf:about="swap://1234567890.jxta#project">
    <rdfs:label xml:lang="en">Project</rdfs:label>
    <swapcommon:location>
        filefolder://windows/c:/Project
    </swapcommon:location>
</swapcommon:Folder>
</rdf:RDF>
```

In a second step, this extracted information can be semantically enriched. This means adding formerly implicit semantics explicitly to the structures as theoretically described by [6] as emergent semantics. We assume for the moment that we can determine the meaning, as intended by the user, and type of a certain information item in an ontological sense and can describe it as either concept, instance or property.

If we extract a "Project"-folder from our file-system and this folder has a subfolder "SWAP" we assume that the user placed these items this way, because SWAP is an instance of project. This aspect is modelled as follows:

```
<rdf:Description rdf:about="swap://1234567890.jxta#SWAP">
    <rdf:type rdf:resource="swap://1234567890.jxta#project"/>
</rdf:Description>
```

Selection: The selection process can be described as a filter on incoming statements. It has to decide which information is useful and therefore should be included into the Local Node Repository. Metadata, e.g. previously collected metadata about the trust in other peers, might prove useful in defining the selection process. The information selected to be included in the Local Node Repository will be annotated with metadata, as described in the next paragraph.

Annotation: Having built an RDF(S) representation of the information sources, in this processing step the "Swabbi"-objects are added. We have to distinguish between information that originated from the extraction process on the local peer and information received from other peers. For extracted structures, a new "Swabbi"-object is created for each resource or statement. To link a "Swabbi"-object to a statement we use the RDF construct of reification. The properties (as presented in 4.1) are filled accordingly and a reference between the resource and the "Swabbi"-object is established with a "hasSwabbi" relation.

The other major source of information are other peers. The selection process has already selected the information to keep. This information is added to the Local Node Repository in the same way as any other information from the peer itself. Additionally, information about the originating peer is included using the 'hasPeer" property of the "Swabbi"-object. The example shows a reified statement with its "Swabbi" information – the first element describes the statement itself, the second one describes the associated "Swabbi"-object, and the last one describes the corresponding peer.

```
<rdf:Statement rdf:about="swap://1234567890.jxta#statement01">
    <rdf:subject rdf:resource="swap://1234567890.jxta#project"/>
    <rdf:predicate rdf:resource="rdfs:subclassOf"/>
    <rdf:object rdf:resource="swap://1234567890.jxta#thing"/>
    <swap:hasSwabbi rdf:resource="swap://1234567890.jxta#swabbiObjectNo01"/>
</rdf:Statement>
<swap:Swabbi rdf:about="swap://1234567890.jxta#swabbiObjectNo01">
    <swap:hasPeer  rdf:resource="swap://1234567890.jxta#knownPeers0001" />
    <swap:label>Project</swap:label>
    <swap:uri rdf:resource="swap://1234567890.jxta#project" />
    <swap:location>filefolder://windows/c:/Project</swap:location>
</swap:Swabbi>
<swap:Peer rdf:about="swap://1234567890.jxta#knownPeers0001">
    <swap:peerId>1234567890</swap:peerId>
    <swap:peerLabel>Christoph</swap:peerLabel>
</swap:Peer>
```

Merging: One goal of the SWAP system is to have a *single* model. Through addition of resources and statements from other peers the same object might be present in the local repository, but under different names.

The system has to identify these two objects through similarity measures. In the approach of [7] three methods are presented, which we extend with a fourth one:

- Word Matching: By checking the labels one can determine if the objects are similar (e.g. by calculating the edit distance [8]). Alternatively WordNet can be used to find synonyms.
- Feature Matching: If an entity has the same predicates and objects as another one this is a strong indication that the object is the same in both cases.
- Semantic-Neighborhood Matching: This method checks the (contextual) neighborhood of two entities ([9]).
- Instance Matching: We also look for instances and where they are classified in the structure. This indicates similarity of the respective classes.

The first prototype of the SWAP system uses word matching comparisons based on the labels of entities. Instance matching is realized by comparing unique identifiers, e.g. a hash code in the case of files and email addresses in the case of persons. Ongoing efforts are being made to also include the other methods, keeping in mind that some have to be adapted to keep the computational complexity manageable.

The last step is to actually do the merging in the Local Node Repository. Whereas in RDF(S) no explicit relation as "equals" is defined, we derived a relation from the equality relation defined in OWL [10].

5.2   Content Rating Model

Statements made by peers can be incomplete, vague or even false. For this reason, statements are not accepted by a peer as an absolute truth, but are judged based on the previous experience with the sender [11]. For example, if the sender tells the receiver something about youth hostels and the receiver knows that the sender is an expert on hotels, then it can derive from the fact that both concepts (hotel and youth hostel) have a small semantic distance that the sender probably also knows more than an average user about youth hostels. To formalize the expertise we introduce confidence ratings that are meta-statements placed in the 'Swabbi'-object that indicate the confidence in a certain statement. We will now describe the different aspects of the rating methods:

Assigning confidence ratings to statements from a peer. Here we have to distinguish between derived statements from the extraction algorithm described in the previous paragraph and statements received from external peers. In the first case we assume that the user is confident in the statements that are derived and therefore assigned a high confidence rating. In the second case the confidence ratings are calculated from the previous statements from the sender. When a peer a receives information from peer b and b is unknown to a, then the statement from b gets a (low) initial confidence rating. If, however b already provided statements before to a then the new confidence is calculated out of these statements. The value is a weighted average where the weighting factor is determined by semantic distance between an old statement and the new one. The similarity measure we use is adapted from [12].

Updating confidence ratings. If other peers that are different from the original sender confirm the statement by repeating it, the statement gains higher confidence. The amount of gain depends of the confidence in the confirming source. This recursive definition of rating is also used in PageRank in Google [13] where the rank of a source depends on the ranks of the sources voting for that source.

Determining the experts to be queried. When a query is received, the receiver first tries to answer the query itself. If it doesn't have a satisfying answer, it tries to find experts on the topic of the query based on the information that has been received from other peers. The system tries to find experts on topics that have a close semantic distance to the topic of the query. Again, we use the similarity measure described above for this aspect.

Aging mechanism to devaluate confidence ratings in time. A SWAP peer can retrieve large set of statements from other peers and from the generated statements by the ontology extractor. To keep the local repository scalable, we use an aging mechanism that removes statements that are too old in combination with a low rating.

6   Related Work

Knowledge management in Peer-to-Peer systems is the topic of various active research projects. Edutella [14], [15] provides an RDF-based infrastructure for exchanging metadata in P2P applications. The Edutella Query Service is intended to be a standardized query exchange mechanism for RDF metadata stored in distributed RDF repositories. The Edutella project focuses on the education community. The Edamok project [16] also deals with distributed knowledge management in Peer-to-Peer systems. It does not use an ontology premise though. Emergent Semantics [17] builds on lightweight (e.g. a file structure with files as instances) and/or heavyweight ontologies that different participants have created. [18] describes an approach for obtaining semantic interoperability among data sources without relying on pre-existing, global semantic models. It enables the participating data sources to incrementally develop global agreement in a completely decentralized process that relies on pair-wise, local interactions, such as in P2P-systems.

7   Conclusion

The completely distributed nature and the high degree of autonomy of individual peers in a P2P system comes with new challenges for the use of semantic descriptions. If we want to benefit from the advantages that normally accompany the use of ontologies as specifications of a shared vocabulary we have to find ways to dynamically align the semantic models of different peers. In this paper, we described a model that combines features of ontologies with rich metadata about the origin of information and the reliability of sources. Furthermore, we introduced methods for creating, integrating and assessing metadata. Our model has several advantages over traditional ontologies in the context of Peer-to-Peer information exchange. The most important feature is the fact that statements in the semantic models are not seen as being the truth as in most traditional models. We rather see the semantic model as a collection of opinions supported by different sources of information. Opinions that many sources agree on are more likely to be true than opinions that are not shared across the system or that even contradict with other opinions. This makes it possible to directly extract semantic models from information sources even if these are not completely compliant with the existing model. Furthermore, we can use heuristic methods to align and update semantic models. If the result of such an update is shared by many peers it will persist.

A key issue for the acceptance of such heuristic methods of course is a careful evaluation of their performance in general and in concrete applications. In order to evaluate the model and the methods on a general level, test procedures are developed in the SWAP project that use simulation techniques to experiment with large scale Peer-to-Peer systems [19]. Furthermore, case studies for the SWAP system in the tourism and finance domains are planned. These case studies will show how much benefit the developed methods provide in real world applications.

One of the most fundamental questions that has to be answered by the case studies is whether it is sufficient to rely on structures that have been extracted from information sources instead of hand-crafted knowledge structures and metadata. It may turn out that in addition to the extraction approach, we also need to annotate information by hand. In this case we have to investigate how methods for supporting semantic annotation can be integrated in the system in order to build up the knowledge structures described in this paper.

Acknowledgements. SWAP is a project funded by the EU under contract no. EU IST-2001-34103.

References

1. Kan, G.: Gnutella. In: Peer-to-Peer: Harnessing the Power of Disruptive Technologies. O'Reilly (1999) 94–122
2. Traversat, B., Abdelaziz, M., Duigou, M., Hugly, J.C., Poulouy, E., Yeager, B.: Project JXTA Virtual Network. Technical report, Sun Microsystems Inc. (2002)
3. Gruber, T.R.: Towards Principles for the Design of Ontologies Used for Knowledge Sharing. In Guarino, N., Poli, R., eds.: Formal Ontology in Conceptual Analysis and Knowledge Representation, Deventer, The Netherlands, Kluwer Academic Publishers (1993)
4. Brickley, D., Guha, R.: RDF Vocabulary Description Language 1.0: RDF Schema (1999), http://www.w3.org/TR/rdf-schema/.

5. Broekstra, J., Klein, M., Decker, S., Fensel, D., van Harmelen, F., Horrocks, I.: Enabling knowledge representation on the web by extending rdf schema. In: Proceedings of the tenth World Wide Web conference WWW'10, Hong Kong (2001)
6. Maedche, A., Staab, S.: Ontology learning for the semantic web. IEEE Intelligent Systems **16** (2001) 72–79
7. Rodríguez, M.A., Egenhofer, M.J.: Determining semantic similarity among entity classes from different ontologies. IEEE Transactions on Knowledge and Data Engineering **15** (2003) 442–465
8. Levenshtein, I.V.: Binary codes capable of correcting deletions, insertions, and reversals. Cybernetics and Control Theory (1966)
9. Maedche, A., Motik, B., Silva, N., Volz, R.: Mafra - a mapping framework for distributed ontologies. In: Proceedings of the EKAW (Knowledge Engineering and Knowledge Management) 2002. Volume 2473 of Lecture Notes in Computer Science, Springer (2002)
10. Dean, M., Connolly, D., van Harmelen, F., Hendler, J., Horrocks, I., McGuinness, D.L., Patel-Schneider, P.F., Stein, L.A.: Owl web ontology language 1.0 reference, Internet:http://www.w3.org/TR/owl-ref/. (2002)
11. Siebes, R., van Harmelen, F.: Ranking agent statements for building evolving ontologies. Proceedings of the AAAI-02 workshop on meaning negotiation, Alberta, Canada (2002)
12. Resnik, P.: Semantic similarity in a taxonomy: An information-based measure and its application to problems of ambiguity in natural language. Journal of Artificial Intelligence Research **11** (1999) 95–130
13. Page, L., Brin, S., Motwani, R., Winograd, T.: The pagerank citation ranking: Bringing order to the web. Technical report, Stanford Digital Library Technologies Project (1998)
14. Nejdl, W., Wolf, B., Qu, C., Decker, S., Sintek, M., Naeve, A., Nilsson, M., Palmér, M., Risch, T.: Edutella: A P2P networking infrastructure based on rdf. In: Proceedings to the Eleventh International World Wide Web Conference, Honolulu, Hawaii, USA (2002)
15. Nejdl, W., Wolpers, M., Siberski, W., Schmitz, C., Schlosser, M., Brunkhorst, I., Lser, A.: Super-peer-based routing and clustering strategies for rdf-based peer-to-peer networks. In: Proceedings of the 12th International World Wide Web Conference, Budapest, Hungary. (2003)
16. Bonifacio, M., Cuel, R., Mameli, G., Nori, M.: A peer-to-peer architecture for distributed knowledge management. In: Proceedings of the 3rd International Symposium on Multi-Agent Systems, Large Complex Systems, and E-Businesses MAL-CEB'2002, Erfurt, Germany. (2002)
17. Maedche, A.: Emergent semantics for ontologies – support by an explicit lexical layer and ontology learning. IEEE Intelligent Systems – Trends and Controversies **17** (2002) 78–86
18. Aberer, K., Cudré-Mauroux, P., Hauswirth, M.: The Chatty Web: Emergent Semantics Through Gossiping. In: Proceedings of the 12th International World Wide Web Conference, Budapest, Hungary. (2003)
19. Ehrig, M., Schmitz, C., Staab, S., Tane, J., Tempich, C.: Towards evaluation of peer-to-peer-based distributed knowledge management systems. In: Proceedings of the AAAI Spring Symposium "Agent-Mediated Knowledge Management (AMKM-2003)". (2003)

An Ontology for Production Control of Semiconductor Manufacturing Processes

Lars Mönch and Marcel Stehli

Technical University of Ilmenau,
Institute of Information Systems,
Helmholtzplatz 3, 98684 Ilmenau, Germany
{Lars.Moench,Marcel.Stehli}@tu-ilmenau.de

Abstract. In this paper, we describe an ontology for a hierarchically organized production control system in semiconductor manufacturing. The semiconductor manufacturing domain is characterized by reentrant product flows, sequence dependent setup-times, prescribed due-dates, a diverse product mix, a mix of different process types including batch processes and preventive maintenance issues because of complex technological processes. Starting from a hierarchical decomposition of the manufacturing system, we use an agent-based architecture for implementing the resulting production control system. In order to coordinate the autonomous entities of the hierarchy, we suggest an ontology that is appropriate to the hierarchical control approach. We illustrate the use of the suggested ontology.

1 Introduction

A complex system is defined as a system whose components are systems in their own right, i.e., a complex system is a relation of interconnected sub-systems (cf. [7] for a formal description of this concept). In this paper, we use the term complex manufacturing system for systems that can be decomposed into a set of manufacturing sub-systems that have their own goals and rights for decision-making.

We consider complex manufacturing systems that are also characterized by

- a diverse product mix,
- reentrant process flows,
- parallel machines with complicated dedication practices,
- sequence-dependent setup-times,
- a mix of different process types, including batch processes,
- inclusion of preventive maintenance issues into production control,
- prescribed due-dates for the lots,
- concurrence of production and engineering lots for scarce machine capacities.

Examples of this type of complex manufacturing systems are semiconductor wafer fabrication facilities (wafer fabs). The development of efficient planning and control strategies is highly desirable in the semiconductor manufacturing domain, because the improvement of operational processes creates the best opportunity to realize the nec-

M. Schillo et al. (Eds.): MATES 2003, LNAI 2831, pp. 156–167, 2003.

essary cost reductions. For a more detailed description of the semiconductor manufacturing domain and related production control issues we refer to [8].

We describe an ontology that takes the hierarchical structure of the control system (and, of course, the resulting multi-agent-system) into account. The ontology is designated for the implementation of a content language in the multi-agent-system FAB-MAS (cf. [2], [10] for the architecture of the FABMAS system). Ontologies for the manufacturing domain have been revisited by many authors (cf. [13], [16], [11]). However, so far an ontology for a hierarchically organized production control system in the semiconductor manufacturing domain has not developed yet.

This paper is organized as follows. In Section 2, we describe the manufacturing domain that is relevant for our research. We also give an outline of the hierarchical production control approach including an agentification. In Section 3, we develop an ontology for hierarchically organized production control systems. We finish the paper by describing the use of the ontology by means of an example.

2 Hierarchical Production Control Approach

We consider a manufacturing system that consists of different work areas. Each of the work areas includes several groups of parallel machines (called work center). The work areas can organize their work in an autonomous way, i.e., there is only a very weak form of central control. Based on the described physical decomposition of the manufacturing system, we suggest a hierarchical multi-layer approach (cf. [7], [12] for the general theory behind this type of approach).

We consider the full wafer fabrication facility as an upper level of the hierarchy. We use a beam-search-type algorithm (cf. [5]) for minimizing the deviation of the completion time of the lots from their planned due date. As a result of the algorithm, we obtain start and end dates for the lots for each single work area.

The middle layer is formed by the different work areas. We use an area-based shifting bottleneck type algorithm (ABSBH) in order to minimize the total weighted tardiness for each single work area. We measure the tardiness with respect to the work area-related start and end dates that are given by the upper level. This layer results in schedules for each single work area. Note that we can treat each single work area separately because of the decoupling effect of the beam-search algorithm.

The lower level is basically formed by work centers. The work centers should implement the schedules obtained from the mid level. In the case of invalid schedules we suggest the use of a modified contract net with properly chosen costs (cf. [9] for the implementation of a machine hour-rate (MHR)-based resource allocation algorithm).

The solution of the decision-making problems on the three levels requires communication and intra- and inter-layer coordination across the decision-making units. For example, it is required to send information on machine break-downs from the manufacturing process up to the upper level in order to update the used models for decision-making. Agents are an appropriate way of implementing the described production control approach because, by definition, agents are decision-making entities. The agents need to communicate. The key elements of an agent communication language are suggested by FIPA. However, it is not possible to specify the content of such a language in a generic way, because it is highly domain- and task-dependent. An appropriate ontology is a prerequisite for the development of a content language for hierarchically organized complex manufacturing systems.

Starting with the PROSA architecture [17], we distinguish between decision-making agents and staff agents. Decision-making agents solve decision problems, while the staff agents support them in the course of the decision-making process. We identify seven decision-making agent types in our application scenario. It is summarized in Table 1.

Table 1. Agentification Due to PROSA Reference Architecture

Agent Type	Description
Lot agent	- represents a single lot
PM agent	- represents a preventive maintenance order
Tool agent	- represents a certain auxiliary resource
Work center agent	- represents a single group of parallel machines on the shop floor
Work area agent	- represents a set of work centers
Fab agent	- represents all work areas
Technology agent	- represents the product knowledge

We also define different staff agents that encapsulate scheduling and monitoring functionality. In Table 2, we summarize the basic functionality of the members of the agency that corresponds to the different hierarchy levels. For a more detailed description we refer to [8].

3   Ontology for Production Control of Wafer Fabs

We define an ontology as a model of a particular field of knowledge, the concepts and their attributes, as well as the relationships between the concepts [4]. An ontology always includes always

1.   a conceptualization of a domain, i.e. how to view and model a domain,
2.   a specification of this conceptualization, i.e. basically a formal description.

Both conceptualization of the domain and specification of the conceptualization are influenced by the used modeling technique, i.e. slots or frames [11]. In this paper, we describe an ontology for a hierarchically organized multi-agent-system. As pointed out in [1], we have to describe the underlying predicates, i.e. expressions that can be true or false, and also the agent actions beside the domain concepts. Following this point of view, we have to develop an application ontology that contains both domain- and task-related parts (cf. [3] for a classification of ontologies).

Table 2. Functionality of the Members of the Agency (Fab, Work Area, Work Center Level)

Layer of the Hierarchy	Corresponding Member of the Agency	Task Description
Entire Fab	Fab Agent	- coordination of the work of the fab scheduling agent, the monitoring agent and the work area agents - decision-making through sequencing the lots for the application of the beam-search algorithm
	Fab Scheduling Agent	- preparation of beam-search algorithm run - running the algorithm - providing scheduling information
Work Area	Work Area Agent	- coordination of the work of the corresponding work area scheduling and monitoring agent - decision-making through choosing the proper machine criticality measure for ABSBH - information providing services
	Work Area Scheduling Agent	- preparation of ABSBH algorithm run - running the heuristic - providing scheduling information
Work Center	Work Center Agent	- implementing the work area schedules in a dispatching manner - works as mediator in case of the contract-net-type allocation algorithm

The ontology to be developed should support scheduling, rescheduling and control activities in a hierarchically organized multi-agent-system. In particular, it should allow for interactions between the agents that represent the units of the manufacturing system in the following situations:
1.   Treatment of exceptions,
2.   Start of scheduling activities,
3.   Exchange of information that is required for scheduling,
4.   Transfer of scheduling results back to the decision-making agents,
5.   Start of monitoring activities,
6.   Transfer of monitoring results back to the decision-making agents,
7.   Negotiations between lot agents and machine agents via mediator,
8.   Exchange of data and information that is required for distributed scheduling according to the ABSBH algorithm.

To develop an appropriate ontology, we start from a data model suitable for the treatment of this type of manufacturing processes. We have to distinguish between static data, describing the shop-floor and products, dynamic data, i.e. the state of lots and single machines, and various kinds of control data, i.e. schedules and information on certain events on the shop-floor. A data model must therefore contain the data given in Table 3.

The basic data model (without control data) is shown in UML (Unified Modeling Language) notation in Figure 1. Here, we describe the association of the data by using

Table 3. Data Required in the Semiconductor Manufacturing Domain

Type of Data	Examples
Static Data	- Structure of the manufacturing system (i.e. machines, segmentation into machine groups, work areas) - Product information - Setup information - Route information (i.e. information on the process flow)
Dynamic Data	- Lot release information - Lot states - Machine states - Setup states of the machines
Control Data	- Lot Plans - Schedules of different degrees of detail

the aggregation and composition techniques for class diagrams. We use the data model as a starting point to derive important concepts for the domain under discourse. Most of these concepts are covered by the Enterprise Ontology [16] and by the OZONE ontology [13]. However, we can only use the abstract concepts (such as activity, resource, order, product, plan), and we have to add several refinements (sub-concepts) necessary to apply the concepts from [13] and [16] to our domain and the hierarchical production control approach. Most of the necessary extensions are caused by the hierarchical decomposition of the shop-floor and the process flows (called routes).

Based on the data model, we derive the following important basic concepts of the domain.

1. **Activity:** An activity represents a process that can be executed over a time interval. We have to distinguish between controllable activities that can be arranged by a decision-maker, uncontrollable and predictable activities and uncontrollable and unpredictable activities. Important controllable activities are production steps and production operations that are formed by a set of consecutive production steps for one work area. The concept activity and related concepts are shown in UML notation in Figure 2. We include domain-specific concepts like rework activities (cf. [14] for a classification of activities in semiconductor manufacturing).

2. **Resource:** A resource is an entity that enables the execution of activities. According to the OZONE ontology [13] we have to distinguish between single machines and aggregated resources. We consider the special aggregated resources Fab machinery, work area machinery and machine group due to the hierarchical decomposition of the production control problem as described in Section 2. Furthermore, we consider batch and non-batching machines.

3. **Tool:** A tool (also called auxiliary resource) is an entity that supports the execution of activities by resources. Photolithography masks (patterns that contain

the information of an integrated circuit) are important examples of auxiliary resources in semiconductor manufacturing.

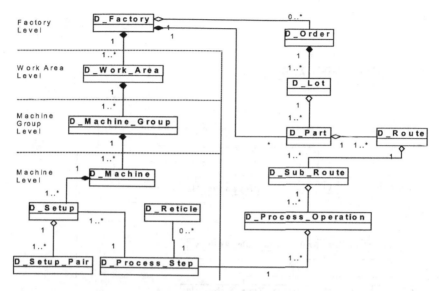

Fig. 1. Data Model for Hierarchically Organized Manufacturing Systems

4. **Order:** An order is a request for a certain number of integrated circuits. An order is characterized by a delivery date, a weight (priority), an order state and the quantity of integrated circuits associated with the order. Each order consists of a certain number of lots. A batch is a temporary collection of lots with the aim to process them at the same time on the same machine.

5. **Product:** A product (also called part) is a piece of goods that meets a set of prescribed requirements. A product is associated with a certain technology. A technology is defined by a sequence of processing steps called route. Usually a product is also associated with a set of auxiliary resources. The route consists of several sub routes that corresponds to the process steps of a certain work area and mask level in the case of the occurrence of reentrant flows.

6. **Event:** An event is a process that starts instantaneously and has no duration. We consider, for example, machine failure events, machine repair events and rework events.

7. **Plan:** A plan is an activity specification with an intended purpose. A plan may include entities that are not released into the manufacturing system yet. A lot plan is a special plan that determines the start and end dates for each production operation of a single lot (released or not).

8. **Schedule:** A schedule is an activity specification with an intended purpose. A schedule only includes entities that are already released into the manufacturing system. In correspondence with the hierarchical production control approach, we consider work area schedules, machine group (work center) schedules and single machine schedules.

Note, that the concepts activity, resource, product, plan, and schedule are highly influenced by the used hierarchical production control approach.

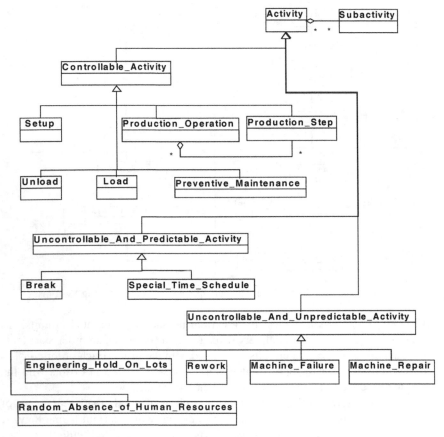

Fig. 2. Concept Activity and Related Sub Concepts of the FABMAS Ontology

In the course of developing the FABMAS ontology we combine techniques described in [15] in order to derive sub-ontologies from a broader ontology (i.e. using the OZONE and Enterprise ontology) with necessary extensions due to the specific semiconductor manufacturing domain.

After deriving important concepts we have to identify predicates. We can distinguish between domain- and task-related predicates. Domain related predicates are facts about a concrete manufacturing system (called basic system), whereas task predicates are closely related to the fulfillment of the goals of the production control system (called control system). In Table 4 we present examples for both domain and task predicates.

Agent activities are important in order to ensure the design goals of the FABMAS multi-agent-system. In most cases we use the agent activities in order to submit instructions from a decision-making agent to its corresponding staff agent. We show examples of agent activities in Table 5. We use the tool Protégé in order to develop and maintain the proposed ontology.

Table 4. Predicates in the FABMAS Ontology

Predicate	Description
Domain-related	
- CONTAINED_IN_WORKAREA	Determines whether a given machine is contained in a given work area or not.
- PROCESS_STEP_ALLOWED_ON_ MACHINE	Determines whether a given process step can be performed on a given machine or not.
Task-related	
- SCHEDULE_VALID	Determines whether a given schedule is valid or not.
- LOT_COMPLETED	Determines whether a given lot is completed or not.
- LOT_LATE	Determines whether a given lot is late with respect to a given segment of the manufacturing system or not.

4   Interactions between the Agents Using the Ontology

We identify certain scenarios for agent interaction. Interaction diagrams are part of efforts to design a coordination language. Here, an appropriate coordination language consists of a set of speech acts, a set of interaction protocols and a suitable ontology.

We consider the request of a work area schedule as an example of using the FABMAS ontology. In this particular case interactions between a lot agent, the work area agent and the work area scheduling agent are required. The lot agent asks the corresponding work area agent for a schedule for its work area. Consequently, the lot agents specify a certain maximum amount of time for determining the schedule (schedules are determined usually in a time-driven manner). The work area agent makes decisions on the scheduling horizon, an appropriate performance measure and a strategy for considering sub problems of the scheduling on a work center level. After this decision-making process the work area agent requests a schedule from the work area scheduling agent. We present the overall scenario in form of an UML sequence diagram in Figure 3.

In Figure 4 we present a more detailed model of the interaction between work area agent and work area scheduling agent. We use SDL (Specification and Description Language) diagrams in order to describe the interactions.

We use agent activities, predicates and concepts of the FABMAS ontology for the above scenario. We start with describing the interaction between lot agent and work

area agent. The lot agent sends a message to the corresponding work area agent with
following content
     (RECEIVE_SCHEDULE_BY_LOT
     :WORK_AREA
     :LOT
     :SCHEDULING_HORIZON)(NOT(TIME_REACHED :MAX_TIME).
The message content starts with the keyword RECEIVE_SCHEDULE_BY_LOT, an
agent activity from the FABMAS ontology. The agent activity is followed by a more
detailed description provided by the concepts WORK_AREA, LOT and
SCHEDULING_HORIZON from the FABMAS ontology. The agent activity depends
on a predicate, in this example, we ask for the maximum scheduling time
MAX_TIME.

The interaction between work area agent and work area scheduling agent is more
sophisticated (cf. Figure 4 for the complete interaction). In a first step the work area
agent initiates the calculation of a schedule by the work area scheduling agent. Therefore, it sends a message with the following content
     (START_CALCULATE_SCHEDULE
     :WORK_AREA)(NOT(TIME_REACHED:MAX_TIME)).
If the scheduling agent agrees to the request for determining a schedule, the work
area agent submits a message with content
     (PREPARE_SCHEDULING
     :WORK_AREA
     :SCHEDULING_HORIZON
     :PERFORMANCE_MEASURE
     :SCHEDULING_METHOD)(NOT(TIME_REACHED:MAX_TIME)).
Again, PREPARE_SCHEDULING is an agent activity from the FABMAS ontology
that is followed by the relevant concept identifiers from our ontology. After obtaining

Table 5. Agent Activities in the FABMAS Ontology

Agent Activity	Description
START_CALCULATE_SCHEDULE	Asks a special scheduling agent to de-termine a schedule.
START_MONITORING	Asks a special monitoring agent to pre-pare a certain monitoring report.
SEND_SCHEDULING_RESULTS	Asks a scheduling agent to transfer schedules back to the requesting agent.
PREPARE_SCHEDULING	Asks a scheduling agent to read all the necessary information in order to calcu-late a schedule.
START_EXCHANGE_INFORMA-TION_FOR_ABSBH	Asks to initiate an information exchange in course of the area-based shifting bot-tleneck heuristic (ABSBH).
START_MHR_NEGOTIATION	Asks to initiate the machine hour-rate-based contact net (in case of an invalid schedule).

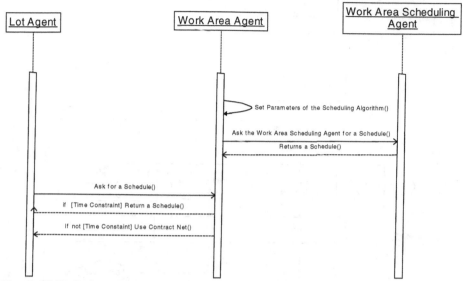

Fig. 3. UML Sequence Diagram for Interaction between Lot, Work Area, and Work Area Scheduling Agent

this message, the work area scheduling agent starts reading all the required information in order to calculate the schedule. Next, the work area agent sends a message with the following content to the work area scheduling agent in order to start the determination of the schedule:

    (CALCULATE_SCHEDULE
    :WORK_AREA
    :SCHEDULING_HORIZON
    :PERFORMANCE_MEASURE
    :SCHEDULING_METHOD)(NOT(TIME_REACHED:MAX_TIME)).

The content of this message is given by the agent activity CALCULATE_SCHEDULE. In a last step, the work area agent asks for the final schedule by using the content:

    (SEND_SCHEDULING_RESULTS
    :WORK_AREA
    :WORK_AREA_SCHEDULE
    :SCHEDULING_HORIZON
    :PERFORMANCE_MEASURE
    :SCHEDULING_METHOD).

After successful calculation of a schedule, the work area scheduling agent sends the message

    (SUCCESSFULLY_DONE:CALCULATE_SCHEDULE)

with predicate type content to the work area agent. In the case of errors during the scheduling determination, other types of content information are necessary (cf. Figure 4).

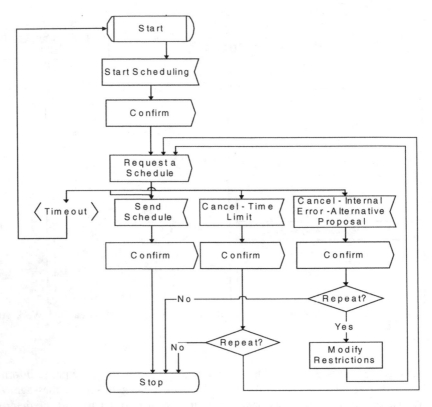

Fig. 4. SDL Diagram for Interaction between Work Area and Work Area Scheduling Agent

5 Conclusions

We present an ontology for production control of semiconductor manufacturing processes. Starting from a brief description of the underlying manufacturing domain and the used hierarchical production control approach, we suggest a data model for the present situation. Using this data model and certain reference ontologies we developed an ontology for the present situation. We describe the use of the ontology in an example.

As an important part of future research we identified the use of the suggested ontology for the construction of a domain-dedicated content language. This language has to be embedded in the FABMAS multi-agent-system. Similar to [6], we do not follow the more generic way of FIPA languages like SL0 or SL1 [1] in order to make the parser for the content language as simple as possible.

Acknowledgement. This research was supported by a grant from the Deutsche Forschungsgemeinschaft (DFG) Priority Research Program 1083 "Intelligent Agents and Realistic Commercial Application Scenarios".

References

1. Caire, G.: Jade Tutorial: Application-defined Content Languages and Ontologies. TILab S.p.A. (2002)
2. FABMAS Project Web Site: http://www.tu-ilmenau.de/fabmas (2003)
3. FIPA Ontology Specification: http://www.fipa.org/specs/fipa00006/ (1998)
4. Gruber, T. R.: Towards Principles for the Design of Ontologies Used for Knowledge Sharing. Int. J. Hum. Comp. Studies 43 (5/6) (1995) 907–928
5. Habenicht, I., Mönch, L.: A Finite Capacity Beam-Search Algorithm for Production Scheduling of Semiconductor Wafer Fabrication Facilities. In: Yücesan, E., Chen, C.-H., Snowdown, J. L., Charnes, J. M. (eds.): Proceedings of the 2002 Winter Simulation Conference, San Diego, USA (2002) 1406–1413
6. Heikkilä, T., Kollingbaum, M., Valckenaers, P., Bluemink, G.-J.: An Agent Architecture for Manufacturing Control: ManAge, Computers in Industry 46 (2001) 315–331
7. Mesarovic, M. D., Y. Takahara: Abstract System Theory, Lecture Notes in Control and Information Sciences, Springer-Verlag, Berlin, Heidelberg, New York, London, Paris, Tokyo (1989)
8. Mönch, L.: Analyse und Design für ein agentenbasiertes System zur Steuerung von Produktionsprozessen in der Halbleiterindustrie. In: Proceedings Verbundtagung Verteilte Informationssysteme auf der Grundlage von Objekten, Komponenten und Agenten (vertIS 2001) 99–112
9. Mönch, L., Stehli, M., Schulz, R.: An Agent-Based Architecture for Solving Dynamic Resource Allocation Problems. In: Verbraeck, A., Krug, W. (eds.): Proceedings of the 14ᵗʰ European Simulation Symposium. Simulation in Industry, Dresden (2002) 331–337
10. Mönch, L., Stehli, M., Zimmermann, J.: FABMAS – an Agent-Based System for Production Control of Semiconductor Manufacturing Processes. To Appear in Proceedings of the First International Conference on Industrial Application of Holonic and Multi-Agent-Systems (HoloMAS 2003). Prague, Czech Republic (2003)
11. Obitko, M., Mařík, V.: Ontologies for Multi-Agent-Systems in Manufacturing Domain. In: Proceedings of the 13ᵗʰ International Workshop on Database and Expert Systems Applications (2002)
12. Schneeweiß, C.: Hierarchies in Distributed Decision-Making. Springer-Verlag (1999)
13. Smith, S., Becker, M.: An Ontology for Constructing Scheduling Systems. In: Working Notes of the 1997 Symposium on Ontological Engineering, AAAI Press (1997)
14. Srivatsan, N., Bai, S. X., Gershwin, S. B.: Hierarchical Real-Time Integrated Scheduling of a Semiconductor Fabrication Facility. Control and Dynamic Systems (61) (1994) 197–241
15. Wouters, C., Dillon, T., Rahayu, W., Chang, E.: A Practical Walkthrough of the Ontology Derivation Rules. In: R. Cichetti et al. (Eds.): DEXA 2002, LNCS 2453, 259–268, Springer-Verlag, Berlin Heidelberg (2002)
16. Uschold, M., King, M., Moralee, S., Zorgios, Y.: The Enterprise Ontology, http://www.aiai..ed.ac.uk/~enterprise/enterprise/ontology.html#papers, (1997)
17. Van Brussel, H., Wyns, J., Valckenaers, P., Bongaerts, L., Peeters, P.: Reference Architecture for Holonic Manufacturing Systems: PROSA. Computers in Industry, Special Issue on Intelligent Manufacturing Systems 37(3) (1998) 225–276

Ontology-Based Capability Management for Distributed Problem Solving in the Manufacturing Domain

Ingo J. Timm[1] and Peer-Oliver Woelk[2]

[1] Technische Universitaet Ilmenau, Institute of Information Systems,
P. O. Box 10 05 65, 98684 Ilmenau, Germany
`itimm@acm.org`
[2] University of Hannover, Institute of Production Engineering and Machine Tools,
Schlosswender Str. 5, 30159 Hannover, Germany
`woelk@ifw.uni-hannover.de`

Abstract. Providing services within multiagent systems, an agent has to register itself with a distinct description of its main capabilities in yellow page services. If another agent is requesting to solve a specific task, it has to be decided whether or not the requested agent is capable of performing the task successfully. We are assuming that task requirements as well as capabilities are specified using ontologies. Decision is easy if the concepts of requested task requirements are directly mapping to concepts of provided capabilities. However, concept inequality may occur. Especially in production engineering with its increasing concern of knowledge about sophisticated manufacturing processes, relying on simple concept equality is not suitable to fulfill demands of current industrial applications. Thus, enhanced methods like ontology-based capability management presented in this paper have to be established to address this problem. For the case of indifferent concepts we are introducing a conflict-based approach for capability negotiation as well as an application scenario for this approach in the manufacturing domain.

1 Introduction

Cooperative distributed problem solving (CDPS) is one of the main features of multiagent systems. Communication facilitates a very flexible way of organizing collaborative work among agents [1]. The coordination follows either the assumption of *benevolence*, i.e. agents are (implicitly) sharing common goals, or *self-interest*, i.e. agents pursue potentially conflicting local goals [2]. For multiagent systems in the manufacturing domain the assumption of benevolence is not suitable, esp. if not only processes within single enterprises but also inter-enterprise cooperation are in question.

The process of CDPS can be divided into three stages: (i) problem decomposition, (ii) sub-problem solution, and (iii) answer synthesis [10]. In this paper, we are focusing on the first aspect: problem decomposition. An implicit assumption

M. Schillo et al. (Eds.): MATES 2003, LNAI 2831, pp. 168–179, 2003.

here is, that each of the problem solving agent has knowledge on its capabilities. A more sophisticated approach would rather ask the question: *How does a problem-solving agent knows whether or not it is capable of solving the requested problem?*

1.1 Distributed Problem Solving in the Manufacturing Domain

Several applications of agent technology in manufacturing focus on digital marketplaces where intelligent agents act on behalf of enterprises, customers or other organizations to achieve goals like to acquire a specific good for the smallest possible price. Since enterprises began to consider several departments as individual profit centers, market-based coordination mechanisms became of increasing concern not only for inter-enterprise relationship but also for internal processes of enterprises like e.g. scheduling tasks at the shop floor.

With respect to manufacturing of customized products in small lot sizes in batch job production, scheduling becomes a distributed problem: Orders have to be manufactured by different resources located at different places at the shop floor. Each resource possesses its own schedule, its own capabilities to perform different manufacturing operations and its own economical profile (e.g. specific machining costs). On the other hand, orders need to be manufactured according to customer requirements and due dates. From point of view of the shop floor, an order schedule must be "calculated" in cooperation of order and resources, where each individual resource decides about the price it will offer its capabilities to the order. Unfortunately, the structure of the shop floor and the orders is not a static one since new machines are taken into operation, other suffer a breakdown, or typical orders change due to altered customer demands: The shop floor for customized manufacturing is a very dynamic environment. Hence, this problem may be solved by methods of CDPS. Intelligent software agents turn out to be a suitable approach to develop dynamic, marketplace-based systems in the manufacturing domain.

Recent research projects deal with shop floor planning problems, e.g. by improving scheduling with respect to robustness and dynamic distributed environments. However, agent technology may be used to overcome existing traditional limitations in today's manufacturing systems, too [3]. For example, the "IntaPS" project implements a system of intelligent agents, which is capable of integrated process planning and production control to enhance the flexibility of planning at the shop floor. It is not bound to the restrictions of simple linear process plans any longer [13]. Since process plans are the result of agent communication, new alternative processing sequences can be found, e.g. in case of re-planning caused by unexpected machine breakdown. Order agents need knowledge about constraints related to the product's features and the necessary capabilities to manufacture these features. In addition, resource agents need knowledge about their capabilities. Thus, management of capabilities is important for negotiation of process plans.

1.2   Problem Decomposition

Problem decomposition is the first stage in CDPS. The coordination of agents in this approach is based on message passing, which fits well into the application domain under the assumptions made above. The contract net protocol is a common representative for task decomposition algorithm in a message passing setting [9]. The problem solving process may be described step-wise: in each step, the problem solving agent provides a complete solution by itself or it decomposes the task. For the next step, it changes the role and requests solutions for each sub-task. Thus, an distributed task decomposition algorithm can be realized. Of course, a problem solving agent has to be able to decide whether or it has the capability to solve a specified task. In real-world applications, there are methods to solve a problem, which are not equal but equivalent. E.g. drilling is the standard operation for creating a whole in a product, but in some cases and with specific machine tools milling may produce an equivalent result. Nevertheless, both actions are not equal. In this context, the mapping of capability to task and vice versa, which is not based on simple concept or string equality is an open issue.

2   Discourse Agent

The Discourse Agent approach specifies an architecture for agent behavior, knowledge representation, and inferences for application in eBusiness, esp. in the manufacturing domain. This basic approach strictly separates internal and external aspects due to privacy and security issues. A three layer architecture is introduced consisting of *communicator*, working on a low-level realization of speech acts, *controller*, determining general agent behavior, and *executor*, i.e. an interface to existing components, e.g. enterprise resource planning (ERP) systems and further information sources [12].

Nowadays, the communicator should be implemented with respect to standardization efforts, like FIPA [6]. In the case of our research project, the communicator is realized on top of a FIPA compliant agent toolkit (JADE, developed by CSELT S.p.A.[1]). The executor has to be implemented according to its directly connected resources, e.g. machine tools. While the communicator and executor layer is constructed in a straight forward manner, the design of the controller layer is more sophisticated implementing two innovative concepts: conflict-based agent control (*cobac*) and open, adaptive communication (*oac*).

The controller layer determines the behavior, strategy, and state of the agent. That means an agent behaves in the way the functions and procedures in the controller decide. It can only learn from experience acknowledged in the controller. The architecture presented here is based on the deliberative agent architecture BDI [8]. The formal foundation is introducing a new (multi-) modal logic, which integrates the formal approaches VSK-logic [16] for inter-agent behavior and the LORA-logic [17] for deliberative agent behavior. In the following, we are

---

[1] http://sharon.cselt.it/projects/jade/

focusing on the internal behavior of an agent, where decisions on proposing for requested tasks are computed[2]. For further definitions, let Ω be the set of any well-formed formulas with respect to the grammatical definitions of this logic; $\mathcal{B} \subset \Omega$ is denoting the set of any possible belief. The main concepts needed for the definition of *Discourse Agents* are introduced in the following paragraphs:

1 DEFINITION (DISCOURSEAGENT) *A discourse agent is given by a 7-tuple:*
$Ag = \langle L, Act, see, reflect, decide, execute, l_0 \rangle$,
where $l_0 \in \mathcal{L}$ is denoting the initial state.

While L, Act, and *decide* are introduced in the next section, *see* (perception function, cf. [16]) , *reflect* (knowledge revision function), and *execute* (action selection function) are not in the focus of this paper.

2.1 The Local State

As basic concepts within an agent controller we define *actions*, the agent is capable of, *plans* as dynamic action sequences and *local states* as explicit state representations.

2 DEFINITION (ACTION) *Let α^c be a communicative action executed in the communicator layer and α^e an executive action performed in the executive layer, then the sets $Act^c = \{\alpha_0^c, \ldots, \alpha_m^c\}$ and $Act^e = \{\alpha_0^e, \ldots, \alpha_n^e\}$ are denoting the communicitave resp. executive actions of an agent. Together they are building the action potential $Act = Act^e \cup Act^c$.*

Following the definition of *Discourse Agent*, plans are tuples consisting of pre and post conditions, a set of available actions as well as mappings *status* and *select*.

3 DEFINITION (ACTIONPLAN) *Let $\varphi_{pre}, \varphi_{post} \in \Omega$ be a pre resp. post condition, $\mathcal{B} \subset \Omega$ the set of possible beliefs of the agent, and $A \subset Act$ a set of available actions, then plan $= \langle \varphi_{pre}, \varphi_{post}, A, status, select \rangle$ is called action plan, if*

- *status $: B \times \varphi_{pre} \times \varphi_{post} \mapsto x$, with $x \in \mathbb{R}_0$ and $B \in \mathcal{B}$, is a mapping denoting the execution status of the plan and*
- *select $: status \times \mathcal{B} \to A$ is a mapping, which selects an action as a next step of the plan.*

The set Pln is denoting the set of all action plans of an agent.

A local state is defined using the mental categories *beliefs*, *desires*, and *intentions* as follows:

4 DEFINITION (LOCALSTATE) *The local state is defined as 5-tuple:*
$L = \langle B, D, I, Plan, \gamma \rangle$ *if*

---

[2] For a detailed introduction to the architecture, esp. the open, adaptive communication approach, refer to [12].

- $B \subset \mathcal{B}$ *is the set of current beliefs,*
- $D \subset \mathcal{B}$ *is the set of current desires,*
- $I \subset D \times Pln$ *is the set of active intentions,*
- $Plan \subset Pln$ *is the set of available plans, and*
- $\gamma : \mathcal{B} \times D \rightarrow \mathbb{R}$ *is a mapping computing the relevance of a desire in the current situation*[3].

2.2   Conflict-Based Agent Control (*cobac*)

The main decision function within a Discourse Agent's controller is *decide*. If this function is computed, the following four steps are processed:

1. Intention reconsideration,
2. Option generation and assessment,
3. Conflict management and resolution, and
4. Option selection.

In the first step, current intentions of the agent are reconsidered. The result of intention reconsideration is a revised set of intention, which does not include intentions, which are not fitting the criteria of the pre-defined level of commitment (blind, single-minded or open-minded commitment) [7].

In the deliberation process an option is defined as a tuple of a desire and a plan (cf. intention, $o = \langle des, plan \rangle$, with $des \in D$ and $plan \in Pln$). The option generation process is building a set of options O, which contains the complete set of intentions I and new options. New option is created for a desire, if no intention is pursuing it and the desire is accessible. The accessibility relation is defined in consideration of the branching temporal structure [17]; modifications on this relation are done with respect to decidability and efficiency. During the creation of a new option a plan is selected for pursuing the desire in question using a plan allocation function.

An evaluation function is assessing each option of the option set O, using the desire assessing function γ and the current state of the plan, such that an option with an almost completed plan will receive high priority within the option filtering process. Next to the intention reconsideration, this evaluation function is implementing the commitment to an intention and should ensure, that important and almost completed tasks will be finished first.

In the next step the options have to be filtered. The filtering is using conflict assessment and resolution introduced with the *Discourse Agent* architecture. For each pair of options, a synergy as well as a conflict value is calculated. Two options are receiving a high synergy value if they are pursuing similar desires and the plans are not contradictory, e.g. the post condition of plan A is not prohibiting the pre condition of plan B. Figures 1 and 2 are showing the conceptual idea of synergy and conflict.

---

[3] The mapping is simplified for this paper, the *Discourse Agent* approach does define a more sophisticated set of mappings, which are assessing desires with respect to user relevance, potential, and risk.

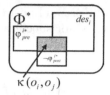
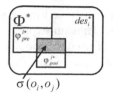

Fig. 1. Conflict Value   **Fig. 2.** Synergy Value

A conflict and synergy potential is calculated as the sum of each conflict and synergy value and used as a performance indicator within the process of conflict resolution. The conflict classification and resolution algorithm is motivated from the field of inter-personal conflict studies [14]. A conflict taxonomy is introduced in [12], where each pair of options is classified as a leaf in this taxonomy. For each type of leaf, there is a resolution strategy taking the cooperation or conflict potential into account. E.g. if two objectives are very similar, they can be merged in a cooperative setting and two objectives pursuing conflicting post conditions can be removed.

The last step of the *decide*-function is filtering the options to create a new set of intentions. Thus, each option must meet a minimum evaluation to be treated as an intention. The *decide*-function is formally defined as follows:

5 DEFINITION (DECIDE) *The mapping: decide* $: \mathcal{L} \to \mathcal{L}$
with decide$(\langle B, D, I, Pln, \gamma \rangle) \mapsto \langle B, D, I^*, Pln, \gamma^* \rangle$ *is called conflict-based agent control if*

- $irf : \langle B, I \rangle \mapsto I^0$ *is intention reconsideration function,*
- $go : \langle B, D, I^0, Pln, \gamma \rangle \mapsto O$ *is option generation function,*
- $crf : \langle \langle B, D, I^0, Pln, \gamma \rangle, O \rangle \mapsto \langle \langle B, D, I^0, Pln, \gamma^* \rangle, O^* \rangle$ *is conflict resolution function, and*
- $filter : O^* \mapsto I^*$ *is option filtering function.*

3   Task Decomposition Using Ontologies

The first step in CDPS for a problem solving agent is, to decide whether or not, it is capable of decomposing or solving the task. In this section we are proposing an algorithm to solve this decision using an ontology for the problem specification as well as an explicit specification of capabilites. This algorithm is using and extending the formal framework of *Discourse Agents*, presented in the last section.

3.1   Formal Remarks on Ontologies

In the definition of local states, we introduced desires as statements, which should become true in future states. Moving this approach to specification of problems, a problem is specified using statements, which describe pre and post conditions. We assume, that an explicit, formal ontology is provided for specification of the semantics of used symbols in these conditions. Ontologies can be formally specified as a 3-tuple, which consists at least of concepts, attributes, and relations.

6 DEFINITION (ONTOLOGY) *Let C be a set of concepts, A a set of attributes, and R be a set of relations on these concepts, then a tuple $Onto = \langle C, A, R \rangle$ is called ontology.*

In the following we are also assuming that an ontology $Onto^t$ used for specification of problems contains at least one taxonomic relation without multiple inheritance ($r^t \in R$). As abbreviation we use *length* as a symbol for the amount of edges between two nodes, $length(n)$ for the length from the root node to node n, and $length(n, m)$ for the length from node n to node m. The mapping $mscc$ is mapping a pair of concepts to the most specific common concept.

3.2 Capabilities

The capability management is using a problem description, an ontology, as well as an agent specified as a *Discourse Agent*. The agent receives a problem description and is performing the *cobac** algorithm to decide how appropriate the agents capabilities are for the specified problem.

Following the definition of *Discourse Agent* the agent's capabilities are determined by its set of available plans. An action plan is describing a capability to transform a state which supports its pre condition into a state supporting its post condition. Taking ontological relations into account, an agent's capabilities could be extended, e.g. including super-concepts from taxonomic relations. The approach of capability management is not only extending capabilities but also problem descriptions. If a problem description is using a specific concept and the capability of an agent matches to the super-concept, the capability may be sufficient. The next paragraph is introducing a conflict-based approach to compute solutions as the above mentioned.

3.3 cobac*

The *cobac* algorithm specified for the conflict-based agent control is using a specific conflict and synergy measure, which is based on partial correspondence and contrast of complex expressions. In opposite to this, the *cobac** algorithm is introducing a conflict measure based on the evaluation of proximity and distance in an ontology, i.e. taxonomic relation.

The goal of the algorithm is to find that capability resp. plan, which is fitting *best* to the requested problem. A requested problem is formalized as a tuple consisting of pre conditions denoting the starting state and a post condition denoting the goal state, such that $problem = \langle \varphi^p_{pre}, \varphi^p_{post} \rangle$. *cobac** is considering the mapping of problem to capability as a conflict and synergy assessment problem. The algorithm should return that capability, which has maximum synergy value and minimum conflict value. Therefore, the algorithm consists of the following three steps:

1. Option generation,
2. Conflict and Synergy assessment, and
3. Option selection.

The computing of $cobac^*$ is using a taxonomy r^t from the underlying ontology as reference relation. Starting the algorithm, a set of options is build, including all plans, which are available for the agent and which pre conditions are supporting the pre conditions of requested problem.

7 DEFINITION (OPTIONGENERATION) *A set of options Opt is constructed for a problem* $\langle \varphi^p_{pre}, \varphi^p_{post} \rangle$ *as specified by:*
$$Opt = \{\langle \varphi_{pre}, \varphi_{post}, A, st, se \rangle | \varphi_{pre} \to \varphi^p_{pre} \text{ and } \langle \varphi_{pre}, \varphi_{post}, A, st, se \rangle \in Plan\}$$

In the next step conflict and synergy between options and problem are assessed. Therefore, each option i is put into relation to the problem and the conflict and synergy values are calculated for each pair of concepts in $\varphi^p_{post}, \varphi^i_{post}$. The conflict $\kappa(p, o_i)$ and synergy $\sigma(p, o_i)$ potential is computed for each option as a sum of all of its conflict and synergy values.

8 DEFINITION (CONFLICT AND SYNERGY) *For each option* $o_i \in Opt$ *and problem* $p = \langle \varphi_{pre}, \varphi_{post} \rangle$ *with a taxonomy* $r^t \subset C^t \times C^t$, *the conflict* κ *and synergy* σ *potential are calculated as follows:*
$$\kappa(p, o_i) = \sum_{c_i, c_p \in C^t \wedge c_i \in \varphi^p_{post} \wedge c_p \in \varphi^i_{post}} k(c_p, c_i) \text{ (conflict) and}$$
$$\sigma(p, o_i) = \sum_{c_i, c_p \in C^t \wedge c_i \in \varphi^p_{post} \wedge c_p \in \varphi^i_{post}} s(c_p, c_i) \text{ (synergy).}$$
The conflict and synergy values of a tuple of concepts c_i, c_j *are determined by the distance in the taxonomic relation (cf. section 3.1):*
$$k(c_i, c_j) = length(c_i, c_j) \text{ and}$$
$$s(c_i, c_j) = length(mscc(c_i, c_j)).$$

The option selection is using these conflict and synergy potentials to select *most* appropriate option for the requested problem. This is determined by the quotient $\psi(p, o_i) = \frac{\kappa(p, o_i)}{\sigma(p, o_i)}$ of conflict and synergy potential, which is minimal if no conflict is found and maximal if no synergy is found. The option with the lowest quotient ψ is used as resulting capability, which is proposed as solution to the task agent. If this quotient is zero, the proposed problem solving capability is equal to the requested problem.

The algorithm presented here is using a taxonomic relation without multiple inheritance. This restriction can easily be overcome by introducing a slightly modified conflict and synergy assessment. Instead of using length of path – which assumes that there is exactly one path – longest path could be used for synergy assessment resp. shortest path for conflict assessment.

3.4   Accepting an Approximate Problem Solver

In this paper, we are focusing on the decision, if a problem-solving agent should propose for solving a requested problem or not. If an agent is proposing a solution to an approximate problem, the task agent has to decide, whether or not it is accepting this solution. We are proposing to use the conflict-based agent control *cobac* algorithm for identifying valid solutions with respect to its desire and the adaptive communication *oac* for cost bargaining if the solution is only similar and not equal to the requested problem.

Alternatively, *cobac** can be used to build an equivalence relation within the ontology. A simplified approach is using the taxonomic relation and a maximum distance value mdv. This value is determining if a solution provided with the capability c_i is valid for the problem c_p: $(length(c_i, c_p) < mdv)$.

4   Scenario: The Gear Wheel

As described above, ontologies resp. a taxonomic relations are used as a basis for capability. In order to illustrate this approach, two quite simple ontologies will be used. The presented example ontologies reflect a small cut-out of the domain only and are tailored in order to represent the concepts needed for the following use cases. Figure 3 is showing an ontology for manufacturing features, the figure 4 focuses on manufacturing processes.

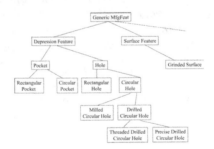

Fig. 3. Ontology of Manufacturing Features

4.1   Use Case A: An Order on Its Way to a Machine

The first use case illustrates how an order agent determines the sequence of necessary manufacturing operations based on capabilities offered by resource agents. It is assumed, that an order agent is requesting the manufacturing of a gear wheel by a cutting process out of forged raw material. In this context, an appropriate process for the tooth flanks is needed, but several cutting processes are available. However, conflicts may occur between different processes since the appropriate cutting process depends on the applied forging process.

Conventional forging processes lead to raw parts with rough surfaces and large allowance (amount of material to removed in final manufacturing steps). Since grinding processes can remove small amounts of material for suitable costs only, they must not be applied to those parts: a conflict arises. On the other hand, conventionally forged parts may be milled by gear hobbing and gear hobbed parts may be grinded: a synergy exists. A different situation occurs in case of precision forged raw parts, which are characterized by small allowance and hardened, semi-rough surfaces. No specific synergy of conflict exists to the process combination hobbing/grinding, but specialized processes like hardfinishing exist for these parts. Knowing about the existence of these different manufacturing processes and their specific pre- and post-conditions, an order agent is able to select appropriate process combinations out of the available capabilities of the resources.

Fig. 4. Ontology of Manufacturing Processes

4.2   Use Case B: How to Make a Gear Wheel

The last paragraph illustrated how ontologies can be used to identify suitable sequence of available manufacturing processes. This identification depends on the propagation of available capabilities from the resource agent to the order agent and thus the ability of the resource agent to determine, if it possesses capabilities to perform a requested manufacturing task. Manufacturing tasks can be represented by manufacturing features (comparable to "design features" used as an object-oriented representation of product-related information like geometry in 3D-CAD systems). In addition, the resource agent may have knowledge to decide, if a manufacturing feature can be processed by a specific capability or not. If applicable, the requesting order agent is notified about specific capability. In this example, features e.g. for assembly operations of multiple parts into the whole product are not considered.

5   Conclusions and Future Work

We have described an approach for capability management in cooperative distributed problem solving. The explicit integration of ontologies for deciding whether or not an agent is capable of solving a problem enables an agent to propose a solution for a similar problem. The use of taxonomies as basic concepts is a first step, only. We are assuming that, there is a benefit of using a simple conflict measure than using no measure at all. The main benefit of the algorithm proposed here is, that a static link from a specific task to a specific capability is no longer needed. These enables multiagent systems to solve problems using alternatives in solving (sub-) tasks. In the manufacturing domain, the system is more flexible in planning and scheduling as more alternatives are available and the mapping from feature to machine tool can be solved dynamically. Furthermore, the algorithm is simple, such that an efficient implementation is possible.

The problem of capability management is still an open problem and will probably not be solved soon. One of the main restrictions of the approach proposed here lays in the assumption, that only unique and shared ontologies between agents exists. Using multiple ontologies may be necessary in real distributed scenarios, but is leading to the problem of equality or equivalence of concepts. Further shortcomings arise from using a simple length evaluation (amount of edges), such that taxonomic relations have to be designed carefully as its quality is corresponding to accuracy of this algorithm.

In the intelligent information integration as well as the semantic web community multiple approaches of estimating similarity of concepts in ontologies or semantic matchmaking are under research, e.g. [4], [15], [5]. We are going to integrate approaches of approximate reasoning, as applied to adaptation of communication vocabularies [11].

The use cases are showing high potential for application of "weak" mapping of cababilities to problems in the domain of distributed systems in cooperative manufacturing settings. Future work of us is focusing on the design and implementation of realistic application scenarios for capability management. Of course, more research and sophisticated algorithms for conflict assessment but also for building equivalence relations within the task agents are needed.

Acknowledgement. The authors would like to thank the reviewers for their valuable and helpful remarks. Parts of the presented work are funded by the Deutsche Forschungsgemeinschaft (DFG) within the projects He 989/5-2 and To 56/149-2 as part of the Priority Research Program 1083 "Intelligent Agents and Realistic Commercial Application Scenarios".

References

1. CONEN, W., AND NEUMANN, G. *Coordination Technology for Collaborative Applications*. No. 1364 in Lecture Notes in Artificial Intelligence. Springer, Berling, 1998.
2. DURFEE, E. H., AND ROSENSCHEIN, J. S. Distributed problem solving and multi-agent systems: Comparisons and examples. In *Proceedings of the 13th International Distributed Artificial Intelligence Workshop* (1994), pp. 94–104.

3. MAREK, V., Ed. *Knowledge and Technology Integration in Products and Services, Proceedings Balancing Knowledge and Technology in Product and Service Life Cycle (BASYS '02)*. Kluwer Academic Publishers, Cancun, Mexico, September 2002.

4. NOY, N. F., AND MUSEN, M. A. Evaluating ontology mapping tools: Requirements and experience. In *Proceedings of the Workshop on Evaluation of Ontology Tools at EKAW'02 (EON2002)* (Siguenza, Spain, October 2002).

5. PAOLUCCI, M., KAWAMURA, T., PAYNE, T. R., AND SYCARA, K. Semantic matching of web services capabilities. In *Proceedings of the 1st International Semantic Web Conference (ISWC2002)* (2002).

6. POSLAD, S., AND CHARLTON, P. Standardizing agent interoperability: The FIPA approach. In *Multi-Agent Systems and Applications: 9th ECCAI Advanced Course, ACAI 2001 and Agent Link's 3rd European Agent Systems Summer School, EASSS 2001, Prague, Czech Republic, July 2-13, 2001: Selected Tutorial Papers* (New York, NY, USA, 2001), M. Luck, Ed., Springer-Verlag Inc., pp. 98–117.

7. RAO, A. S., AND GEORGEFF, M. P. *Proceedings of the Second International Conference on Principles of Knowledge Representation and Reasoning (KR & R-91)*. Morgan Kaufmann Publishers, San Mateo, CA, 1991, ch. Modeling Rational Agents in a BDI-architecture, pp. 473–484.

8. RAO, A. S., AND GEORGEFF, M. P. BDI-agents: from theory to practice. In *Proceedings of the First Intl. Conference on Multiagent Systems* (San Francisco, 1995).

9. SMITH, R. G. The contract net protocol: High-level communication and control in a distributed problem solver. In *Readings in Distributed Artificial Intelligence*, A. H. Bond and L. Gasser, Eds. Morgan Kaufmann, San Mateo, 1988.

10. SMITH, R. G., AND DAVIS, R. Frameworks or cooperation in distributed problem solving. *IEEE Transactions on Systems, man and Cybernetics 11*, 1 (1980).

11. STUCKENSCHMIDT, H., AND TIMM, I. J. Adapting communication vocabularies using shared ontologies. In *Proceedings of the Second International Workshop on Ontologies in Agent Systems, Workshop at 1st International Conference on Autonomous Agents and Multi-Agent Systems* (Bologna, Italy, 15-19 July 2002 2002), S. Cranefield, Ed., pp. 6–12.

12. TIMM, I. J. Enterprise agents solving problems: The cobac-approach. In *"Informatik 2001" – Tagungsband der GI/OCG Jahrestagung, 25.-28. September 2001* (Universitaet Wien, 2001), K. Bauknecht, W. Brauer, and T. Mueck, Eds., pp. 952–958.

13. TOENSHOFF, H. K., WOELK, P.-O., TIMM, I. J., AND HERZOG, O. Planning and production control using co-operative agent systems. In *Proceedings of the International Conference on Competitive Manufacturing (COMA '01)* (Stellenbosch, South Africa, 31st January — 2nd February 2001), D. Dimitrov and N. du Preez, Eds., pp. 442–449.

14. VAN DE VLIERT, E. *Complex Interpersonal Conflict Behaviour – Theoretical Frontiers*. Essays in Social Psychology. Psychology Press, East Sussex, UK, 1997.

15. VISSER, U., STUCKENSCHMIDT, H., SCHLIEDER, C., WACHE, H., AND TIMM, I. Terminology integration for the management of distributed information resources. *Kuenstliche Intelligenz 16*, 1 (2002), 31–34.

16. WOOLDRIDGE, M., AND LOMUSCIO, A. *Proceedings of the Seventh European Workshop on Logics in Artificial Intelligence (JELIAI-2000)*. Springer-Verlag, Berlin, 2000, ch. Multi-Agent VSK Logic.

17. WOOLDRIDGE, M. J. *Reasoning about Rational Agents*. The MIT Press, Cambridge, Massachusetts, 2000.

Using the Publish-Subscribe Communication Genre for Mobile Agents

Amir Padovitz, Seng Wai Loke, and Arkady Zaslavsky

School of Computer Science and Software Engineering, Monash University,
Caulfield East, VIC 3145, Australia
padovitz@bigpond.com, swloke@csse.monash.edu.au,
a.zaslavsky@monash.edu.au

Abstract. We advocate the event-based communication genre for mobile agent communities, which is useful for exchanging and disseminating large volumes of small lightweight messages. We propose that the publish-subscribe model complements the proprietary or standard agent communication languages. We describe how we implemented the event notification mechanism for mobile agents, and analyse experiments that demonstrate the Elvin-based event notification mechanism for communication between heterogeneous agents, in particular, Grasshopper agents and Aglets. We also discuss experiments for measuring message losses due to agent migration.

1 Introduction

Various Internet-scale applications have found mobile agents advantageous [2]. The problem of agent communication at run-time is very much a challenge, and communication between heterogeneous agents in multi-agent systems or, in other words, agents from diverse platforms or environments poses even a bigger challenge [11].

A different paradigm, which has been useful for asynchronous communication between loosely coupled components of distributed systems, is publish-subscribe event notification mechanism. In this paper, we investigate the use of Elvin, a typical stateless content-based event communication system [5] in a dynamic mobile agent environment. While implementations of publish-subscribe models may differ, the fundamental principles remain the same, and in this paper we use the name Elvin both as the name of a specific implementation and more significantly as a generic representative of the class of event notification systems.

We highlight below three benefits of event-based mechanisms in dynamic mobile agent environments:

- The concept of an event is a natural abstraction for the activities within the environment and the interactions among places and agents. We see the event mechanism as a communication genre complementary to other means of inter-agent communication. For transfer of large data chunks between agents or more structured conversations, other inter-agent communication mechanisms (e.g., FIPA

M. Schillo et al. (Eds.): MATES 2003, LNAI 2831, pp. 180–191, 2003.

- ACL, www.fipa.org) can be used. The event service only serves as a means of communicating (potentially large volumes of) short messages among agents or to agents about events, in a lightweight manner.
- Event-based models provide implicit invocation [1]: a component A can invoke another component B without A being required to know B's *name* or B's *location*. Components such as B 'register' interest in particular 'events' that components such as A 'announce'. When A announces such an event, the event system notifies (or invokes) B, even though A doesn't know that B or any other components are registered. This suits a dynamic environment, where A need not know B's location since B might be continually moving, and A can interact with other components in the environment without knowing their details (e.g., their name, or how many agents there are, thereby providing scalability). Elvin's mechanism to achieve implicit invocation is *content-based addressing* (or *undirected addressing*) where a notification is not explicitly directed by the producer to specific consumers, but is simply multicast to consumers whose subscriptions match the notification description.
- The Elvin paradigm is independent of agent toolkit – there are APIs implemented for C, C++, Perl, Python, and Java languages, and so can be used for communication between agents built using different toolkits.

We discuss design, implementation and experiments that were conducted to investigate the potential and practicality of integrating a publish-subscribe communication mechanism such as Elvin with mobile agents, as first suggested in [3].

The rest of this paper is organized as follows. Section 2 discusses relevant background concepts. Section 3 discusses our implementation together with technical hurdles. Using the event-based mechanism, however, has one drawback, which is the loss of messages during agent migration. Section 4 describes the experiments we conducted on event-based communication between agents from two different toolkits, and the extent of message loss due to agent movement. Section 5 concludes with future work.

2 Background and Related Work

2.1 Publish-Subscribe Model

A common model for performing asynchronous communication in component-based environments is the publish-subscribe model [1]. Generally, entities that wish to send messages "publish" them as events, while entities that wish to receive certain types of messages (or events) "subscribe" (or register) to those events. A publisher of a message is not aware of the recipients requesting that message and might not even be aware of their existence. Similarly, components that receive messages may not be aware of other components that may also listen to the same event and can only receive messages they are registered for. Often, an entity may become both a publisher and subscriber, sending and receiving messages within the system.

To accomplish the event-based model, a separate entity is deployed between the producer and consumer of a message, which decouples the connection between those entities and provides the necessary mechanism for distributing a message to registered subscribers.

We observe the stateless nature of the publish subscribe model, which is characterized as fast, efficient and relatively simple implemented mechanism, and distinguish it from a state-full implementation such as message queuing that uses a different style for performing communication. A weakness of the stateless model is the potential loss of messages. In contrast, message queues use the store-and-forward technique, which guarantees the delivery of messages but results in high latency, greater overheads and slow message delivery [6]. Examples of message queuing systems are IBM's MQSeries [12], BEA MessageQ [13] and a range of applications that are built using the Java Message Service (JMS) [7], such as the Oracle Message Broker [8].

Further distinction of event-based systems is the evolution from subject-based systems, in which a message relates to a group of subjects, towards content-based systems, where a subscriber can search for content that appears within a message. A content-based communication mechanism, used in heterogeneous multi-agent systems can become a powerful means of communication between agents that share similar interests (content) without having prior knowledge of each other.

Several content-based event systems, such as Elvin [5], LeSubscribe [9] and Gryphon [6] exist, offering a selection of services and attempts to overcome the undelivered messages problem [6].

2.2   The Elvin Event Notification System

Elvin provides a scalable and dynamic publish-subscribe event notification mechanism. It is built and used in a client-server architecture, in which an Elvin server is responsible for managing client connections and transferring messages between publishers and subscribers. Consumers of notifications register their interest in specific events with the server. Upon receiving a notification (message) from a producer, the Elvin server forwards the notification to the relevant client subscribers by comparing the message content with the list of subscriptions it holds. As the routing of a message is based on its content, it provides the flexibility to operate in a dynamic environment and is independent of the need to configure information relating to the recipients of a notification. The notification itself is encapsulated within an object and contains a list of key-value pairs. A consumer expresses its interest with a subscription element, which is built with a special subscription language containing predicates.

2.3   Agent Toolkits – Aglets and Grasshopper

Two mobile agent toolkits were used during this study: IBM's Aglets (www.trl.ibm.com/aglets/index_e.htm) and IKV++ GmbH Grasshopper (www.grasshopper.de). Although different in other aspects, both toolkits provide an internal communication mechanism used to send messages between agents implemented in the same toolkit. The Grasshopper communication mechanisms are of particular interest as they provide a variety of messaging facilities including message multi-casting. Both toolkits expose a set of Java classes as an API to facilitate mobile agent implementation.

In Aglets, mobile agents live and act within an environment (object) termed context. The context (located in specific host/s) manages the active agents. Grasshopper's execution environment is more complex and consists of several elements, termed regions, agencies and places.

3 Implementation

Prior to this research, Elvin was successfully used in several applications, such as CSCW environments to achieve mutual awareness between different parties. However, application objects that were utilizing the Elvin mechanism in those applications were static, in the sense that they were located at the same host for their entire lifetime.

In contrast, mobile agents may be active and migrate between different hosts. During the lifetime of a mobile agent, it can execute on several agent places in different times and may need to communicate with other mobile agents as well as with static objects.

As Elvin's original focus is to provide an event-notification based communication for traditional distributed applications and architectures, in which objects that are using Elvin remain in the same location, it was initially unfit to be used as part of mobile code. Hence, new functionality had to be added to facilitate such integration. Furthermore, the newly developed capabilities were targeted to be used by any mobile agent toolkit and not be restricted to a specific one.

The new functionality that supports the use of Elvin in mobile code was developed to integrate easily with the regular mobile agent's code, requiring only minimal changes in the agent's program. As mobile agent toolkits mostly operate on a Java Virtual Machine, development of new functionality was done in the Java Environment.

3.1 Basic Elvin Client Constructs and Mobility Hurdles

Two fundamental constructs for performing Elvin communication are the *consumer* and *producer* objects. These objects are part of the Elvin Client library, which enables *consumer* objects to register callback methods that are activated for specific notifications, and allow *producer* objects to publish new notifications intended for listeners (that use the *consumer* object). The Elvin Server behavior dictates that an application that consumes notifications (by using the *consumer* object) must exist in the same location in which it originally subscribed for the particular notification/s at the time the notification is sent by the server. An Elvin *connection* object describes the communication details and exists for each *consumer* object. Upon receiving an event, the server will broadcast a notification for that event to subscribing objects, in the location in which the original subscription took place (and as maintained by the Elvin *connection* object).

Mobile agents cannot use these Elvin constructs since they often change their location and still require receiving notifications. In such a scenario, the Elvin server is not aware of their new location and continues to send messages to the old location. It is also infeasible for them to return to their original subscribing location, and even if they do so, they will lose many of the notifications sent to them, while in transit or executing in other nodes. We will discuss solutions to this problem later.

In Figure 1, which illustrates this problem, a mobile agent first subscribes for events (stage 1), and then migrates to another location (stage 2). An Elvin Server contains a subscription registration from the agent, and a connection that is identified with the old location, thus sending new notifications to the wrong host.

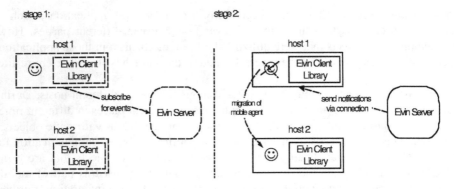

Fig. 1. The connection problem between the Elvin Server and a mobile agent.

A second important mobility problem is concerned with the nature of migration of mobile agents. While in transit, a mobile agent has no concrete existence on a particular host and is therefore unable to receive Elvin messages. We consider this problem in more detail later.

A third hurdle in implementing a solution for mobile agents is the fact that all Elvin Client objects are implemented as non-serializable objects. As such, they cannot migrate as part of the mobile agent code to new locations. This imposes obvious restrictions on the way mobile agents can use existing Elvin objects.

3.2 MobileConsumer

To solve the mentioned mobility problems, new functionality, represented by a *MobileConsumer* class was developed and added to the Elvin Client Library. The *MobileConsumer* class supports Java Serialization, and thus, can be transported to different hosts as part of the mobile agent. The functionality implemented in this class follows the approach suggested in [3], in which an agent removes all existing subscriptions before migrating to a new location and re-subscribes to the same notifications after arriving at the new location.

The class embeds this kind of behavior and performs the required operations on behalf of its client (the mobile agent). A *MobileConsumer* object keeps information such as a serializable representation of Elvin subscriptions and Connections, and is implemented as a single object per client. Consequently, a mobile agent client needs only to use the *MobileConsumer* object in two predefined states: before the migration, and right after the migration.

Two public methods are provided for this purpose:
```
NotifyPreMigration()
NotifyNewLocation(...)
```

The client uses the first function just before migrating to a new location, and the second is activated immediately after arriving at the new location. Ideally, these functions are implemented in callback functions that are activated just before and after migration (by the agent's toolkit execution environment). Such a feature is common in most mobile agent toolkits. The following code snippet demonstrates the use of *MobileConsumer* and other Elvin classes in a basic scenario, in which a mobile agent subscribes for notifications:

```
MobileConsumer mc =
  new MobileConsumer(ElsvinServerURL);

public void onCreation(Object itin) / init(Object[] crea-
tionArgs){
    Subscription sub = new Subscription(strSubscription);
    // NotificationHandler → class to handle
    // notification events
    NotificationHandler nh = new NotificationHandler();
    sub.addNotificationListener(nh);
    mc.addSubscription(sub);
}

public void onDispatching(MobilityEvent m) / beforeMove(){
    mc.notifyPreMigration();
}

public void onArrival(MobilityEvent e) / afterMove(){
    NotificationHandler nh = new NotificationHandler();
    mc.notifyNewLocation(nh, strSubscription);
}
```

The '/' separates the different names in the Aglet and Grasshopper toolkits for callback methods of similar purpose.

4   Experimental Evaluation

4.1   Communication between Mobile Agents of Different Toolkits via Elvin

The current limitation on various mobile agents communication mechanisms is their inability to perform outside the agent's toolkit environment. As previously described, implementing the *MobileConsumer* class in the Elvin Client Library enables easy integration of Elvin Client on different mobile agent platforms. Consequently, different vendors' mobile agents can communicate (peer to peer), share knowledge and receive broadcasted notificaions, all with the use of Elvin.

The following experiment examined the capability to perform communication via Elvin by migrating mobile agents. The communication was performed between agents running on two different platforms: Grasshopper and Aglets. The architecture consisted of four Grasshopper agencies and four Aglet servers representing eight different hosts. Two mobile agents, one for each toolkit, were migrating between these hosts (Grasshopper agents to Grasshopper agencies and Aglets to Aglet servers). The mobile agents were listening and sending Elvin notifications to each other, and to a static service called *Simulation Monitor*, which was also receiving Elvin notifications.

The *Simulation Monitor*'s task consisted of obtaining the state of the experiment at a given time, in terms of the agents' locations and messages sent and received by those agents. This information could then be visually expressed and verified against the expected results.

An Elvin Server process was also running to facilitate the communication. The Elvin Server conducted all communications between the agents themselves and the monitor service. Elvin does not restrict the amount of subscriptions applications can have, or the amount of events they produce.

As a result of the messages exchanged via Elvin, the *Simulation Monitor* is always aware of the current locations of the agents, as well as to the messages received by them (the monitor can also obtain the messages sent between the agents by simply subscribing to them). However, in this experiment, the monitor serves as a control unit to provide us information on the agents' actual capabilities of communicating and receiving messages.

Figure 2 (A, B and C) illustrates the basic communication scenarios that together formed the whole process in the experiment. In Figure 2A, at time t1, the agents and *Monitor* service subscribe for events. Then at time t2, the agents activate the `Noti-fyPreMigration()` functionality. On arrival to a new location (Figure 2B), agents activate the `NotifyNewLocation()` method call (at time t3). At time t4, the agents send Elvin notifications - publishing their arrival (for the monitor) and sending Hello messages to each other.

In Figure 2C, agents and the monitor accept Elvin notifications (time t5). Upon receiving a peer notification, an agent sends an Elvin message to the monitor (time t6).

Successful results of the experiment have proven the ability of Elvin to serve as a communication mechanism between mobile agents that perform migration, independent of platform considerations.

4.2 Measuring Message Delivery

Most Elvin related procedures are activated just before or after migration. We conducted performance measurements of the total time of Elvin related procedures vs.

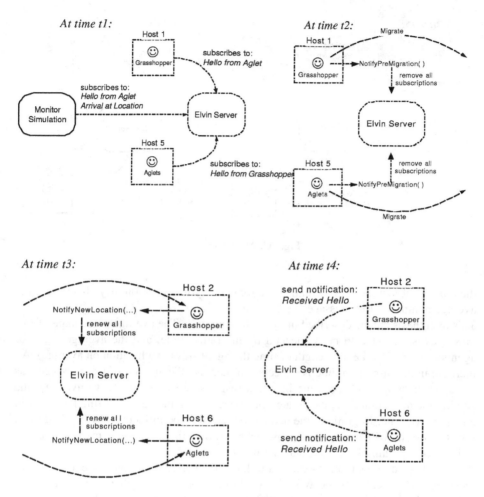

Fig. 2. Figure 2 (A and B). At time t1, t2, t3 and t4. (t1<t2<t3<t4<t5<t6<t7)

the total time of migration (excluding Elvin procedures) in Grasshopper mobile agents in a single machine. The results of the test suggest that a relatively small amount of time is consumed by Elvin procedures compared with migration time. The average ratio of the time for Elvin procedures to migration time was about 1 to 16. Despite the seemingly good performance of Elvin, the results imply a relatively long duration of migration, which can result in lost messages. Mobile agents are not responsive during migration (transfer of code and state); hence messages that are sent to those agents during that time are lost. A relatively long migration time can mean that considerable amount of messages may be lost during the life-cycle of an agent. Other factors that also affect the delivery of messages are bandwidth and communication latency, and duration of stay of an agent in a location. The greater the bandwidth the less the migration time (i.e. the time an agent spends in migration), and consequently, the fewer

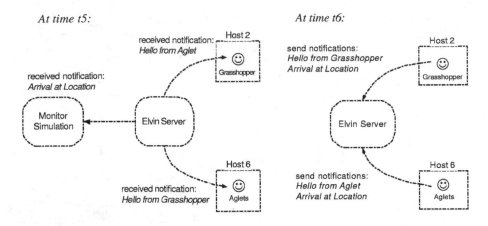

Fig. 2C. At time t5, t6

the number of lost messages. Similarly, a longer stay in a location may also reduce the average number of lost messages.

This hypothesis can be described in the following way. The average percentage of lost messages is expected to be influenced by migration time, and the average delay of agents at a location (i.e. the length of time the agent stays at a location on average). An increase in the migration time is expected to increase the amount of lost messages, as the agent then spends more time in a non-responsive (transit) state. Conversely, the smaller the migration time, the greater the chance that a message will find the agent in a responsive state. Migration time itself is expected to be influenced by bandwidth. A low bandwidth will cause an increase in migration time, as agent migration is the transfer of a stream of code and state between two hosts.

Agents' delay at a location is expected to have a negative effect on the amount of lost messages. The greater the delay in the location, the greater the chance that a message will find the agent in a responsive state. Consequently, on average, fewer lost messages are expected when agents stay longer at a location.

An experiment that examines the effect of various parameters on the amount of lost messages was conducted by simulating mobile agent behaviour.

The experiment consisted of six different hosts located on four physically separated machines, five Aglets mobile agents, an agent *creator* process, and a *monitor* service process. Mobile agents, created by the *creator* process, migrate to other hosts, and send Elvin notifications to each other. In order to produce a close-to-reality simulation, the agents' behaviors are randomized. Each agent obtains a randomly chosen migration path between the hosts and sends arbitrary number of messages to randomly chosen agents in each new host it arrives at. Consequently, each agent operates a different migration path and receives a different total number of messages from different agents. Agents receive messages from other agents by subscribing to Elvin. An agent can utilize content-based addressing, and subscribe to messages with certain attributes (without explicitly specifying the identity of agents it would like to receive messages from), or might use agent identifiers in the subscription to subscribe to messages (intended for itself) from a particular agent (thus emulating point-point message delivery).

The *Monitor* service subscribes to all the messages produced by each agent. Hence, it continuously receives messages that are sent between the agents. The *Monitor* aggregates the total messages sent to each agent, and compares those with the number of messages that were actually received by the agents. A mobile agent internally counts messages it receives and at the end of its migration process sends the count to the *Monitor*, via Elvin.

Two parameters - delay per location, i.e. the time spent by an agent at a location, and (bandwidth) delay in agent migration, i.e. the time spent by the agent in transit – were dynamically configured to measure their effect on the percentage of lost messages.

Each agent would calculate a random location delay time based on an upper bound, for every new location it arrives at. By choosing a higher upper bound for an experimental run, we would expect a greater average delay per location for the agents.

Delay in agent migration was simulated by postponing the notification of an agent's new location to Elvin, thus appearing to the system as a delay in migration.

Communication between agents was performed in a networked environment using a remote Elvin server, denoting a true representation of communication bandwidth.

4.3 Results and Interpretation

An initial set of experiments was conducted, measuring different delays per location while simulating high bandwidth (small delay in migration). The results indicate a clear trend of decrease in lost messages for greater delays (of agents) per location.

Figure 3 shows the effect of the agent's location delay (i.e. the upper bound) on the average percentage of lost messages. The greater the average delay, the fewer messages lost.

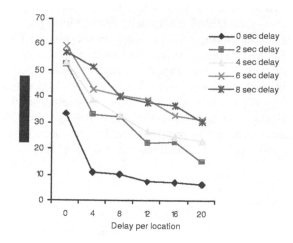

Fig. 3. Effect of different migration delays

A second stage of the experiment added a simulation of low bandwidth to examine the influence of long migration periods on the percentage of lost messages. This operation did not affect, however, the speed of Elvin communication between the agents (since the messages are small). Bandwidth's effect was than examined with added delays in migration time ranging between 0 and 8 seconds. The figure also shows the effect of different migration delays (i.e., the different graphs), against delay per location.

On average, the rate of decrease of lost messages is initially high and gradually declines, often resembling an asymptotic curve. The increase in migration delay leads to an increase in the percentage of lost messages.

5   Conclusions and Future Work

We have proposed a content-based publish subscribe communication genre for mobile agents in heterogeneous multi-agent systems, which is useful in the case of exchanging and disseminating short communications about events. We have demonstrated the applicability of the idea by experimenting with the Elvin system and developing functionality that enables the integration of Elvin with mobile code. Our current implementation suffices when guaranteed point-to-point delivery of messages is not required, e.g. applications where information about events are disseminated and whoever is listening might take advantage of it. On one hand, this is not a problem as point-to-point delivery between specific senders and receivers is not the intention of this genre, and there are other communication genres (e.g., the traditional agent communication language implementations) that handle that. Other event-based systems such as Gryphon [6] have tried to address the message loss issue, with a limited amount of success. It can also be argued that guaranteeing the delivery of messages is not part of the stateless publish subscribe paradigm and should be dealt with in the application layer. We have considered three solutions in [14] for the problem of messages not being received by the agent while in transit.

In conclusion, we mention the DEMS (Distributed Event Messaging System) [4] developed for mobile agent monitoring, control, and communication. DEMS is based on the Java event model of event objects, event listeners, and event sources, and is used with the EMAA toolkit. Our Elvin-based approach can be used for the same purpose – to monitor and control mobile agents – but we leverage on the Elvin publish-subscribe infrastructure, including Elvin's scalable architecture of being able to handle thousands of events efficiently, and the rich subscription language. In addition, our approach is toolkit independent, and in principle, can be programming language independent, as long as there is an Elvin client library for that language.

References

[1]   Dingel, J., Garlan, D., Jha, S., and Notkin, D. Towards a Formal Treatment of Implicit Invocation. *Proceedings of the 1997 Formal Methods Europe Conference*, 1997. Available at http://www-2.cs.cmu.edu/afs/cs/project/able/www/paper_abstracts/implicit-invoc-fme97.html

[2]   Loke, S.W. An Overview of Mobile Agent Technology for Distributed Applications: Possibilities for Future Enterprise Systems. *Informatica: An International Journal of Computing and Informatics*, Vol. 25(2), July 2001, pp 247–260.

[3]   Loke. S.W., Rakotonirainy, A., and Zaslavsky, A. Enabling Awareness in Dynamic Mobile Agent Environments (short paper). *Proceedings of the 15th Symposium on Applied Computing (SAC 2000)*, Como, Italy, March 2000, ACM Press.

[4]   McCormick, J., Chacón, D., McGrath, S. and Stoneking, C. A Distributed Event Messaging System for Mobile Agent Communication, March 2000, TR-01-02. Available at http://www.atl.external.lmco.com/overview/papers/986.pdf

[5]   Segall, B., Arnold, D., Boot, J., Henderson, M., and Phelps, T. Content Based Routing with Elvin4,*Proceedings AUUG2K*, Canberra, Australia, June 2000
       Available at http://elvin.dstc.edu.au/doc/papers/auug2k/auug2k.pdf

[6]   Sumeer Bhola Robert Strom Saurabh Bagchi Yuanyuan Zhao, Joshua Auerbach fsbhola, robstrom, sbagchi, yuanyuan, Exactly-once Delivery in a Content-based Publish-Subscribe System, IBM T.J. Watson Research Center

[7]   Sun Microsystems. *Java Message Service*, November 1999.

[8]   Oracle Message Broker 1.0, Datasheet October 1999

[9]   M. K. Aguilera, R. E. Strom, D. C. Sturman, M. Astley, and T. D. Chandra, Matching Events in a Content-Based Subscription Systems, *Proc.18th ACM Symp. Principles of Distributed Computing (PODC '99), 1999*.

[10]   F. Fabret et al., Filtering Algorithms and Implementation for Very Fast Publish /Subscribe Systems, *SIGMOD Conf., 2001*.

[11]   Labrou, Y.; Finin, T.; and Peng, Y. 1999. The interoperability problem: Bringing together mobile agents and agent communication languages. In Ralph Sprague, J., ed., *Proceedings of the 32nd Hawaii International Conference on System Sciences*. Maui, Hawaii: IEEE Computer Society.

[12]   IBM MQSeries online overview and documentation
       http://www-3.ibm.com/software/integration/mqfamily/

[13]   BEA MessageQ online overview and documentation
       http://edocs.bea.com/tuxedo/msgq/

[14]   Padovitz A., Zaslavsky A, Loke S.W. Awareness and Agility for Autonomic Distributed Systems: Platform-Independent Publish-Subscribe Event-Based Communication with Mobile Agents. Accepted for publication in the *1ˢᵗ International Workshop on Autonomic Computing Systems*, to be held at DEXA 2003.

Multiagent Matching Algorithms with and without Coach

Frieder Stolzenburg[1], Jan Murray[2*], and Karsten Sturm[2]

[1] Hochschule Harz (University of Applied Studies and Research), Automation and Computer Sciences Department, Friedrichstr. 57–59, D–38855 Wernigerode, GERMANY, fstolzenburg@hs-harz.de
[2] Universität Koblenz-Landau, Campus Koblenz, Computer Science Department, Artificial Intelligence Research Group, Universitätsstr. 1, D–56070 Koblenz, GERMANY, {murray,schlumpf}@uni-koblenz.de

Abstract. A matching is a (one-to-one) mapping between two sets, satisfying some given constraints. In a multiagent scenario, i.e. in a setting where at least one of the sets corresponds to a group of agents, a number of interesting facets are added to this general matching problem. Therefore, in this paper, we discuss several different matching criteria, where preference between elements is based on their distance (not on rankings), and state their relationship to well-known criteria, e.g. Pareto efficiency. We also introduce algorithms for computing matchings. The first one (*LocalMatch*), a decentralized algorithm, requires only communication between pairs of agents. The second algorithm (*GlobalMatch*) with a central control agent, called coach, computes a globally maximal matching, i.e., where the maximal distance in the matching is minimized not only for the whole set of elements, but also for each submatching, in $O(n^{2.5} \log n)$ time. Especially this kind of matching has applications in multiagent systems for solving transportation problems, coordination of rescue robots, and marking in (simulated) robotic soccer, which is addressed in this paper.

Introduction

A problem that is frequently encountered in computer science and other contexts is to find a mapping of the elements of one set to the elements of another one satisfying some given constraints. These *matching problems* have been studied extensively, and a number of matching algorithms for different needs have been proposed throughout the years, e.g. for the well-known *stable marriage problem* [4] which finds matchings between two sets based on preference lists or rankings. Many different real-world matching tasks such as marking in (simulated) robotic soccer, public transportation problems etc. can be seen as instances of theoretical matching problems.

---

* This research is partially supported by the grant *Fu-263/8-1* from the German research foundation *DFG*.

M. Schillo et al. (Eds.): MATES 2003, LNAI 2831, pp. 192–204, 2003.

In a multiagent scenario, i.e. in a setting where at least one of the matching sets represents a group of autonomous agents, a number of interesting facets are added to the general matching problem. First of all, the matching process may be centralized or decentralized. In the former case, one distinguished agent, called *coach*, calculates a matching for the whole group and then informs the other agents of the generated matching. Alternatively, a matching can be computed in a decentralized (or local) way, if all agents participate actively in the process. In this case, an agent communicates with some or all of its mates to calculate an appropriate matching. Both, the centralized and the decentralized methods have advantages and drawbacks. A central control instance may always be a bottleneck and a potential point of failure in a system. A decentralized approach, however, may be infeasible because of time constraints or high communication costs.

Another interesting scenario arises, if *both* matching sets represent groups of agents, that do not necessarily have the same interests or preferences for a matching. Such a scenario may lead to a variety of the stable marriage problem [4], as a solution that satisfies the rankings of the members of both groups as good as possible has to be found.

However, in this paper we concentrate on settings where one matching set consists of agents and the other represents passive entities (which may also be agents, that are not actively participating in the matching process). Here, we examine matchings that are based upon distances in $\mathbb{R}^d$, especially $\mathbb{R}^2$, as distance-based matching problems frequently arise in real-world applications. Therefore, in Sect. 1 three possible application scenarios are presented, namely robotic soccer (RoboCup), public transportation problems, and rescue actions in a disaster area.

Section 2 presents various criteria for computing (distance-based) matchings and examines the relations among them. After that, algorithms for decentralized matching and globally maximal matchings (where the maximal distance in the matching is minimized not only for the whole set of elements, but also for each submatching) are given. The decentralized algorithm (Sect. 3) determines a possibly partial matching between two sets, which locally satisfies one of the matching criteria. This algorithm only requires communication among pairs of agents. The algorithm for computing a globally maximal matching between two sets by means of the coach agent (Sect. 4) extends the one presented in [3].

One of the matching algorithms has been implemented in the RoboLog Koblenz simulated soccer team. It is an algorithm for computing a (ranking-based) stable marriage [6,9] (also called globally minimal matching here), by making use of the coach agent that computes matchings in order to optimize opponent marking. Section 5 finishes the paper with some concluding remarks.

1 Application Scenarios

1.1 RoboCup

The RoboCup Initiative [7] aims at fostering research in robotics, artificial intelligence, and multiagent-systems. As a sample domain *robotic soccer* has been chosen, because soccer combines many interesting problems, e.g. dealing with uncertain and incomplete information, cooperation and coordination in a team of autonomous agents, or planning and acting in a highly dynamic environment.

Annual world competitions and a number of local events provide benchmarks and opportunity to present results of current research. The RoboCup is divided into different leagues, which focus on different research aspects. One of those leagues is the *Simulation League*, which does not deal with real robots. As the software agents in this league are not hampered by any of the mechanical problems of real robots, research focuses on the aspects of situated multiagent-systems like team work, learning, opponent modeling and similar topics.

In the simulation league two teams of 11 autonomous agents compete in a simulated soccer match. The two dimensional, discrete-time simulation is carried out in a client/server style by the *RoboCup Soccer Simulator* (or *Soccer Server* for short) [2]. The Soccer Server maintains a model of the world containing the positions of all objects on the field, as well as additional information about them, e.g. the velocities of moving objects or the remaining stamina of all players. In each simulation step clients may send *one* command for moving or manipulating the ball, e.g. *dash*, *kick* or *turn*, and several minor commands to the server. The effects of these commands are taken into account by the simulator when the world model is updated for the next step. Sensory input simulating a vision system is sent to the agents at regular intervals. This input contains noisy data about the objects in an agent's view range, as well as information about its bodily state. Three different kinds of agents can be distinguished, the *fielders*, the *goalie*, and the *(online) coach*. The fielders and the goalie form the actual team. They are almost identical in the way they perceive the environment and the actions they can execute, but the goalie has the additional ability to pick up the ball. With the help of different *player types* the agents' capabilities are parameterized, e.g. the maximum strength of a kick or the rate of recovery may vary.

The coach agent, however, is different. It gets global and noiseless information from the Soccer Server about the position and speed of all players and the ball. But the coach cannot physically interact with its environment. It can only support its team by giving advice or information to its players. To this end the coach sends messages in the special language *Clang* [2] to the players. To prevent the coach from controlling its team in a (too) centralized fashion its messages reach the players with a substantial delay if the ball is in play. In addition to that, the number of messages a coach can send during the game is limited.

1.2   Public Transportation

Consider a taxi service in a big city. At a given time the cars are spread throughout the city. From various spots in the city customers call the headquarters to order a taxi. The headquarters then have to assign each free car to a waiting customer in such a way that the customers are satisfied with the service. Clearly this is a setting in which a centralized matching procedure should be preferred because of the time bounds. A decentralized matching requires the taxi drivers to first spread the available information among themselves and then find a matching, which usually takes a substantially longer time than the centralized approach.

1.3   The Rescue Scenario

In the unfortunate event of a major disaster (e.g. an earthquake) extensive rescue actions have to be taken as soon as possible. The disaster area has to be searched, injured or buried people must be found and saved, fires have to be extinguished. One severe problem is that the disaster area still holds lots of dangers for human rescue squads, so having support from autonomous robots is strongly desired.

The tasks of robots in this scenario includes exploring buildings, finding buried or injured persons to establish contact to them and provide information to the human rescue forces. While this is a task that is usually controlled from a central headquarters, it may very well be that the communication lines break down, so that the headquarters are out of reach. But (a subset of) the rescue robots may still be reachable by radio. As time is of utmost importance in such a rescue scenario, it would be desirable, that the robots are able to coordinate and go on with their exploration tasks until the connection to the headquarters is re-established. Therefore they must be able to find a mapping between robots and target locations in a decentralized way.

2   The Matching Problem

Let us now introduce some formal notation and formalism for the matching problem. The most interesting case in our context is maximal matching, where the maximal distance is minimized, because this is best-suited for the application scenarios just mentioned. But beforehand, we have to introduce the concept of matching in general (Def. 1) and optimality criteria for them (Def. 2 and 3).

Definition 1 (Matching). *Let* $P = \{p_1, \dots, p_{n_1}\}$ *and* $Q = \{q_1, \dots, q_{n_2}\}$ *be two sets of agent positions in* $\mathbb{R}^d$. *A* partial matching *M is a set of edges between P and Q, such that each vertex from P or Q has at most one edge incident in M. If M is of maximal cardinality, it is called* complete matching *or just* matching *for short.*

Usually, P and Q have the same cardinality n (i.e. $n_1 = n_2 = n$), and the most interesting case is where the agent positions are points in the plane (i.e. $d = 2$). In our context, P represents positions of agents that each have to reach one of the positions in Q as quickly as possible. As distance $d(p, q)$ between two points $p \in P$ and $q \in Q$, we simply take their Euclidean distance (i.e. the L_2 norm). We also make use of the following notation: if M is a matching with $(p, q) \in M$, then we write $d_M(p)$ for $d(p, q)$. A well-known optimality criterion for matchings is stability [4,5], which is defined next.

Definition 2 (Stable matching). *A matching M between P and Q is stable iff for all pairs* $(p_i, q_i) \in M$ *and* $(p_j, q_j) \in M$ *(with* $i \neq j$*), we have* $d(p_i, q_j) \geq$

$\min(d(p_i, q_i), d(p_j, q_j))$, *i.e., there is no pair* $(p_i, q_j) \notin M$ *of agents where both agents prefer each other more than their current partners. Therefore,* M *is also called a* stable marriage *(in this context with distance-based ranking).*

But the stability of a matching is usually not enough for real world applications. Some other kind of optimality criterion is needed. In Fig. 1 (a), for example, the stable (distance-based) matching is indicated with dashed lines. But in most applications the solution indicated by the solid lines would be preferred, because the sum of lengths (5 vs. 7) and the maximal distance (3 vs. 6) is better. Note that, if we just consider rankings and not the concrete distances, then both solutions in Fig. 1 (a) are stable and even ranking-optimal according to [5], where the rankings have to be summed up as in the Borda voting protocol [8]. Let us now introduce other interesting properties of rankings.

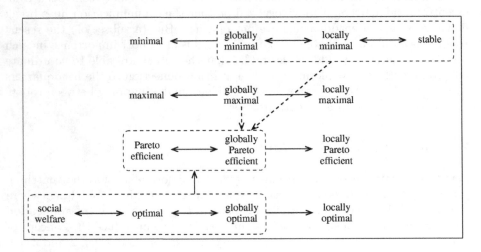

Fig. 1. Matching (counter)examples. Boxes denote elements of P, circles stand for elements of Q. Only relevant properties of the solutions are given. The respective distances are annotated at the connecting edges. Different line styles (solid, dashed, or dotted) indicate different matchings whose properties are summarized. Dash-dot lines count for both the dashed and dotted solutions.

Definition 3. *A matching* M *between* P *and* Q *is*

1. minimal *iff* $\min_p d_M(p) \leq \min_p d_{M'}(p)$, *i.e., the minimal distance is minimized,*
2. maximal *iff* $\max_p d_M(p) \leq \max_p d_{M'}(p)$, *i.e., the maximal distance is minimized,*
3. Pareto efficient *iff* $d_{M'}(p_1) < d_M(p_1)$ *for some* $p_1 \in P$ *implies* $d_{M'}(p_2) > d_M(p_2)$ *for some* $p_2 \in P$, *i.e., nobody can be better off unless at least another one is worse off, and*

4. optimal iff $\sum_p d_M(p) \leq \sum_p d_{M'}(p)$, i.e., the sum of distances is minimized,

for all matchings M' between P and Q. Note that P and Q have to be restricted to the respective elements occurring in M.

A maximal matching is also called *bottleneck matching* [3], and an optimal matching clearly optimizes the *social welfare*. Pareto efficiency is a well-known property studied in competitive multiagent systems [8]. Unfortunately, all these properties are different, as Figures 1 (a) and 1 (b) demonstrate.

For all these settings, there are many known algorithms in the literature. The optimal solution among the stable (ranking-based) matchings can be found in $O(n^4)$ time [5]. [1] provides an $O(n^{2+\epsilon})$ algorithm for the optimal matching problem, which is called minimum-weight bipartite Euclidean matching there. Bottleneck matching is considered in [3], which presents an algorithm in $O(n^{1.5} \log n)$ time.

The problem, however, is that all these algorithms need central control or negotiation among more than two agents. What happens if we allow only communication and exchange of partners among at most two agents? — This leads us to the following definition, that gives us stronger versions of the properties from Def. 5 (global matchings), or allows us to restrict attention to submatchings only (pairs of agents in local matchings).

Definition 4. *Let M be a matching between P and Q, and $\mathcal{P}$ be one of the properties from Def. 3. Then, we define:*

1. *M globally satisfies $\mathcal{P}$ iff $\mathcal{P}$ holds for all submatchings $M' \subseteq M$, and*
2. *M locally satisfies $\mathcal{P}$ iff $\mathcal{P}$ holds for all submatchings $M' \subseteq M$ with $|M'| = 2$, i.e. for all subsets of cardinality 2.*

Clearly, global properties imply the simple properties from Def. 3 and their local versions. But local properties, in general, do not imply the respective (simple) property, as Figures 1 (c) and 1 (d) demonstrate. The following theorem states some relationships among the properties. Fig. 2 summarizes the relationships among the properties.

Theorem 1. *A matching M is Pareto efficient iff it is globally Pareto efficient. It is optimal iff it is globally optimal. If a matching M is optimal, then it is also Pareto efficient, but not vice versa.*

Proof: We only address the last part of the theorem here, by proving its contraposition. Thus, if M is not Pareto efficient, there exists another matching M' such that $d_{M'}(p_1) < d_M(p_1)$ for some $p_1 \in P$ and $d_{M'}(p_2) \leq d_M(p_2)$ for all $p_2 \in P$. But this implies immediately $\sum_p d_{M'}(p) < \sum_p d_M(p)$. Hence, M cannot be optimal.

To see that the converse does not hold (i.e., Pareto efficiency does not imply optimality), look at Fig. 1 (a). The dashed solution is Pareto efficient, but not optimal. ∎

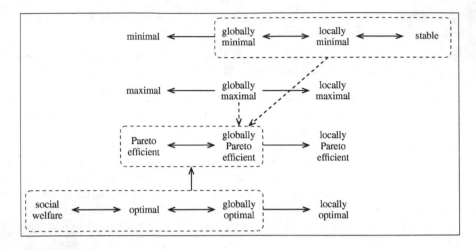

Fig. 2. Implication graph for matching properties. Solid arrows indicate (bi)implications. For dashed arrows, the condition that all distances are different is additionally required. Equivalent concepts are comprised in dashed boxes.

3 Decentralized Matching

In this section we provide a decentralized algorithm *LocalMatch* for calculating local matchings. The algorithm is able to deal with partial matchings and requires only communication between pairs of agents. For this, we first have to reformulate the local matching definitions from Def. 4 for use in the pairwise algorithm.

Definition 5. *Let* $M = \{(p_1, q_1), \ldots, (p_n, q_n)\}$ *be a matching between* P *and* Q. *Then, a pair* $(p_i, q_j) \notin M$, *but* $(p_i, q_i) \in M$ *and* $(p_j, q_j) \in M$, *is called*

1. *locally minimal iff* $\min(d(p_i, q_j), d(p_j, q_i)) \geq \min(d(p_i, q_i), d(p_j, q_j))$,
2. *locally maximal iff* $\max(d(p_i, q_j), d(p_j, q_i)) \geq \max(d(p_i, q_i), d(p_j, q_j))$,
3. *locally Pareto efficient iff* $d(p_i, q_j) > d(p_i, q_i)$ *or* $d(p_j, q_i) > d(p_j, q_j)$, *or* $d(p_i, q_j) = d(p_i, q_i)$ *and* $d(p_j, q_i) = d(p_j, q_j)$, *and*
4. *locally optimal iff* $d(p_i, q_j) + d(p_j, q_i)) \geq d(p_i, q_i) + d(p_j, q_j)$.

Alg. 1 states the algorithm for local matching in pseudo-code. We now explain some new notation used in it. A vertex $v \in P \cup Q$ incident with an edge in the (possibly partial) matching M is called *matched*. Otherwise, it is called *exposed*. Following the lines of [3], we define:

Definition 6. *A path* $\pi = (v_1, \ldots, v_k)$ *is a sequence of positions in* $P \cup Q$. *It is identified with its set of edges* $\{(v_1, v_2), (v_2, v_3), \ldots, (v_{k-1}, v_k)\}$. π *is called an* alternating path *iff for* $1 \leq i < k$, *we have* $v_i \in P$ *iff* $v_{i+1} \in Q$, *and, for any two subsequent edges* (v_{j-1}, v_j) *and* (v_j, v_{j+1}) *in* π, *for* $1 < j < k$, *it holds* $(v_{j-1}, v_j) \in M$ *iff* $(v_j, v_{j+1}) \notin M$. *(In this context, an edge* (q, p) *with* $q \in Q$ *and* $p \in P$ *has to be read as* (p, q).) π *is called an* augmenting path *iff it is* *alternating and v_1 is an exposed vertex in P and v_k is an exposed vertex in Q. Finally, we define $M \oplus \pi = (M \backslash \pi) \cup (\pi \backslash M)$, i.e. as symmetric difference between sets of edges.*

Intuitively the algorithm works as follows: An agent $p_i \in P$ selects a partner from $q_j \in Q$ if it is free (i.e. not matched), preferring closer ones. If p_i already has a partner q_i, but q_j is closer (and not matched so far), then p_i will take q_j instead of q_i. If q_j is already matched and one of the properties $\mathcal{P}$ from Def. 5 is not satisfied, the relevant partners are swapped (in the procedure *Swap*). This can be realized by communication among pairs of agents. The algorithm exploits the following theorem.

Theorem 2. *A matching M is locally minimal, locally optimal, locally Pareto efficient, or locally optimal, respectively, (according to Def. 4) iff the respective property holds for all pairs $(p_i, q_j) \notin M$ (according to Def. 5).*

---

funct *LocalMatch*(P, Q)
  begin
    $M \leftarrow \emptyset$
    while $\mathcal{P}(M) \implies Partial(M)$ **do**
        Swap(p_i, q_j) **where** $p_i \in P, q_j \in Q$
    od
    return(M)
  end

proc *Swap*(p_i, q_j)
  begin
    if $(p_i, q_j) \in M$ **then** *exit* **fi**
    if *Exposed*(p_i)
      then if *Exposed*(q_j) **then** $M \leftarrow M \oplus (p_i, q_j)$
                else let $(p_j, q_j) \in M$
                    if $d(p_i, q_j) < d(p_j, q_j)$ **then** $M \leftarrow M \oplus (p_i, q_j, p_j)$ **fi**
        fi
      else let $(p_i, q_i) \in M$
        if *Exposed*(q_j) **then if** $d(p_i, q_j) < d(p_i, q_i)$ **then** $M \leftarrow M \oplus (q_j, p_i, q_i)$ **fi**
                        else let $(p_j, q_j) \in M$
                            if $\neg \mathcal{P}(p_i, q_j)$ **then** $M \leftarrow M \oplus (p_i, q_j, p_j, q_i, p_i)$ **fi**
        fi
    fi
  end

Algorithm 1: Pseudo-code for algorithm *LocalMatch* for local matching.

In the procedure *LocalMatch*, the test $\mathcal{P}(M)$ means, that all $(p_i, q_j) \notin M$ satisfy $\mathcal{P}$. Note that, for ranking-based preference relations (stability), *LocalMatch* might not always terminate. The example from Fig. 1 (a) would oscillate between both solutions. But for distance-based preference, we have the following theorem:

Theorem 3 (Termination). *The procedure LocalMatch from Alg. 1 terminates for every property $\mathcal{P}$ from Def. 5.*

Proof: We first consider the properties local minimality and local maximality. For this, let L be the list of distances $d(p, q)$ for all $(p, q) \in M$, sorted in increasing order or decreasing order, respectively. The *lexicographic ordering* $\ll$ for lists $L = \{l_1, \ldots, l_n\}$ and $L' = \{l'_1, \ldots, l'_n\}$ is defined as follows: $L \ll L'$ iff for all j such that $l_j > l'_j$ there exists $i < j$ (with $1 \leq i, j \leq n$) such that $l_i < l'_i$. Since the length of the lists is constantly n, and there are only finitely many different lengths l that are possible, $\ll$ is a well-ordering. If now L is a result of one application of the *Swap* procedure with property $\mathcal{P}$ being one of locally minimal (i.e. stable) or locally maximal, respectively, and $L' \neq L$ is the list before this application, then it must be $L \ll L'$. Hence the procedure will terminate.

For Pareto efficiency termination is clear, because at least one distance $d_M(p)$ is decreased for one $p \in P$ in each step, while the others remain the same. If $\mathcal{P}$ is local optimality, then simply the sum of lengths decreases monotonically.   ■

Unfortunately, locally maximal and even locally optimal matchings can be infinitely worse than (globally) maximal and optimal ones (and hence it is worthwhile to consider global matching algorithms, see Sect. 4). In order to see this, we consider a regular n-gon ($n \geq 3$) with unit edges. The angle in each corner is then $\varphi = \pi(n-2)/n$. We add now lines of length x in each corner, the length y remains from each side, and z is as shown in Fig. 3. Now, by the intercept theorems, we get:

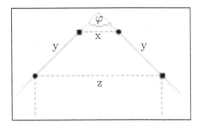

Fig. 3. N-gon example.

$$\sin(\varphi/2) = \frac{z/2}{(1+y)/2} = \frac{x/2}{(1-y)/2}$$

The solution with n times distance x is clearly a maximal and optimal matching. But the solution with n times distance y is locally maximal and locally optimal, if the conditions $z \geq y \geq x$ and $z + x \geq 2y$ hold. If we take $z + x = 2y$ which implies both conditions, we have $y = \sin(\varphi/2)$. But in this case, the ratio between x and y converges to zero:

$$x/y = 1 - y = 1 - \sin(\varphi/2) = 1 - \sin(\pi(1/2 - 1/n)) \xrightarrow[n\to\infty]{} 0$$

4   Globally Maximal Matching

In this section, we will focus on the problem of computing a globally maximal matching. The problem of computing a maximal (or bottleneck) matching has been treated in the literature [3]. However, maximal matchings can often be improved, as Fig. 1 (f) shows, because they are not even locally maximal in general. Since only *global* maximality implies Pareto efficiency, we concentrate on the problem of computing globally maximal matchings. However, this implication is only valid if all possible distances between points of P and Q are different, look at Fig. 1 (e). This is summarized in the following theorem. A similar theorem holds for globally minimal matchings.

Theorem 4. *If M is a globally maximal matching between P and Q, and $d(p, q)$ is different for all $p \in P$ and $q \in Q$, then M is Pareto efficient.*

Alg. 2 shows the procedure for computing locally maximal matchings. It extends and refines the procedure in [3] for computing bottleneck matchings by one additional loop, namely the one in the function *GlobalMatch*. There, we make use of the list L of all pairs $p \in P$ and $q \in Q$, that is sorted by ascending distances $d(p, q)$. Note that, with p_k, q_k, and d_k, we denote the respective components of the k-th element in L. Obviously, L contains n^2 elements.

The function *Bottleneck* with index m computes a maximal matching M for the given point sets P and Q according to the procedure in [3], taking into account only the distances less or equal than d_m. It returns the index $k \leq m$ of the edge with maximal length d_m in the maximal matching M just computed. After that, we consider the submatchings without this maximal element. In this context, we assume that all distances are different, and hence the maximal element is uniquely determined.

The function $Augment_k(\pi)$ returns an augmenting path π if possible, where all distances are smaller than the given bound d_k, starting from the exposed vertices in P, by constructing a layered graph according to [3]. Note that, its good complexity can only be obtained by making use of an abstract data structure $\mathcal{D}_r(Q')$ for a set of objects $Q' \subseteq Q$ and a fixed length r, supporting the operations $neighbor(\mathcal{D}_r(Q'), p)$ (returns an element $q \in Q'$ whose distance from $p \in P$ is at most r) and $delete(\mathcal{D}_r(Q'), q)$ (deletes the object q from Q'). In the Euclidean planar case (i.e. $d = 2$), this can be implemented efficiently by means of unit disks, see [3, Sect. 5]. Exploiting this result, we get the following theorem:

Theorem 5. *The procedure GlobalMatch requires time $O(n^{2.5} \log n)$ for computing a globally maximal matching M between P and Q.*

5   Conclusion

In this paper we presented various types of distance-based matchings for situated multiagent systems. We defined different criteria for determining the quality of such matchings and related them to well-known concepts in multiagent-systems, e.g. Pareto efficiency. Several application scenarios have been given to motivate our work, including public transport, rescue scenarios and robotic soccer.

We described algorithms for calculating local and global matchings in a decentralized and centralized way. As another example for centralized matchings calculated by a special agent, a so-called coach, we described the online coach of the RoboLog Koblenz soccer simulation team, where a ranking-based algorithm

```
funct GlobalMatch (P, Q)                    funct Bottleneck_m(P, Q)
  begin                                       begin
    M ← ∅                                       i ← 0
    m ← n²                                       j ← m
    L ← SortedList(d(p,q))                       while i < j do
          p∈P, q∈Q                                  M ← ∅
    for k ← 1 to n do                              k ← ⌈(i+j)/2⌉
       m ← Bottleneck_m(P, Q)                      while Augment_k(π) do M ← M ⊕ π od
       P ← P\p_m                                   if Partial(M) then i ← k else j ← k fi
       Q ← Q\q_m                                od
       M ← M ⊕ (p_m, q_m)                       return(k)
    od                                        end
    return(M)
  end
```

Algorithm 2: Pseudo-code for globally maximal matching.

for computing stable matchings is already integrated in the marking procedure [9].

With this algorithm, players are assigned to opponents they have to mark during a free kick or kick in. First, sets of players from both teams are selected based on their relevance for the current situation (e.g. distance to the ball and position on the field) and their player types. For a brief discussion of the latter, see the appendix. With those sets, a minimal matching between teammates and opponents is calculated. The players are then told which opponent to mark based on this ranking. Test games revealed that the team performance (measured by goal difference) can be slightly improved by this.

In the near future we plan to implement other methods for calculating matchings between teammates and opponents for marking, as well. We will also examine the relationship of the presented methods for matching and certain kinds of contract nets, namely those which allow a *swap-operator* for agents (see [8]).

References

1. P. K. Agarwal, A. Efrat, and M. Sharir. Vertical decomposition of shallow levels in 3-dimensional arrangements and its applications. *SIAM Journal on Computing*, 29(3):912–953, 1995.
2. M. Chen, K. Dorer, E. Foroughi, F. Heintz, Z. Huang, S. Kapetanakis, K. Kostiadis, J. Kummeneje, J. Murray, I. Noda, O. Obst, P. Riley, T. Steffens, Y. Wang, and X. Yin. *RoboCup Soccer Server*, 2003. Manual for Soccer Server Version 7.07 and later (obtainable from sserver.sf.net).
3. A. Efrat, A. Itai, and M. J. Katz. Geometry helps in bottleneck matching and related problems. *Algorithmica*, 31:1–28, 2001.
4. D. Gale and L. Shapely. College admissions and the stability of marriage. *American Mathematical Monthly*, 1962.
5. R. W. Irving, P. Leather, and D. Gusfield. An efficient algorithm for the "optimal" stable marriage. *Journal of the ACM*, 34(3):532–543, 1987.

6. J. Murray, O. Obst, and F. Stolzenburg. RoboLog Koblenz 2001. In A. Birk, S. Coradeschi, and S. Tadokoro, editors, *RoboCup 2001: Robot Soccer World Cup V*, volume 2377 of *Lecture Notes in Artificial Intelligence*. Springer, Berlin, Heidelberg, New York, 2002. Team description.
7. Official homepage of the RoboCup Federation. http://www.robocup.org/.
8. T. W. Sandholm. Distributed rational decision making. In G. Weiss, editor, *Multi-agent Systems. A Modern Approach to Distributed Artificial Intelligence*, chapter 5, pages 201–258. MIT Press, Cambridge, MA, London, 1999.
9. K. Sturm. Der RoboLog-Coach – Ein Online-Coach für Fußballmannschaften der Simulationsliga der RoboCup-Initiative. Diplomarbeit D 690, Fachbereich Informatik, Universität Koblenz-Landau, 2003.

Appendix: Recognizing Player Types

As has been mentioned above a matching algorithm has been implemented in the RoboLog coach. This coach also has the ability to determine opponent *player types* with an extraordinary reliability [9]. Based on this, players are selected for participation in the actual matching process, which assigns a player to an opponent to be marked. In this section we will briefly describe, how the player types are determined.

In the RoboCup Simulation League the players' abilities to run or handle the ball are the same in terms of *what* a player can do. But with the help of so-called *player types* the abilities are varied slightly. At the beginning of each match the simulator constructs six different player types (so-called *heterogeneous players*) by randomly setting some parameters influencing a player's speed, ball handling, ability to recover, etc. within fixed bounds. The generated player types are made known to all players and the online coaches, who may then substitute default players for heterogeneous ones. Thus one of the problems that must be solved during a simulated soccer match is determining the types of the opponent players, because knowing their player types provides knowledge about their strengths and weaknesses. This task is usually given to the online coach of a team because of its complete and noiseless sensor data.

The coach observes the opponents' positions $\vec{p}_t$ and velocities $\vec{v}_t$. From these values the coach can calculate a player's *player_decay*, i.e. its slow down rate, which depends on the player type. This is done with the help of the following formulæ, which are part of the server's update mechanism. If a player's position and velocity are $\vec{p}_t$ and $\vec{v}_t$, respectively, in simulation cycle t, then the values of $\vec{p}_{t+1}$ and $\vec{v}_{t+1}$ for simulation step $t+1$ are calculated as follows:

$$\vec{v}'_t = \vec{v}_t + \vec{a}_t + \vec{n}_t + \vec{w}_t \tag{1}$$

$$\vec{p}_{t+1} = \vec{p}_t + \vec{v}'_t \tag{2}$$

$$\vec{v}_{t+1} = \vec{v}'_t \cdot player\_decay \tag{3}$$

where the vectors $\vec{a}_t$, $\vec{n}_t$, and $\vec{w}_t$ denote the acceleration, noise, and wind at time t. Note that in the Soccer Server all these measurements are not real physical values but are considered lengths (normalized to one time unit). These vectors are not observable by the coach. From the player's position $\vec{p}_{t+1}$ at time $t+1$, vector $\vec{v}_t'$ can be derived by means of (2). Together with (3) we get:

$$player\_decay = \frac{\|\vec{v_{t+1}}\|}{\|\vec{v}_t'\|} = \frac{\|\vec{v_{t+1}}\|}{\|\vec{p_{t+1}} - \vec{p_t}\|}, \quad \text{if } \|\vec{v}_t'\| \neq 0 \tag{4}$$

At time $t+1$ the coach knows the player's current position and velocity and its position at time t. Thus, the value of *player_decay* can easily be calculated with the help of (4). By comparing this value with the *player_decay* parameter values of the player types, the coach determines a player's type, where a player is accepted, if the difference between the calculated and the exact value is less than 0.005.

With this method implemented in the RoboLog Koblenz online coach [9] we conducted several experiments. We discovered that the above method achieves better results if players run fast. Therefore, our coach only tries to detect the type of a player that has moved more than 10^{-4} m from the previous to the actual simulation step. With this adjusted method our online coach was able to determine opponents' player types of different teams with an average reliability of 99.5 % in several test games.

Improving Evolutionary Learning of Cooperative Behavior by Including Accountability of Strategy Components

Jörg Denzinger and Sean Ennis

Department of Computer Science, University of Calgary, Canada
{denzinge,ennis}@cpsc.ucalgary.ca

Abstract. We present an improvement to evolutionary learning of cooperative behavior which incorporates some accountability measure for strategy components into the evolutionary learning process. Our evolutionary approach is based on evolving sets of prototypical situation-action pairs (strategies) that together, with the nearest-neighbor rule, represent the decision making of our agents. The basic idea of our improvement is to collect data for each pair showing the results of its applications. We then choose those pairs in the parent strategies that had positive results for the construction of new sets of pairs for our strategies. Our experiments within the OLEMAS system show that the incorporation of accountability results in substantial improvements of both on- and off-line learning when compared to the basic evolutionary approach. In nearly all experiments, either the agent teams required less learning time or found better strategies. In many cases both were observed.

1 Introduction

Having the ability to learn is often viewed as a very important feature of an agent in a multi-agent system. Adapting to new (resp. slightly changed) environments, dealing with new agents, or relieving the human developer from having to develop all details of a cooperation concept are just a few of the consequences we hope for when agents are able to learn. Naturally, different agent architectures require different learning methods, but a lot of the research done on learning in multi-agent systems has focused on rather reactive agents. Two general ideas for such learning have surfaced: reinforcement learning (see [11], [10], or [6]) and evolutionary learning.

In this paper, we focus on evolutionary learning of cooperative behavior. Evolutionary learning (EL) concentrates on finding whole strategies (in contrast to the reinforcement approach that focuses on all possible situations and all possible actions in these situations). Working on a pool of strategies, evolutionary techniques are used to generate new strategies (mostly out of the better strategies in the pool) that hopefully combine positive aspects from the parents. Over time, strategies evolve that come progressively closer to achieving the intended behavior (for examples, see [8], [5], or [3]). The evolved strategies are usually

M. Schillo et al. (Eds.): MATES 2003, LNAI 2831, pp. 205–216, 2003.

much more compact than the weight matrices or graphs of reinforcement learning. Due to this, substantially fewer experiences are necessary to evolve working strategies when compared to reinforcement learning (even if we combine the experiences obtained by every strategy tried out in the evolutionary process). On the negative side, so far, even the successful strategies often include elements that are not needed (resp. wrong) and are therefore simply not used in the solution. In addition, since experiences are attributed to whole strategies and not individual actions (or small action sequences) the learning is less focused than it is in reinforcement learning (which sometimes can be a positive asset, but can also hinder the progress of learning).

In this paper, we present an improvement of the evolutionary learning method of [3] and [4] that integrates an accountability aspect to deal with the problem mentioned above, namely statistics about single pairs of situations and actions, into the evolutionary learning process. More precisely, our learning approach is based on prototypical situation-action pairs (SAPs) and the nearest-neighbor rule as the agent architecture. A strategy of an agent is then a set of such prototypical SAPs. In the basic version, the fitness of a strategy is obtained by measuring how near a strategy comes to solving the given problem during simulations of the whole multi-agent system and its environment.

Our improvement idea is to not only compute the fitness of a strategy out of the simulations, but also statistics about the use and consequent success of the SAPs in the strategy. We then use these statistics to influence the application of the genetic operators that generate new strategies. In the basic version of the learning algorithm, after selecting parent strategies based on their fitness (and some random decisions), picking SAPs to either be included or excluded from the new strategy is done purely at random. In our improved version, this picking is now performed based on the statistics about the pairs (and again, some random decisions), thus repeating the selection idea of the strategy level. The general idea we use is that SAPs whose application often resulted in better situations should be selected with a higher probability than pairs that generally did not improve the situation of agent and agent team and the pairs that made the situation worse.

We implemented this improvement into the OLEMAS system (see [4] and [2]). Our experiments in the area of Pursuit Games show that the new version including accountability aspects clearly outperforms the basic version of OLEMAS for almost all game variants and for both usage in off-line and on-line learning. Outperforms in this context means that either less generations of the GA are needed to find a successful strategy (thus also reducing the learning time) or that the found strategies are better than those found by the basic version (i.e. less actions are performed by the agent team until success) or both.

2   Learning with SAPs

In this section, we present the method of evolutionary learning of [3] and [4], as realized in the OLEMAS system (**O**n-**L**ine **E**volution of **M**ulti-**A**gent **S**ystems), that is the basis for our work. We start by presenting the agent architecture used, followed by the GA we use for learning, and finally we briefly discuss the use of this basic learning method for off- and on-line learning.

2.1   Agent Architecture: SAPs and NNR

Very abstractly, an agent $\mathcal{Ag}$ can be described by a triple $\mathcal{Ag} = (Sit, Act, Dat)$, where Sit is the set of situations $\mathcal{Ag}$ can be in, Act is the set of actions $\mathcal{Ag}$ can perform, and Dat is the set of possible values of the internal data areas of $\mathcal{Ag}$. $\mathcal{Ag}$ then realizes a function $f_{\mathcal{Ag}}$: $Sit \times Dat \rightarrow Act$. In reactive agents, the emphasis of $f_{\mathcal{Ag}}$ is mainly on Sit.

In our agent architecture, $f_{\mathcal{Ag}}$ bases its decisions on a set of prototypical situation-action pairs, its strategy, that are part of an area in Dat. As the name suggests, an SAP contains an element of Sit^{1} and an action from Act. For determining what action to perform in a situation s, the agent computes the similarity (resp. distance) of all situations in its strategy and s, and performs the action of the SAP whose situation is most similar to s (i.e. it applies the nearest-neighbor rule, NNR). Naturally, there usually are different possible definitions for similarity. Also, we have to describe situations in such a way that the definition of a sensible similarity measure is possible.

The behavior B of an agent $\mathcal{Ag}$ starting with a situation s_0 can be described as a sequence $B(\mathcal{Ag}, s_0) = s_0, sap_1, s_1, ..., s_{i-1}, sap_i, s_i, ...$, where sap_j is an element of its strategy and the action associated with it leads $\mathcal{Ag}$ from situation s_{j-1} to s_j. Naturally, if there are other agents in the system, then s_j also depends on the actions they perform in s_{j-1}.

2.2   The Basic GA for Learning

Our evolutionary learning method is based on a Genetic Algorithm for sets (since we use sets of SAPs as strategies). This means that for learning we always consider a set of strategies. New strategies are generated out of old strategies by applying so-called Genetic Operators, which in our case are Crossover and Mutation. The initial set of strategies (initial population) is generated randomly (although in [2] we presented a variant that makes use of previous knowledge), i.e. by generating random SAPs.

Crossover requires two parent strategies, $st_1 = \{sap_{11}, ..., sap_{1n}\}$ and $st_2 = \{sap_{21}, ..., sap_{2m}\}$, and generates a new strategy st_{new} by picking randomly the needed number of SAPs out of $st_1 \cup st_2$ (without duplicates). *Mutation* requires only one parent st_1 and in order to generate a st_{new}, it allows for three possibilities, namely deleting a random SAP of st_1, i.e. $st_{new} = st_1 - sap_{1j}, j \in \{1, ..., n\}$, generating a SAP sap randomly and adding it to st_1 (provided that st_1 does not already have the maximal allowed number of SAPs), i.e. $st_{new} = st_1 \cup sap$, or exchanging a SAP in st_1 by a randomly generated one (sap), i.e. $st_{new} = st_1 -$

---

[1] Situations might be extended to also contain data from the current value of Dat of the agent.

$sap_{1j} \cup sap$ (which combines the other two possibilities; again, duplicates are not allowed). We have organized generating new strategies into so-called "generations", i.e. we generate a given number l of new strategies and then form a new generation by deleting the l worst strategies from the old generation and adding to it the l newly generated ones.

The last sentence already referred to another basic requirement of GAs: the ability to measure the quality, or the *fitness*, of the individuals in a population. The fitness is not only needed to delete strategies, it also is a key component in selecting the parent strategies, although it is combined with a random influence. There are many different ways to combine fitness and randomness, and in OLE-MAS we have chosen a variant in which the probability of a strategy for being selected as parent is proportional to its fitness.

For measuring the fitness of an individual strategy (in fact, for the strategies of all agents of a team) we measure the success it produces in every step of its application (for a given limited number of steps, either in the real world or in a simulation of it), except if the strategy is totally successful, in which case the fitness is just the number of steps (length of the action sequence) needed to fulfill the given goal. More precisely, since the success obviously is related to the application, we need a function $\delta : Sit \rightarrow \mathbb{N}$ measuring how far away a situation is from success. Then we take the behavior of the agent $\mathcal{A}g$ employing the strategy from the start situation s_0, i.e. $B(\mathcal{A}g, s_0)$, and sum up $\delta(s_j)$ for all s_j in $B(\mathcal{A}g, s_0)$.

If the agents have to deal with effects out of their control (for example, random effects or other agents that cannot be predicted) then, starting from s_0, different behaviors can be observed in different runs. The fitness is then computed as the sum of the elemental fitnesses generated by each of the observed behaviors in a given number of runs of the strategy.

If we want to learn strategies for several agents, then an individual in our Genetic Algorithm contains an individual strategy for each of the agents. The fitness of an individual is still the summed up $\delta(s_j)$ for all situations in the behavior of one agent, since each s_j is the consequence of the actions of all agents taken in the previous situation.

2.3   Offline and Online Learning

With regard to learning, one very often finds the distinction between on-line and off-line learning with the later meaning that learning and applying the learned knowledge are separated in different phases. In contrast, the former means that the learning, and the application of what is learned are interleaved so that problems like when to learn, or what to do when learning is not finished, have to be solved. For learning cooperative behavior for a team of agents that has to learn to solve a certain problem/task, pure off-line would mean that learning takes place first and then the agent team has to perform a run that solves the task without doing any more learning. Consequently, an on-line learning agent or agent team will also learn during the run. These are only the extremes, however, and a lot of combinations of them are also possible.

Our evolutionary learning, as described in the previous subsection, can be used for both, off- and on-line learning. If the start situation s_0 is the situation the team has to start from when solving the given task, and if the number of steps allowed for the fitness evaluation is the number of steps allowed for the task, then our learning approach can be used for off-line learning. This is to say that at the end of the learning we will have a strategy (for each learning agent) that then will be used for solving the task (see [3]). In [4], we presented a way to use our approach for on-line learning as well by introducing a special action "learn" for the agents. Its application leads to executing our learning GA for a rather small number of steps, starting from a situation that the agent thinks it will be in after executing "learn", and using models of the other agents to predict their behavior. So, in on-line learning the individuals in our Genetic Algorithm contain only the one strategy for the agent executing "learn", even if several agents are doing on-line learning. With regard to learning, every agent "is on its own". As we will see in Section 5, our improvement of the basic GA will improve both the use for off- and on-line learning.

3   Adding Accountability of SAPs

One of the big advantages of evolutionary learning as described in the last section is that it partially avoids having to solve the credit assignment problem (i.e. having to determine how much a particular action contributed to the success of an action sequence, a basic problem in reinforcement learning). Since a fitness is computed for a whole strategy (a posteriori), it is not necessary to develop a sophisticated mechanism for deciding a priori how much a particular action and its immediate outcome will be responsible for the final outcome of an action sequence (although our fitness uses some crude estimation of the success of each action in a sequence to compare strategies that were not totally successful). In the case of off-line learning for several agents, we also do not have to decide which agent contributed how well to the team effort. Unfortunately, this means that very good actions (or good strategies for other agents) can compensate for not-so good ones, as long as we achieve success in the end. Even worse, with our particular agent architecture we can have useless SAPs in very successful strategies and their uselessness is not detected due to the fact that they were never responsible for an action taken.

Our idea for improving our evolutionary approach is to add some accountability to the prototypical SAPs of a strategy (not to all possible SAPs) and to use this accountability to influence the Genetic Operators. This influence will be in such a way that "bad" or useless SAPs are less likely to appear in offspring of strategies (only less likely, because together with another set of SAPs they might be valuable; see our experimental evaluation in Section 5 that compares this approach to an approach were the SAP selection is purely based on the observed quality of the SAPs). Each action occurring in the observed behavior of an agent will provide feedback, and this feedback will be used to determine good, indifferent, bad, and unused SAPs. This idea combines the a posteriori evaluation of whole strategies, provided by the basic evolutionary learning, with the advantage of accountability of strategy parts.

More precisely, we extend a SAP in a strategy by a so-called statistic-tuple stat(sap) = (use-nr, good, bad, indiff). Whenever a new strategy st is created, the statistic-tuples of all its SAPs $\{sap_1^{st},..., sap_n^{st}\}$ are initialized to $(0,0,0,0)$. For each run of st as agent $\mathcal{A}g$ (starting with a situation s_0), we use the resulting behavior $B(\mathcal{A}g,s_0) = s_0,sap_1,s_1,...,s_{i-1},sap_i, s_i$ to update the statistic-tuples in st as follows:

For all s_{k-1},sap_k,s_k in $B(\mathcal{A}g,s_0)$, $1 \leq k \leq i$:

$$stat(sap_j^{st}) = \begin{cases} stat(sap_j^{st}), \text{if } sap_j^{st} \neq sap_k \\ (\text{use-nr} + 1, \text{good} + 1, \text{bad}, \text{indiff}), \text{if } \delta(s_{k-1}) > \delta(s_k) \\ (\text{use-nr} + 1, \text{good}, \text{bad}, \text{indiff} + 1), \text{if } \delta(s_{k-1}) = \delta(s_k) \\ (\text{use-nr} + 1, \text{good}, \text{bad} + 1, \text{indiff}), \text{if } \delta(s_{k-1}) < \delta(s_k) \end{cases}$$

for all $j \in \{1, ..., n\}$. Naturally, the last 3 cases require that $sap_j^{st} = sap_k$. Note that we have chosen to reuse the δ-function we already use in the fitness function. Obviously, other functions can also be used. This is also the case for several other decisions we already have made and will make in the following. So, we judge the impact that each use of a SAP has, but we only use three categories, namely positive, negative, and indifferent impact. Note that, by using δ, the impact of a SAP is measured relative to the decisions the other agents did make, since they also influence what the successor situation of a situation is, but for learning of cooperative behavior, this should obviously be the case!

The statistic-tuples of SAPs are then used to modify our Genetic Operators. For Crossover, we have strategies $st_1 = \{sap_{11},..., sap_{1n}\}$ and $st_2 = \{sap_{21},...,sap_{2m}\}$. We take $st_1 \cup st_2$ and divide its SAPs into three pools:

good_pool = $\{sap \in st_1 \cup st_2 \mid$ use-nr > 0 and good - bad $>$ good_min$\}$
indiff_pool = $\{sap \in st_1 \cup st_2 \mid$ use-nr > 0
            and good_min $\geq$ good - bad $\geq$ bad_max$\}$
bad_pool = $\{sap \in st_1 \cup st_2 \mid$ use-nr $= 0$ or use-nr > 0
            and bad_max $>$ good - bad$\}$

Here, good_min and bad_max are parameters that allow us better control over which SAPs go into which pool. One obvious value for both of them is 0, which results in having in good_pool all SAPs that more often resulted in better situations than worse. Then indiff_pool is usually rather small. By having good_min $>$ 0 and bad_max $<$ 0, we can broaden indiff_pool a little bit and make it tougher to get into good_pool. The same three pools can also be defined for only one strategy, which we have in case of Mutation.

For generating a new strategy st by Crossover, we use the pools as follows. We use two parameters p_{good} and p_{indiff}, $p_{good} + p_{indiff} \leq 1$, that define the percentages for the SAPs taken from the pools. If st is supposed to have q SAPs, then we randomly select

  − $\lceil p_{good} \times q \rceil$ SAPs out of good_pool,

- $\lceil p_{indiff} \times q \rceil$ SAPs out of good_pool $\cup$ indiff_pool, and
- $q - \lceil p_{good} \times q \rceil$ - $\lceil p_{indiff} \times q \rceil$ SAPs out of good_pool $\cup$ indiff_pool $\cup$ bad_pool.

This means that for each of the q SAPs needed, SAPs in good_pool have a chance to be selected, while SAPs in the other pools are eligible for less "positions" in the new strategy. Note that in the case of a pool containing less SAPs than needed, all SAPs of this pool are selected and the remaining allotment for this pool will be selected out of the next lower pool.

The intent of having Mutation is to add new SAPs to the gene pool (i.e. the SAPs occurring in any strategy of the population). Therefore accountability aspects are not so important for Mutation. So, we still use the three kinds of Mutation we discussed in Section 2.2, but we can also add variants of the delete and exchange Mutations, in which we delete/exchange not a random SAP, but a random SAP of bad_pool.

After having seen the usage of statistic-tuples, one might ask if it is really necessary to initialize the tuples for the SAPs in a new strategy to a zero-vector. Why not inherit the statistics from the parent? Due to using the nearest-neighbor rule for action selection, the statistic-tuples have a certain dependency on the other SAPs in a strategy, especially with respect to the bad and indiff numbers in the tuple. If a particular SAP is put into a new strategy, in situations it previously was responsible for the action taken now another SAP might become responsible for the action (if its situation is more similar). In addition, if we learn strategies for several agents in one individual, the statistic tuples reflect accountability of actions with respect to the actions of the other agents (as already mentioned). In a new individual, some of the other agents will act differently. Therefore SAPs should not inherit their statistics from their parents.

4   Pursuit Games and the OLEMAS System

In order to test our improvement of evolutionary learning with accountability of SAPs, we integrated our approach into the OLEMAS system (see [4] and [2]). OLEMAS presents many variants of Pursuit Games as an application domain.

4.1   Pursuit Games

Pursuit Games were first introduced in multi-agent systems in [1]. Since then, many variants of them have been introduced, see [3] for a list of features that can be varied. The general idea of a Pursuit Game is to have a group of hunter agents and one or several prey agents that move on a playing field consisting of connected grids. The goal of the game is to have the hunters catch the prey within a given limit of so-called turns, where the "catch" can be defined in several ways (see Section 5).

Due to the many features that can be varied –like number of agents involved, obstacles, possible actions agents can take, their size, shape and speed, many possible random influences– very different game variants can be defined, some favoring the hunters, some the prey. Developing good strategies for the hunter agents that achieve the necessary cooperative behavior to win the game, is, even for a single variant, not always easy. However, given the enormous number of possible variants, letting the hunters learn their strategies becomes a must.

4.2 Instantiating Our Approach for OLEMAS

In OLEMAS, a situation is described by a vector providing the coordinates of all visible agents relative to the agent for which the situation is described, in a fixed agent order. In addition, for each of these agents we also provide in the vector their type and orientation. The set of actions of an agent can contain, in addition to moves in the different directions and staying put, turns and for on-line learning agents "learn". Associated with each action of an agent is the number of turns this agent needs to perform the action.

For measuring the similarity of two situations, we sum up the squares of the difference in numbers of the corresponding coordinate fields and the orientation fields of the two situation vectors. The function δ, that is used for both, fitness computation and updating the statistic-tuples, is the sum of the Manhattan distances between each hunter agent and each prey agent.

5 Experimental Evaluation

We have performed experimental series with a number of variants of Pursuits Games to evaluate the general usefulness of our improvement. Due to lack of space, we cannot present all experiments and therefore selected the most different ones with regard to the different features. We tested both the on- and off-line versions of OLEMAS. In our experiments, we examined the (average) time needed for learning and the quality of the found solution. The later is expressed by the (average) number of steps (turns) needed by the hunter agents to catch the prey and by the success rate, i.e. the percentage of system runs that have a positive result (i.e. hunters catching the prey within the given limit of steps). Naturally, the success rate is only of interest if either the game variants include random factors or we perform on-line learning.

In addition to comparing the base learning algorithm of [3], resp. [4], with our improvement, we also compared our improvement described in Section 3 with an obvious variant of our general idea of including accountability into EL. This variant is selecting the SAPs from the parent strategies totally controlled by the success of the SAPs with the parents, without the additional random influences that we proposed in Section 3. As we will see, this variant, that we call *pure success-based*, is already better than the base algorithm and sometimes also better than what we proposed in Section 3, which in the following we will call *success-influenced*. The overall performance of the success-influenced version is better than the pure success-based one (see later).

The general setting of all experiments is that we defined a game variant, the basic parameters of our GA and the basic learning parameters, and between the

Table 1. Experimental results for off-line learning, times in minutes

Variant	Base algorithm			Pure success-based			Success-influenced		
	time	steps	success	time	steps	success	time	steps	success
1	**555.00**	**99**	-	-	-	-	-	-	-
2	1144.00	77	50%	1071.00	82	**60%**	**971.00**	**51**	60%
3	20.18	73	60%	20.70	37	70%	**9.18**	**30**	85%
4	34.25	51	70%	17.18	47	**80%**	**12.07**	**45**	80%
5	-	-	-	544.00	326	**20%**	**375.00**	**272**	15%
6	0.38	73.5	**100%**	**0.18**	**59.4**	**100%**	0.23	59.9	**100%**
7	375.00	107	30%	281.00	47	**55%**	**244.00**	**51**	55%
8	5.18	190	-	**4.85**	**109**	-	5.03	177	-
9	82.07	43	-	79.05	44	-	**74.00**	**31**	-
10	69.10	71	-	41.18	69	-	**40.67**	**57**	-
11	135.18	117	-	82.07	91	-	**60.00**	**72**	-

Table 2. Experimental results for on-line learning, times in minutes

Variant	Base algorithm			Pure success-based			Success-influenced		
	time	steps	success	time	steps	success	time	steps	success
1	**6.65**	**153.4**	**90%**	8.58	232.9	80%	7.38	197.4	**90%**
2	448.00	97.3	60%	464.00	79.2	**70%**	**419.00**	**65.4**	70%
3	0.36	59.8	90%	0.33	50.4	**100%**	**0.24**	**48.1**	100%
4	0.32	54.1	95%	0.30	50.4	**100%**	**0.28**	**41.5**	100%
5	177.12	61.3	65%	105.00	71.9	85%	**92.23**	**60.9**	**90%**
6	0.29	35	**100%**	**0.19**	**29.4**	**100%**	0.20	32.4	**100%**
7	132.08	72.5	55%	111.23	51.7	70%	**103.98**	**40.1**	**80%**
8	2.70	214.5	**80%**	**2.34**	**199.3**	**80%**	2.37	201.3	75%
9	5.78	141.9	90%	**2.59**	**68.8**	**100%**	2.90	65.5	**100%**
10	14.05	73.5	55%	11.08	61.8	65%	**10.68**	**39.7**	**70%**
11	7.00	171.3	45%	5.13	116.7	55%	**3.53**	**64.9**	**90%**

three tested learning algorithm variants the only differences are whether and how the statistical data of the SAPs was used in the Genetic Operators. For the success-influenced variant, the values used for the parameters defining the influence of the different pools are $p_{good}=0.65$ and $p_{indiff}=0.25$. The additional parameters of Section 3 were good_min = 0 and bad_max = 0. For Mutation, we only used the three kinds we discussed in Section 2.2 with the same probability.

The game variants with fixed start positions have these positions depicted in Figure 1. Also in Figure 1, on the right side, we present names for the different agent shapes used in the experiments. In variants 1,8,9,and 11 the goal of the game is to "kill" the prey(s), i.e. a hunter occupying a grid field that is also occupied by the prey (for variant 8, both preys have to be killed at the same time). In all other variants, the game goal is to immobilize the prey. In game variants with only one hunter, this hunter's strategy is to be learned. In variants 2 and 7, both hunters' strategies are learned, resp. both hunters perform on-

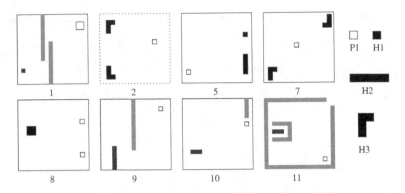

Fig. 1. Start positions for game variants and shapes of agent types

line learning. In variant 3, we have a hunter of type H1 (learning) and one of type H2 with a fixed strategy (simply moving towards the prey, which forces the other hunter to come up with a good support strategy). This fixed strategy is also employed by one hunter of type H2 in variant 4, the hunter of shape H2 in variant 5 and the hunter of type H3 in variant 6. The learning hunter in variant 4 also has shape H2, while the learning hunter in variant 6 has shape H1. The preys in variants 1,3,4,6 and 8 to 11 use a strategy that tries to evade the nearest hunter, while in the other variants the preys move randomly. If not otherwise depicted, the preys are of type P1. Note that variants 2 and 11 have an infinite grid, while all other variants are played on a 30×30 grid.

Let us first look at the results for off-line learning in Table 1. With the exception of the maze variant 1, both the pure success-based and the success-influenced modifications outperform the original algorithm. For many variants, we have large improvements in run (i.e. learning) time and where the improvements are not so big, we see large reductions in the number of steps, i.e. in the quality of the found strategies. Comparing our two modifications, for 8 of the variants the success-influenced approach is faster (often substantially), while for the other two it is not much slower.

For on-line learning (see Table 2), we again have no improvement by either of our modifications for the maze variant 1, while for all other game variants the success-influenced algorithm has better run times, better average number of steps and (with one exception) a higher success rate. The pure success-based method is always better than the base algorithm in at least one measure, but not consistently with all measures. If we compare our two modifications then the success-influenced one has the upper hand for most variants and for those where it does not, it is very close (for variant 9, the run time is not so close, but the average number of steps is better, instead).

So, with the exception of variant 1 (in fact, we tried several other, more complex mazes and variant 1 is typical for the outcome), including accountability of SAPs into EL leads to substantial improvements with regards to both learning time and quality of the found (cooperative) strategies. Why do our modifications lead to worse performances for mazes? Looking at the difference in definition and performance between the pure success-based approach and the success-influenced approach (that we propose as the approach to choose in future) helps us to find the reasons behind it. And these reasons go back to the general problem of exploration vs. exploitation that learning approaches of behavior have.

Obstacles in general, but very especially mazes require from an agent a lot of exploration in order to deal with them. Especially with a function δ that does not take into account obstacles or other agents that are in the way, it is very important that agents explore their possibilities long enough to get into situations that are clearly better. With a maze, rather long action sequences are required to reach a situation that obviously leads towards the goal (with some intermediate situations that even might look like they lead away from the goal) and therefore allows for an appropriate reward for the decisions that led to the actions. In our base algorithm, the random effects that an evolutionary algorithm makes use of are responsible for exploring the possibilities. Adding accountability to the approach by using the statistic data counters the random effects, obviously more in the pure success-based approach than in the success-influenced one. Taking away some of the randomness makes it harder to explore and consequently our improvement is not an improvement at all but instead makes learning worse. In less extreme situations, with more realistic obstacles, the success-influenced approach on the one side focuses the randomness, which results in being better than the base algorithm. On the other side, by having the accountability of the SAPs just as an influence and not as the only selection criteria on the SAP level, there is the right amount of randomness there to explore the situations, which results in the success-influenced approach being better than the pure success-based approach.

6   Related Work

While using different learning algorithms on different levels of an agent has been suggested as the future of learning in multi-agent systems (see, for example, [9]), our improvement of EL by adding accountability does tackle just one level of learning (although both, our improvement and different algorithms on different levels can be seen as combinations of learning approaches, see the next paragraph).

Within evolutionary computing, learning classifier systems (LCS) are also used to learn the behavior of an agent. In fact, as pointed out in [7], LCS can be seen as a more general technique than reinforcement learning, being able to mimic it. In LCS, the whole set of individuals (that represent single rules) at any point in time represents one agent strategy, so that the fitness of an individual has to be seen as a measure for a strategy component (this is often referred to as the Michigan approach to evolutionary computing). In contrast, our basic EL approach has as individual still a whole strategy (this is called the Pittsburgh approach) and our improvement adds accountability of components on a lower level. Consequently, we still have the advantages of the basic approach, like not having to completely solve the credit assignment problem and judging a whole strategy after a complete run, but now combined with the accountability advantage of LCS (and reinforcement learning).

7   Conclusion

We have presented an improvement to evolutionary learning of cooperative behavior for agents based on prototypical situation-action pairs and the nearest-neighbor rule. The improvement aims at accountability of all decisions with regard to learning, adding a second layer to learning structure within the basic genetic operators. In our experiments, we used two different ways to make use of this and our evaluation showed that, with the exception of mazes, both improvements achieved better results than the original evolutionary learning algorithm, i.e. the time spent for learning was less or the quality of the learned strategies was better or both. When comparing the two ways of making use of accountability, a success-influenced approach that combines accountability of SAPs with some random influences in most cases achieved better results, due to a better mixture of exploration and exploitation in it, than a pure success-based approach. Since maze-like settings can be easily detected, our results recommend to employ our success-influenced approach whenever the setting is not maze-like.

References

1. M. Benda; V. Jagannathan and R. Dodhiawalla. An Optimal Cooperation of Knowledge Sources, Technical Report BCS-G201e-28, Boeing AI Center, 1985.
2. J. Denzinger and S. Ennis. Being the new guy in an experienced team – enhancing training on the job, Proc. AAMAS-02, ACM Press, 2002, pp. 1246–1253.
3. J. Denzinger and M. Fuchs. Experiments in Learning Prototypical Situations for Variants of the Pursuit Game, Proc. ICMAS'96, AAAI Press, 1996, pp. 48–55.
4. J. Denzinger and M. Kordt. Evolutionary On-line Learning of Cooperative Behavior with Situation-Action-Pairs, Proc. ICMAS'00, IEEE Press, 2000, pp. 103–110.
5. T. Haynes, R. Wainwright, S. Sen and D. Schoenefeld. Strongly typed genetic programming in evolving cooperation strategies, Proc. 6th GA, Morgan Kaufmann, 1995, pp. 271–278.
6. J. Hu and M.P. Wellman. Multiagent reinforcement learning: theoretical framework and an algorithm, Proc. 15th Machine Learning, AAAI Press, 1998, pp. 242–250.
7. P.L. Lanzi. Learning Classifier Systems from a Reinforcement Learning Perspective, Technical Report 00-03, Politecnico di Milano, 2000.
8. M. Manela and J.A. Campbell. Designing good pursuit problems as testbeds for distributed AI: a novel application of genetic algorithms, Proc. 5th MAAMAW, 1993, pp. 231–252.
9. P. Stone. Layered Learning in Multi-Agent Systems: A Winning Approach to Robotic Soccer, MIT Press, 2000.
10. M. Tan. Multi-agent reinforcement learning: Independent vs cooperative agents, Proc. 10th Machine Learning, Morgan Kaufmann, 1993, pp. 330–337.
11. C.J.C.H. Watkins. Learning from Delayed Rewards, PhD thesis, University of Cambridge, 1989.

The C-IPS Agent Architecture for Modeling Negotiating Social Agents

Diemo Urbig, Dagmar Monett Díaz, and Kay Schröter

Humboldt University of Berlin
Department of Computer Science, AI Group
Unter den Linden 6, 10099 Berlin, Germany
{urbig,diaz,kschroet}@informatik.hu-berlin.de

Abstract. The basic concepts in agent negotiation are negotiation object, negotiation protocol and reasoning process. While aiming to transfer sociological concepts into multi-agent systems, where agents coordinate themselves by negotiation, we recognized the need for a more detailed structure. Therefore we developed C-IPS, which is presented in this article. It distinguishes between external constraints and internal reasoning processes. The reasoning process covers decisions regarding the negotiation issue, the partner, and a particular step. Its modularization supports the development of agents with different degrees of autonomy. The components of the C-IPS architecture are modeled according to the BDI approach. As an example for the application of C-IPS we consider agents that are required for the INKA project.

1 Introduction

Within the last years distributed artificial intelligence has been more and more influenced by social sciences. Sociological concepts have been considered as a promising way to describe and construct groups of agents and their interactions, to model and to simulate human societies, and to evaluate computer-human relations. However, in designing multi-agent systems (MAS) sociality is often considered in a very general way, where social refers to the ability and practice of interaction. In the social simulation domain sociality is more deeply addressed. For instance, the domain-independent *PECS* agent architecture incorporates social status as one of four important parts of the agent's reasoning process [18]. Contrary, we believe that social concepts cannot be localized within specific parts of the agent architecture, but they are a property of the complete architecture and its specific implementation.

The transfer of sociological concepts is a vital part of our *INKA* project, which is carried out in the context of the DFG priority program *Socionics*[1]. The project's aim is a system that enables experiments where artificial agents negotiate with humans. For that, we need agents that support different degrees of delegation within negotiations. Our application domain is shift exchanges in

---

[1] It supports research projects that combine sociology and computer science.

M. Schillo et al. (Eds.): MATES 2003, LNAI 2831, pp. 217–228, 2003.

a hospital, but we do not develop a new system for shift plan creation. For the transfer of sociological concepts we have to analyze which parts of the agents' architecture are influenced by which concepts and how do these parts interact. Such an analysis requires a well-structured reasoning process of the agent. Therefore, we propose the C-IPS structure. Combined with the Belief-Desire-Intention (BDI) approach, C-IPS provides a flexible architecture for negotiating agents. It supports a modular development as well as different degrees of agent's autonomy, i.e. different kinds of decisions can be delegated to the agent.

First, the article presents the basic ideas of C-IPS. Then, we enhance C-IPS by adding concepts from BDI architectures. Based on the INKA project the article finally presents an example for agents that follow the C-IPS architecture. The example also shows how C-IPS supports the modeling of sociological concepts within the agent architecture.

2   Structuring the Reasoning Process by Means of C-IPS

In the MAS literature on agent negotiations the negotiation object, the negotiation protocol, and the reasoning process are considered as the most important concepts [7]. This does not explicitly include partners nor does it provide a structure for the reasoning process. Consequentially, the design might focus on the selection of negotiation steps and might underestimate the impact of autonomous issue and partner selections. Increasingly, researchers become aware of other reasoning processes negotiating people are involved in, e.g. partner selection processes [8]. C-IPS aims to handle such extensions in a more comprehensive manner (see Figure 1). The starting point is the distinction between external constraints (C) and the agent's internal reasoning process. The reasoning process is divided into three sub processes: issue selection (I), partner selection (P), and step selection (S). The definition of the constraints heavily influences the design of the reasoning process. Their interdependency can be roughly described as follows: The more restrictive the external constraints are, the easier the reasoning process of the agent can be, but also the less flexible the agent is. In fact, an agent might be able to negotiate everything, but the agent's designer usually restricts this by defining the range of *negotiation objects*. From this set the agent selects issues for negotiations. The negotiation issue determines the space of possible deals[2]. Another constraint is the *negotiation protocol*, which limits the sequence of negotiation steps. However, one can also imagine that the protocol is not given and the agents reason about the meaning of messages. C-IPS additionally emphasizes external constraints related to the choice of the *negotiation partner*. Sometimes the designers assume that the partners for conflict resolution are given by the conflict. This is not always true, because sometimes other agents might be helpful to solve the conflict, but have to be identified before, or even the conflict itself is not sufficiently circumscribed.

Within the internal reasoning process an agent has to decide the issue of the intended negotiation, the negotiation partner, and particular negotiation steps.

---

[2] The identity of negotiation objects and issue is the most restrictive constraint.

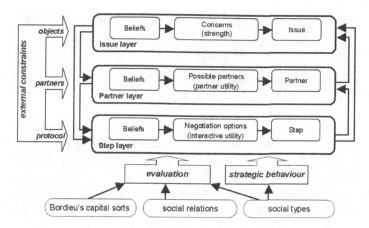

Fig. 1. The C-IPS-BDI architecture and the three sociological concepts we want to integrate into our negotiating agents.

Although these decisions are mutually dependent there is usually no common decision process. An agent architecture with three distinct components representing the three decisions enables and enforces the agents' designer to explicitly define the dependencies between them. For instance, an application may require that agents can change the issue during an ongoing negotiation or the set of partners might change. A structure anticipating the three distinct decisions can simplify the comparison of different negotiation architectures and agents' reasoning processes.

We propose that the structures of the three decision components follow the BDI approach [6,15]. B^k, D^k, I^k, with $k \in \{I, P, S\}$ denote the beliefs, desires, and intentions of the different components. $I = (I^I, I^P, I^S)$ refers to the global intention of the agent, which is interpreted as to do the step I^S in a negotiation on issue I^I towards the partner(s) I^P.

The beliefs B^k of each component contain knowledge about (1) states that might be reached and states that are temporarily recognized to be impossible to reach, (2) intentions chosen in other components, where applicable (3) the history of a ongoing negotiation, and (4) beliefs that are needed for specific implementations of the components. The beliefs are updated based on new perceptions P_t. The states an agent thinks about can either be explicitly given as beliefs or can be a result of a reasoning process based on the beliefs. The constraints limit the space of states. During the evaluation process the agent derives desires D^k, which represent the states it would like to reach. The preference function of each component gives degrees of desires, thus it discriminates between desires. Based on the preferences, the desires, the beliefs, the old intentions, and the knowledge about states that are recognized to be impossible (Imp^k) a component determines its new intention. When all parts of the global intention I have been chosen, the intention is put into action. Similar to [3] we can define:

$$B_{t+1}^k := update(B_t^k, P_t)$$
$$D_{t+1}^k := evaluate(B_{t+1}^k, D_t^k)$$

$$I_{t+1}^k := \text{filter}(B_{t+1}^k, D_{t+1}^k, I_t^k, \text{prefer}^k, \text{Imp}_t^k), \text{ with } \text{prefer}^k : D_{t+1}^k \mapsto \mathbb{R}$$

$$Action_{t+1} := \left\{ \begin{array}{ll} act(I_{t+1}) & if \ I_{t+1}^I \neq \emptyset \wedge I_{t+1}^P \neq \emptyset \wedge I_{t+1}^S \neq \emptyset \\ \emptyset & otherwise \end{array} \right\}$$

If the evaluation cannot find desires or the filter function cannot select an intention, then the agent recognizes that the currently chosen intentions of the other components represent (at least temporarily) states that are impossible to reach[3]. These states are members of the set Imp_t^k. To indicate how long they are assumed to be impossible, the agents assign durations to them. After a negotiation or an unsuccessful request for a negotiation an agent sets the partner for the issue as temporarily impossible[4].

Strategic behavior is a concept often used to describe human negotiations, which goes beyond pure short-term optimization. Defining strategic behavior as a behavior such that agents deviate from the individually most preferable choice to reach better results [4,10], we can locate strategic behavior within the process that selects intentions from desires. Hence, we assume that strategy is not about what is good for an agent, but it is procedural knowledge about useful behavior given some preferences. Strategies are not restricted to one step but have a mid or long term perspective. This knowledge can be acquired in the long run or is implemented by the agent's designer (as it is done in the INKA project). We distinguish isolated strategic behavior from coalitions. Currently we only consider isolated strategic behavior, where agents do not mutually coordinate their deviations from personal preferences.

3   Applying C-IPS in the INKA Project

In this section we describe how C-IPS is applied in the INKA project, where artificial agents and humans negotiate the exchange of shifts in a hospital domain [13]. Let S be the set of all shifts and A be the set of agents. Agents initiate negotiations to solve conflicts between the shift plan and their individual leisure time interests.[5] Let $SP_t \subseteq S \times A$ be the shift plan at time t, which relates shifts to agents and $SP_t(a) = \{s \mid (a, s) \in SP_t\}$ the personal shift plan of an agent a. The function $lt_t : S \mapsto \mathbb{R}$ assigns each shift a value between zero and one, where zero means no interest and one represents the strongest interest to have free. The initiator's goal is to exchange a conflict-raising shift.

---

[3] For instance, if the current global intention I is $(I_1^I, \emptyset, \emptyset)$, i.e. partner and step have not been not chosen yet, and the partner component cannot select a partner, then $(I_1^I, \emptyset, \emptyset) \in Imp^I$.

[4] Thereby we avoid deadlocks when agents initiate negotiations again and again and possibly block other agents.

[5] Although very interesting for human-like negotiations, we currently exclude the concept of argumentation in negotiations, i.e. agents do not explain why they did particular decisions or what preferences they have (e.g. [14,17]).

3.1   Social Concepts to Be Integrated

The INKA project requires the integration of Bourdieu's capital sort theory as a way to evaluate behavioral alternatives. Furthermore, it requires agents to reason about social types and to build and maintain relations to other agents. As the theoretical background of these concepts is not emphasized in this paper we give only a brief overview.

Bourdieu's capital sorts. When people negotiate they may pursue different goals. Before and during a negotiation they have to evaluate different possible agreements, e.g. shift exchanges. These options usually have many properties that may contribute in several ways to the fulfillment of different goals. Such evaluation processes are subject to research in multi-criteria decision-making and multi-attribute utility theory (MAUT). Both provide mechanisms to model and to solve such problems (e.g. [12]). To apply these mechanisms in the agent design process, the agent's designer has to select the most relevant properties and goals. This task can sometimes be very difficult, especially if there are many of them or if they are not easily to identify. This is the case in our application. In sociological theory aggregation and generalization is used to reduce the complexity of the description of humans, their goals, and the properties of opportunities to fulfill them. Similar to [16] we apply Bourdieus' capital sort theory to reduce the complexity of many goals and complex properties. In order to describe the human behavior we assume that a person or an agent would like to accumulate capital. Doing this he has preferences for different capital sorts, while different alternatives of the behavior have different contributions to these capital sorts [1]. The INKA project considers economic, social, cultural, and symbolic capital [13]. The contributions of different shift types, i.e. early, late, and night shifts during working days and at the weekend, were calculated according to [11].

The utility function $U : \mathbb{R}^4_{[0,1]} \times \mathbb{R}^4 \mapsto \mathbb{R}$ maps the capital interests (ci), given as values, which are between zero and one and sum up to one, and a capital equipment (ca) to a real value. This function incorporates concepts of MAUT. Until a refinement by experimental evaluations we calculate $U(ci, ca)$ as the weighted sum $\sum_{i=1}^{4} ca_i \cdot ci_i$. An agent's capital equipment is defined by its personal shift plan. The capital assigned to a shift is given by $ca_S : S \mapsto \mathbb{R}^4$. The value sv of a shift s is defined as the difference between the value of the agent's capital equipment with and without the shift. Because of the additivity of U this can be simplified to $sv(ci, s) = U(ci, cp_S(s'))$. Similarly, the value of an exchange is defined, with s being the shift to give away and s' the shift to take in return: $ev(ci, s, s') = U(ci, cp_S(s') - cp_S(s))$.

Social types. An important sociological concept within the INKA project is the social type. Let the set T contain all social types then the function $st : A \mapsto T$ assigns each agent a social type. For each social type we assume typical values of agent attributes. The attributes of social types can be divided in attributes that guide the evaluation processes and attributes that are related to the actual behavior of an agent. The capital interests ($ci_T : T \mapsto \mathbb{R}^4_{[0,1]}$), the general interest to work ($ww_T : T \mapsto \mathbb{R}_{[0,1]}$), the willingness to negotiate ($wn_T : T \mapsto \mathbb{R}_{[0,1]}$), willingness to compromise ($wc_T : T \mapsto \mathbb{R}_{[0,1]}$), the importance of personal and typified relations ($ipr_T, itr_T : T \mapsto \mathbb{R}_{[0,1]}$), and the typified leisure time interests ($lt_T : T \times S \mapsto \mathbb{R}_{[0,1]}$) belong to the first group. The willingness to give information ($wi_T : T \mapsto \mathbb{R}_{[0,1]}$) directly influences the behavior, hence it belongs to the second group.

The self-perception of an agent, i.e. the class it assigns to itself, is a frame that guides the agent's individual behavior. The only attribute that is not strictly applied within the self-perception is the typified leisure time interest. An agent can have leisure time interests that differ from the ones give by the social type. The social type that is assigned to another agent is used to estimate the other agent's behavior. Such classifications enable people in social contexts, as well as agents in MAS to reduce the complexity of their decision-making process and – much more interesting – it adds a generalization mechanism. In fact, experiences with one agent out of a class might be attributed to all agents in this class. A more detailed introduction to the idea of multi-dimensional social types within MAS can be found in [13].

Social relations and altruism. In human interactions one can frequently observe the formation of relation networks. On the one hand, such relations affect the tendency to negotiate with particular persons. On the other hand people are often more willing to make concessions towards others they have a good relationship with. These concessions can be interpreted as taking the other agents' preferences into account, i.e. behave more altruistically. In our model an agent i assigns a value to each agent $r_t : A \mapsto \mathbb{R}_{[0,1]}$, where, zero (one) denotes a bad (good) relation. Since the relations can change dynamically, and the focus of our modeling is the negotiation itself, we consider the formation of relationships depending on the agents' experiences in past negotiations. Relations improve and get worse on the basis of successful or unsuccessful negotiations. Other examples for experience-based partner selection mechanisms can be found in [5,17].

Consequently applying the concept of reasoning about social types, we introduce typified relations, which represent relations to social types. This implies that agents also maintain values for each social type, i.e. $r_t : A \cup T \mapsto \mathbb{R}_{[0,1]}$. Thereby, we generalize experiences with individual agents to social types, i.e. experiences to single agents are also attributed to its social type. This implies that the typified relation to an agent can contradict the personal relation to it.[6]

Using the C-IPS we can make our interpretation of the two mentioned effects of social relations, preferring particular partners and behaving altruistically, more explicit. The issue component does not depend on social relations. In the partner component partners are chosen, which an agent has good relations with. In both, the issue and partner component, no altruistic behavior is applied. In fact, agents do not explicitly prefer other agents as partners, just because they

---

[6] For instance, an agent might prefer to negotiate with agents of the social type workaholic but does not like to do it with agent Bob, who is a workaholic.

would benefit from a negotiation. In the step component the agents behave altruistically towards agents they have a good relation with. Contrary to our *passive altruists*, active altruist would behave altruistically in the other components, too.

3.2 The INKA Agents

After briefly introducing the sociological concepts we apply, we now present the details of the INKA agents' reasoning processes. Doing this we follow the structure given by the C-IPS architecture. In the reasoning process we focus on the desire and intention selection.

External constraints. Within the hospital there are formal guidelines, e.g. prohibitions to possess certain configurations of shifts or to exchange shifts between people with different hierarchical positions or qualifications. Although these limitations are implemented in the agents there is an administrative instance that has to confirm every exchange. This is especially important for cases when incomplete information exist.[7] The function $allowed : A \times S \times A \times S \mapsto \{true, false\}$ gives for an exchange[8] whether it is formally allowed or not.

The negotiation objects are all formally allowed shift exchanges between two agents. As designer's restrictions we additionally assume that the issue is limited to a single shift that the initiator of a negotiation wants to give away. The negotiation is then on the shift the initiator has to take in turn from the other agent (responder)[9]. We also require that both agents, a and a', have to possess the shift they give away and have to be able to take the shift offered in return:

- $I_t^I = \{(a, s, a', s') \mid (a, s, a', s') \in S \times A \times S \times A \wedge allowed(a, s, a', s')\}$
- $\forall (s, a, s', a') \in I^I : s \in SP_t(a) \wedge s' \in SP_t(a') \wedge s' \notin SP_t(a) \wedge s \notin SP_t(a')$
- $\forall (s_1, a_1, s_1', a_1'), (s_2, a_2, s_2', a_2') \in I^I : s_1 = s_2'$

For the partner component we require that the negotiation partner should be able to contribute to the issue of the negotiation, thus

$$I_t^P \in A \text{ and } \exists (a', s', a'', s'') \in I_t^I : I_t^P = a''$$

A negotiation step consists of a performative and where appropriate of an exchange. The negotiation protocol usually restricts the sequence of performatives, while the negotiation issue restricts the exchange. Informally negotiating people rarely use the contract net protocol; they instead show very flexible negotiation courses. We allow agents to do proposals, to agree on a proposal, and to cancel the negotiation. Additionally, the agents can make an ultimatum, which means that the negotiation is canceled in the next step if the other agent does not agree. A call-for-proposal (cfp) enables agents to ask for another proposal.

---

[7] The agents may be not able to recognize that an exchange is prohibited.
[8] An exchange describes the two agents and their originally assigned shifts.
[9] Further work will be concerned with relaxing these restriction in order to enable more complex exchange-operations like cyclic-exchange.

Agreeing can follow only a proposal or an ultimatum; hence the cfp prevents the other agent from agreeing. Before the exchange of proposals the initiating agent requests the partner for a negotiation. Since our agents cannot yet negotiate with several agents in parallel, the request implies the question whether the other agent is busy or not. It also contains the question whether there have been changes in the other agent's shift plan or interests since the last negotiation on the same issue. Thereby agents can avoid redundant negotiations that may result in negative experiences. After the negotiation, a possible reached agreement has to be confirmed by the administration. The initiator requests this and forwards the answer to the responder.

Layer dependencies. Although the C-IPS architecture allows the definition of complex dependencies between the components, during the first application we follow a simple sequential model. After calculating the issue, the partner is selected. The issue and the partner guide the step layer. From this we get the following conditions $I_t^S \neq \emptyset \rightarrow I_t^P \neq \emptyset$, $I_t^P \neq \emptyset \rightarrow I_t^I \neq \emptyset$, $I_t^I = \emptyset \rightarrow I_t^P = \emptyset$, and $I_t^P = \emptyset \rightarrow I_t^S = \emptyset$. If an agent becomes a responder the received negotiation request determines its issue and its partner.

Issue layer. A need for negotiation always arises when there is a sufficiently strong conflict between the administratively given shift plan and the individual leisure time interests. Variable leisure time interests, which can not really be forecasted by the administration, result from events outside the hospital. They are therefore an aggregate of the agent's goals outside the hospital. Agents not only balance between goals within and outside the hospital, but they also consider the fulfillment of different goals within the hospital. Bourdieu's capital sorts model the second aspect.

The beliefs of the issue component of agent a are its personal shift plan $SP_t(a)$, the own social type $st(a)$, and the leisure time interest $lt_t(s)$. Let $E_{a,s}$ be the set of all exchanges according to the external constraints, where an agent a can give the shift s away. The agent's concerns, i.e. desires of the issue component, are all $E_{a,s}$ such that for shift s there is positive leisure time interest. The strength, i.e. the preference to give a shift away, is determined by weighting the value of the shift and the leisure time interest at the time of the shift. This balancing is influenced by the agent's willingness to work. Let the utility functions su and eu represent this balancing process for shifts and exchanges with capital interests ci, shifts s and s' and leisure time interest l and l', then $su(ci, s, l) = ww_T(st(a)) \cdot sv(ci, s) + (1 - ww_T(st(a))) \cdot l$ and $eu(ci, s, l, s', l') = ww_T(st(a)) \cdot (sv(ci, s') - sv(ci, s)) + (1 - ww_T(st(a))) \cdot (l' - l)$. In the issue component we model only a very simple strategic behavior. We assume that for a negotiation there has to be a minimum leisure time interest, which is given by willingness to negotiate wn_T. Then the strongest concern related to a shift s with an $lt_t(s)$ above this threshold and being not recognized to be impossible is chosen as the intention of the issue layer.

$$evaluate^I(B_{t+1}^I, D_t^I) = \{E_{a,s} \mid lt_t(s) > 0\}$$
$$prefer^I(E_{a,s} \in D_{t+1}^I) = 1/su(ci(st(a)), s, lt_{t+1}(s))$$

$$filter^I(B^I_{t+1}, D^I_{t+1}, I^I_t, prefer^I) = \underset{\{E_{a,s}|E_{a,s}\in D^I_{t+1}\wedge lt_t(s)>wn_T(a)\wedge(E_{a,s},\emptyset,\emptyset)\notin Imp\}}{argmax\ prefer^I(E_{a,s})}$$

Regarding the sociological concepts, in the issue component the agents only use the concept of social types as self-perception. They reason based on Bourdieu's capital sorts, but they do not consider any kind of relations nor do they reason about other agents.

Partner layer. In the partner component, desires are partners that are possible according to the external constraints for negotiations on the given issue, i.e. $possible_t(a', s) = true$. The agents are ranked by a partner utility that depends on the personal and the typified relations as well as on a shift plan value $spv(a', E_{a,s})$ that is a measure for the quality and quantity of exchanges that are possible with another agent according to the given issue $E_{a,s}$. Within the preference function ipr_T and itr_T determine the impact of personal and typified relations. Varying this we can check whether considering generalized experiences can increase the overall performance or not.

$$evaluate^P(B^P_{t+1}, D^P_t) = \left\{a' \mid a' \in A \wedge possible(a', I^I)\right\}$$

$$prefer^I(a' \in D^P_{t+1}) = r_t(a')^{ipr_T(st(a))} \cdot r_t(st(a'))^{itr_T(st(a))} \cdot spv(a', I^I_{t+1})$$

$$filter^I(B^I_{t+1}, D^I_{t+1}, I^I_t, prefer^I) = \underset{\{a'|a'\in D^P_{t+1}\wedge(I^I_{t+1},a',\emptyset)\notin Imp^P\}}{argmax\ prefer^I(a')}$$

In the partner component we have included personal and typified relations. The agent develops experience-based preferences for selecting particular partners. Altruistic considerations are not modeled. After selecting an issue and a partner, the agent can initiate a negotiation.

Step layer. As described in the subsection on external constraints, the agents start a negotiation by requesting a negotiation. Contrary to desires at the other components, the desires in the step component do not concern a particular step. Instead desires are about desirable exchanges. All considered exchanges (exchanges covered by the issue and related to the partner) are ranked by the interactive utility. The interactive utility of an exchange $ie(a, a', s, s')$ incorporates our concept of altruism and is therefore calculated from the own utility of an exchange and from an social type based estimation of the other agent's utility of the exchange. Similar to [2] we calculate a weighted sum of both utilities: $ie(a, a', s, s') = (1 - \alpha_{a'}) \cdot eu(ci(st(a)), s, lt_t(s), s', lt_t(s')) + \alpha(a') \cdot eu(ci(st(a')), s, lt_T(st(a'), s), s', lt_T(st(a'), s'))$. The altruism factor depends on the relations and on a social type specific predisposition to behave altruistically (implemented by willingness to compromise): $\alpha_{a'} = r_t(a')^{ipr_T(st(a))} \cdot r_t(st(a'))^{itr_T(st(a))} \cdot wc_T(st(a))$. Altruism is often regarded as a way to overcome prisoner's dilemma-like situations. But if both agent are excessively altruistic (i.e. $\alpha > 0.5$), then they can experience such situations, too (see also [9]). By relating the cancel decision to the personal utility and the accept decision to the interactive utility we avoid these situations.

For the case a negotiation request is accepted, we assume that the negotiation takes place within a virtual zone: Exchanges are compared with two strategic lines, the accept line and the cancel line. If the other agent's proposal is good enough, i.e. its evaluation is above the accept line and above the cancel line, then it is accepted. If the proposal is too bad, i.e. below the cancel line, then the negotiation is canceled. Over time the accept line descends while the cancel line ascends. Hence the zone where agents further negotiate gets smaller and an end of the negotiation becomes more likely. If the proposal is above the cancel but below the accept line, then the agent does not wish to agree or to cancel, but does another proposal or cfp. The agent itself only proposes exchanges, which it would accept. These are the agent's desires.

From the desires and the knowledge about the protocol the agent derives a particular negotiation step as intention. A step is an appropriate performative according to the protocol (i.e. proposal, agree, cancel, cfp, or ultimatum) and additionally - if necessary - an exchange. Contrary to the issue and the partner component, we have modeled a complex strategic behavior in the filter process of the step component.

$$evaluate^S(B^S_{t+1}, D^S_t) = \{(a,s,a',s') \mid (a,s,a',s') \in I^I_{t+1} \wedge a' = I^P_{t+1} \wedge$$
$$ie(a,s,a',s') > acceptLine(t+1) \wedge$$
$$eu(ci_T(st(a)), s, lt_t(s), s', lt_t(s')) > cancelLine(t+1)\}$$
$$prefer^S((a,s,a',s') \in D^S_{t+1}) = ie(a,s,a',s')$$
$$filter^S(B^S_{t+1}, D^S_{t+1}, I^S_t, prefer^S) =$$
$$strategy(B^S_{t+1}, D^S_{t+1}, I^S_t, prefer^S, \text{set of weighted tactics})$$

The basic concept of our implementation of strategy is a tactic. Tactics contain a precondition, usually referring to past negotiation steps and to both strategic lines, and a body that determines a particular negotiation step. The body can also be influenced by the history of the current negotiation.

While a tactic gives one negotiation step for a specific set of situations, a strategy provides a sequence of steps for a wide range of situations. We create a strategy from a set of tactics and the two strategic lines. To each tactic a weight can be assigned. If the preconditions of more than one tactic hold, the weights are taken into account. If necessary, the weights are temporarily adjusted. Applicable tactics without a weight are only considered if the sum of weights of all applicable tactics is less than 1. In this case the difference to 1 is equally distributed among the applicable tactics. If the sum is greater than or equal to 1, the tactics without a weight are not considered and the weights are normalized such that the sum equals 1. Using these weights as probabilities one tactic is chosen randomly. This flexible model of strategies as a set of partially weighted tactics enables us to merge, extend, or reduce strategies dynamically[10].

In our application we currently define four tactics: Agreeing and Canceling, which compare interactive and personal utilities of the partner's last proposal or ultimatum with the accept line and cancel line. The tactic Step-by-step is

---

[10] Although currently the strategy is fixed we plan to introduce adaptable strategies and learning mechanisms.

a simple heuristic to do a proposal. The agent proposes one negotiation option after the other starting with the one that is ranked highest. If there is no other option the last one is repeated and after 5 repetitions an ultimatum is done. This tactic is only applicable if Agreeing and Canceling are not applicable. The same holds for the fourth tactic, Cfp. These tactics are combined into a strategy. We assign a weight to the tactic Cfp that depends on the social type. It is inversely related to the willingness to give information. The accept line has an initial value that is five percent below the best-ranked negotiation option. It decreases 5 percent of the interactive utility of the best negotiation option each step. The cancel line starts at zero and increases half the absolute value the accept line decreases.

4   Conclusions

In this article we have proposed the C-IPS framework to model negotiating agents. The frequently used concepts of negotiation protocol, object, and reasoning process can be put into a broader context of external constraints and reasoning process. Both can be structured more detailed regarding the negotiation issue, the partner, and a particular negotiation step. This enforces a clear definition of concepts and ideas during the agent design. The three components of the agent's reasoning process we have modeled according to the BDI approach.

Although not being exhaustively, we give a deeper insight into the design of the INKA agents, thereby showing how the C-IPS architecture can be applied and how it can support the analysis and modeling of concepts like social types, social relations, and altruism. C-IPS has made visible that altruism in negotiations can be defined in different ways, e.g. passive and active altruists.

The component-based approach enables different degrees of delegation. By leaving different decisions to humans, we can implement four degrees. First, the human does all decisions; hence the agent is without any intelligence and is, in fact, only an interface. Second, the agent gets the issue and the partner, but negotiates on its own. Third, the agent gets only the issue of the negotiation. And forth, the agent even recognizes the concerns of the user and after several negotiations it just provides a better shift plan.

During the next steps we model more complex negotiations within the C-IPS approach, i.e. relaxing the sequential order of the components' decisions and enabling multilateral negotiations. Further we aim to improve the domain-independent formalization of C-IPS.

References

1. P. Bourdieu. Ökonomisches Kapital, kulturelles Kapital, soziales Kapital. In R. Kreckel, editor, *Soziale Ungleichheiten. Soziale Welt. Sonderband 2*. Schwarz, Göttingen, 1983.
2. S. Brainov. Altruistic cooperation between self-interested agents. In W. Wahlster, editor, *12th European Conference on Artificial Intelligence (ECAI 96)*, pages 519–523. John Wiley & Sons, Ltd., 1996.

3. H.-D. Burkhard. *Handbuch der Künstlichen Intelligenz*, chapter Software-Agenten, pages 943–1020. Oldenbourg Wissenschaftsverlag, München, 3. edition, 2003.
4. D. W. Carlton and J. M. Perloff. *Modern industrial organization*. Harper Collins, New York, 2nd edition, 1994.
5. P. S. Dutta and S. Sen. Identifying partners and sustenance of stable, effective coalition. In *proceedings of the Fifth International Conference on Autonomous Agents (poster paper)*. Montreal, Canada, May 28 - June 01 2001.
6. K. Fischer, J. P. Müller, and M. Pischel. A pragmatic BDI architecture. In M. N. Huhns and M. P. Singh, editors, *Readings in Agents*, pages 217–224. Morgan Kaufmann Publishers, 1998.
7. N. R. Jennings, P. Faratin, A. R. Lomuscio, S. Parsons, C. Sierra, and M. Wooldridge. Automated negotiation: Prospects, methods and challenges. *Int. Journal of Group Decision and Negotiation*, 2000.
8. K. Kurbel and I. Loutchko. Multi-agent negotiation under time constraints on an agent-based marketplace for personnel acquistion. In *Proceedings of the 3rd International Symposium on Multi-Agent Systems, Large Complex Systems, and E-Business (MALCEB2002)*, pages 566–579. Erfurt, Germany, October 2002.
9. C. Landesman. *The Voluntary Provision of Public Goods*. PhD thesis, Princeton University, 1995.
10. H. Laux. *Entscheidungstheorie*. Springer, 4. edition, 1998.
11. E. Lettkemann, M. Meister, A. Hanft, K. Schröter and R. Malitz. The description of practical roles in hospital environments. In G. Lindemann, C. Jonker, and I. J. Timm, editors, *Proceedings of the MASHO Workshop: Modelling Artificial Societies and Hybrid Organizations. 25th German Conference on Artificial Intelligence*, pages 29–36, Aachen, Germany, 2002.
12. J.-L. Marichal. Behavioral analysis of aggregation in multicriteria decision aid. In J. Fodor, B. De Baets, and P. Perny (eds.), Preferences and Decisions under Incomplete Knowledge. Series: Studies in Fuzziness and Soft Computing Vol. 51 (Physica Verlag, Heidelberg, 2000) pp. 153-178
13. M. Meister, D. Urbig, R. Gerstl, E. Lettkemann, A. Osherenko, and K. Schröter. Die Modellierung praktischer Rollen für Verhandlungssysteme in Organisationen. Wie die Komplexität von Multiagentensystemen durch Rollenkonzeptionen erhöht werden kann. Working paper tuts-wp-6-2002, Technical University – Technology Studies, Berlin, 2002.
14. S. Parsons, C. Sierra, and N. Jennings. Agents that reason and negotiate by arguing. *Journal of Logic and Computation*, 8(3):261–292, 1998.
15. A. S. Rao and M. P. Georgeff. Modeling rational agents within a BDI architecture. In R. Fikes and E. Sandewall, editors, *Proceedings of Knowledge Representation and Reasoning (KRR-91)*, pages 473–484, San Mateo, CA, 1991.
16. M. Schillo and G. Vierke. Multidimensional utility vectors in the transportation domain. In I. Timm, editor, *Proceedings of the Workshop on "Agent Technologies and Their Application Scenarios in Logistics" at ECAI 2000*. 2000.
17. L.-K. Soh and C. Tsatsoulis. Agent-Based Argumentative Negotiations with Case-Based Reasoning. AAAI Fall Symposium on Negotiation Methods for Autonomous Cooperative Systems; 2001.
18. C. Urban. PECS: A Reference Model for Human-Like Agents. In Magnenat-Thalmann, N., Thalmann, D. (eds.): Deformable Avatars. Kluwer Academic Publishers, Boston, 2001.
19. M. Wooldridge and N. R. Jennings. Intelligent agents: Theory and practice. *Knowledge Engineering Review*, 10(2), 1995.

Author Index

Lecture Notes in Artificial Intelligence (LNAI)

Lecture Notes in Computer Science